To Philip

CON

CW01522360

KEIJO VIRTAMO

KALEVI AHO – PEKKA JALKANEN
ERKKI SALMENHAARA – KEIJO VIRTAMO

FINNISH MUSIC

Otava
Publishing Company Limited

Photographs:

The Archives of Otava Publishing Company Ltd. and
Finnish Composers' Association p. 83, 120, 133, 217, 224;
Finnish Composers' Association/Maarit Anderzén p. 80, 107, 113, 115,
118, 123, 128, 130, 137, 143, 147, 150, 156, 162;
Lehtikuva p. 191, 193, 195, 227, 238;
Radio Finland Picture Archives p. 175, 181, 185;
Sony Classical Archives s. 172;
University of Helsinki/Department of Musicology p. 211.

English translation: Timothy Binham and Philip Binham

Graphic design: Kari Koski

Otava Printing Works
Keuruu 1996

ISBN 951-1-14477-4

ERKKI SALMENHAARA

BIRTH OF A NATIONAL AND MUSICAL CULTURE IN FINLAND

The history and culture of Finland are deeply marked by the country's geographical location on the East-West divide of Europe's northernmost fringes. The Finnish forests, lakes and seasons have left their imprint on painting and music. The most unusual feature of Finland's culture, however, is no doubt the language. Not an Indo-European language, Finnish belongs to the Finno-Ugric family of languages, setting the the Finns apart from their Nordic and Russian neighbours. It was previously believed, mainly on linguistic grounds, that the home of the ancient Finns was in the region of the Volga Bend in Russia. More recent genetic research, however, has revealed that the Finnish genotype is primarily – perhaps up to three quarters – European. According to this theory, the Finns moved northward gradually, adopting a new language as they went.

Some History

Finnish culture in the form of folk poetry and song originated long before the years for which historical records exist. The adoption of a literary culture and the Christian religion began with the Swedish 'crusades' of the 12th century. The political objective of these expeditions was to establish Finland's position within Sweden's sphere of influence, in the face of the perpetual menace of Novgorod. The Pope confirmed Finland's annexation to Sweden in 1216. Thus Finland became Sweden's eastern bulwark against Russia. Constant warfare between Sweden and Russia led to repeated adjustments of the eastern border of the province of Finland, until in 1809, following the 'War of Finland', Sweden was finally compelled to cede Finland to Russia.

Finland obtained the status of an independent Grand Duchy of the Russian Empire, gaining considerable latitude to promote its national culture despite intermittent periods of oppression. In the midst of the First World War in 1917, Finland gained its political independence, which – unlike the Baltic States – it was able to maintain despite heavy losses during the Second World War. Finland was thus never occupied by enemy Russian forces except for the years of the 'Great Wrath' from 1716 to 1721. Even as a Grand Duchy, Finland always maintained a primarily Western orientation, culminating logically in accession to the European Union in 1995.

The most significant secular event in Finland under Swedish rule was the founding of the first university, the Academy of Turku (Åbo Akademi) in 1640. If only because of their geographical proximity, cultural contacts between Stockholm and Turku were – and still are – close. Turku developed into Finland's first centre of both religious and secular music.

Russia, however, took a dim view of the city's contacts with Sweden, and raised Helsinki – which was farther away from Stockholm – to the status of capital of the Grand Duchy of Finland in 1812. Then, following the great fire of Turku in 1827 – the worst disaster ever to strike a Finnish city – the university (i.e. Academy) was also transferred to Helsinki in 1828.

One might say that music moved to Helsinki with the university. The lovely, 'temple-like' assembly hall of the Neoclassical, Empire-style University of Helsinki became the centre of Finnish music life, a status it retained until the Finlandia Hall was built in 1971. Sibelius conducted the premieres of his principal works at the University; international stars who gave concerts there included Henryk Wieniawski, Pablo de Sarasate, Leopold Auer,

Anton and Arthur Rubinstein, Eugène Ysaÿe, Pablo Casals, Sergei Rakhmaninov, Fritz Kreisler, Alfred Cortot, Yehudi Menuhin, Gustav Mahler, Wilhelm Furtwängler, Serge Koussevitzky, Leopold Stokowski and Igor Stravinsky. Already in the 19th century, Helsinki had a remarkably lively and cosmopolitan music scene. This was partly due to the influence of St Petersburg, the imperial capital: many of the foreign artists who visited St Petersburg stopped on the way in Helsinki. Travel was facilitated by the opening of a regular steamship service between the two cities in 1837, and construction of the St Petersburg – Helsinki railway in 1870.

Besides Turku, another old town with a lively international culture was Viipuri (Vyborg), Finland's third-largest city before the wars. The loss of Viipuri to the Soviet Union following the Second World War was a heavy blow to Finnish music, even though the city's principal music institutions and personalities moved to Finland. Indeed, Karelians evacuated to Finland after the war have played a major role in Finnish cultural circles and the business world.

Musical links with St Petersburg (Leningrad) and Russia continued throughout the Soviet period, however. The Leningrad Philharmonic first visited Finland in 1946, and many worldfamous Soviet artists – including Yevgeni Mravinski, Emil Gilels, Svyatoslav Richter, David and Igor Oistrakh, Leonid Kogan, Mstislav Rostropovich, Vladimir Ashkenazy and Viktoria Mullova – performed in Finland with a frequency and visibility out of all proportion to our small country's rather modest status in the Western music world. Musically and politically, Finland served as a showcase for Soviet performers. The Wihuri Foundation conferred the International Sibelius Award on Dmitri Shostakovich in Helsinki in 1958. On Shostakovich's initiative, the composers' associations of Finland and the Soviet Union concluded a cooperation agreement, which included a programme of regular exchange visits for composers. Shostakovich was elected honor-

Inauguration of the University of Helsinki's renovated assembly hall in 1948.

ary member of the Finnish Composers' Association, and a notable tradition of Shostakovich performances soon developed in Finland. Finns were, of course, well aware of the awkwardness of Shostakovich's position, and he was honoured as a great composer and a courageous man. Some Finnish composers were also influenced by his musical style.

This special status did not, however, entail any break in the historical links with the Western music world, particularly with Scandinavia. Independence enabled Finland to take part in the joint Nordic music festivals, which it did for the first time in Copenhagen in 1919. Previously Finland had not been invited, as this would have meant having to invite Russia as well. Immediately after the Second World War, Finland was involved in founding the Nordic Composers' Council, the joint organization of the national composers' societies in the Nordic countries. Its main mission was to carry on the tradition of the Nordic music festivals, renamed the Music Days and first held in Oslo in 1948. The event has been held, basically every two years, in each of the participating countries in turn. This five-country festival, which concentrates on new music, is unique even by international standards. Contacts have also been cultivated with the world outside by inviting some guest country to each festival. Under 30-year-old Nordic composers also have their own annual event, called Ung Nordisk Musik. Apart from the Nordic Music Days, Finland has been a regular participant at the international music festivals of the ISCM (International Society for Contemporary Music) since the 1950s.

The Language Question

The international status of Old Viipuri is illustrated by the fact that four languages – Swedish, Finnish, Russian and German – were spoken there. Elsewhere in Finland, Swedish was established as the language of the ruling classes by centuries of Swedish rule. Even during the period of the Grand Duchy, the Russian language did not replace Swedish in this role, despite intermittent efforts to 'Russify' the country, whereas the Finnish language was given equal legal status with Swedish in the 1860s. In practice, however, Swedish remained the dominant language of the educated urban population until the end of the 19th century. This was reflected in the music world, which was marked by a language controversy that flared up from time to time, particularly among students' choral societies. Even as late as the 1910s, the 'War of Orchestras' between two competing philharmonic societies in Helsinki was triggered largely by the language question.

Religious literature had been published in Finnish since the country's Lutheran reformer, Bishop Mikael Agricola, published his translation of the New Testament, *Se Wsi Testamenti* (1548), but Finnish-language literature proper dates only from the 1860s, when Aleksis Kivi (1834–72) laid the foundation for the Finnish novel, drama and poetry. And yet Johan Ludvig Runeberg (1804–77), who wrote in Swedish, enjoyed the status of national poet from the 1830s on. The Finnish-speakers, however, had an unbeatable trump card in the epic *Kalevala*, consisting of folk poetry (or 'runes') collected and ordered by Elias Lönnrot. The first edition of the *Kalevala* was published in 1835.

Nowadays Swedish is the mother tongue of only six per cent of the Finnish population. For historical reasons, however, the status of the Swedish language remains strong, and is enshrined in the law. Swedish-speaking individuals and institutions are particularly prominent in Finnish literature, but also in the country's music life, enriching Finnish culture as a whole with their strong contribution.

The *Kalevala* and Music

Although Finland was part of a major political power in the days of both Swedish and Russian rule, it always felt uncomfortable in this role, as the country lacked a political identity. The essential element of national identity is language, for language generates culture. Swedish was the language of the educated class, but the publication of the *Kalevala* gave Finland a national epic in its own vernacular. The *Kalevala* led to the rediscovery of an ancient culture which extended all the way back to a period before written history. The *Kalevala*, as it were, filled a gap in the history of Finnish-speaking Finland. Now that Finland could proudly display a work that was comparable even with the great Classical epics, the country assumed a position as a nation among nations.

The significance of the *Kalevala* to the genesis and shaping of a national identity in the 19th century was immeasurable, not least in the sphere of music. The first musical work inspired by the *Kalevala* was Filip von Schantz's *Kullervo Overture* from 1860, intended as the overture to an opera on the subject, which von Schantz, who died young, never completed. Jean Sibelius created a national musical idiom with his *Kullervo Symphony* in 1892; one hundred years later, Aulis Sallinen's opera *Kullervo* received its world premiere in Los Angeles.

The epic attracted international attention early on – in the music world as well as in literary circles; in fact, an opera on *Kalevala* themes was already being planned in the 1880s in the United States. Planning to compose an opera, E.H. Krehbiel turned to his friend, the well-known author Lafcadio Hearn, for a suitable subject. In a letter to Krehbiel in 1882, i.e. ten years before the first performance of Sibelius's *Kullervo*, Hearn asserted that Krehbiel would find in the *Kalevala* everything he needed for a magnificent opera, including supernatural forces, passion and the eternal struggle of good and evil, darkness and light – a complete world inspiring the composer to produce unprecedented new themes. The sets of such an opera could be more fantastical and wonderful than anything Wagner had ever dreamed up in his creations of Talmudic infinitude.

Hearn returned to the subject two years later, suggesting the most amazing, momentous and Ragnarökian subject that could be imagined – a subject which would surpass Wagner and every trilogy ever written: the wooing of Pohjola's Daughter in the *Kalevala,* the only truly musical epic he had ever read. According to Hearn, Orpheus was a mere idle braggart compared with Väinämöinen and the suitors (!).

The opera project never seems to have materialized, but Krehbiel eventually became an influential music critic who wrote with insight about Sibelius and other composers. Sibelius himself planned to compose an opera on the same subject in the 1890s, but this project also came to nothing in the end. However, in 1906 Sibelius composed the symphonic fantasy *Pohjolan tytär* (Pohjola's Daughter). As for Hearn, northern exoticisim was not his only interest. He moved to Japan in the 1890s and published a collection of Japanese mythical tales, which later inspired Pehr Henrik Nordgren, who had studied in Japan, to compose the piano work *Ten Ballads on Japanese Tales of Horror* (1972–77).

For compositions based on themes from the *Kalevala*, the

relevant anniversary years have always been particularly productive. In 1935 someone suggested that new compositions on *Kalevala* themes should be banned for the next fifty years, but the proposal went unheeded. According to a catalogue drawn up by the Frenchman Henri-Claude Fantapié, some 330 *Kalevala*-based works had been composed in Finland by 1985. The epic itself has been translated into 45 languages. A hypermedia *Kalevala* on CD-ROM was released in 1996.

Folk Music

The songs of the Finnish people do not have the mastery of the skaldic poetry of Iceland, nor are they comparable with the melodious, noble and sagacious songs of the Greeks; but they greatly surpass those insipid rhymes which long brought shame upon the taste of the latter-day Europe. With such songs did the ancient denizens of Finland honour their gods; with their hidden power they believed themselves the masters of a mighty tool for bending almost all nature to their will; with these songs they praised the deeds of their fathers, their heroes and their daring; wreaked vengeance upon their enemies; and amused themselves in company. – These songs all had the same tune, as simple and grave as the people themselves, and were, when the occasion presented itself, accompanied on a kind of harp; with these songs, too, the women eased their heavy toil when grinding flour.

This description of the ancient sung poetry of the Finnish people stems from a lecture held in Stockholm in 1788 by Henrik Gabriel Porthan, an expert on folk poetry, history, languages, geography, literature and aesthetics, who brought into Finland the European Enlightenment and its Neo-Humanist ideals. Porthan's interest in music is shown by the fact that in 1770 he founded the Aurora Society in Turku, which held the first public concerts in Finland in 1773 and 1774.

Although it has later been established that the five-beat '*Kalevala* tune' extended with a minor pentachord is only one of many variant melodies in ancient Finnish folk poetry, it has consolidated its position as the prototype for the two-line verse. It was first used in art music by the Italian explorer Giuseppe Acerbi, who travelled through Finland in 1799. His third clarinet quartet contains a movement bearing the title *Runa finnoise*. The quintuple meter of the melody gave him problems, however, and he had to complement the melody, scored in 2/4 time, with an additional one-quarter rest! The melody has been used right up to the present day by many Finnish composers and a few foreign ones as well.

The "kind of harp" referred to by Porthan was the five-stringed *kantele*, honoured as Finland's national instrument, and again a focus of interest in the sphere of 'world music' as well as in contemporary art music. The old rune-singing tradition has also been revived. At a celebration of Kalevala Day (February 28, also the 'Day of Finnish Culture') in 1996, a world record was set in rune-singing, with 1,512 lines sung consecutively in 2 hours 40 minutes. The full length of the *Kalevala* is 22,795 lines.

Together with incantations, working songs, dirges and the Sámi *joiku* of Lapland, rune-singing represents the oldest stratum in Finno-Baltic folk song, with roots extending at least back into the early Middle Ages. Geographically and ethnographically, the rune-singing area covers Finland, Finnish and Russian Karelia, Estonia, Ingria (the area around present-day St Petersburg), and the nearby lands of the Votic and Veps tribes. The oral tradition survived until the beginning of the 20th century: 32,000 lines were taken down from the Ingrian rune-singer Larin Paraske, who died in 1904. Jean Sibelius was among those who heard her sing.

By the beginning of the 19th century, the alliteration typical of the *Kalevala* meter had given way to rhyme, and epic linearity to strophic structure, in the newer brand of folk song, which took its melodies from the Continent and Sweden rather than improvising them. Instrumental music also exerted an influence. Although the melodies were performed monophonically, they were no longer genuinely monophonic, having a background structure based on major-minor tonality or modality. The lyrics of songs began to be printed as broadside ballads (*arkkiveisut*).

With the national awakening of the late 19th century, widespread interest began to arise in collecting, scientifically ordering and publishing folk tunes. Songs of the newer type, in particular, were disseminated through popular publications and schoolbooks, entering the national heritage. One of the typical features of National Romanticism was its use of folk melodies as thematic material, arranged in keeping with the ideals of art music. Thus the rustic folk song was domesticated, but at the same time some of its original freshness was lost. Moreover, songs with words that were considered obscene were bowdlerized mercilessly.

The earliest phase of instrumental folk music was represented by pastoral instruments and the kantele, which was used for accompanying both rune-singing and dancing. *Pelimannimusiikki*, folk music played by country fiddlers, gained a particularly strong status as wedding music during the 18th century, especially in the western parts of the country. This genre has recently seen a new flowering at the Kaustinen Folk Music Festival, which was founded in 1968 and has grown since into a general forum for world music. Another new development is professional training at the Sibelius Academy for 'folk musicians', who often combine elements of folk and pop.

The Estonian folk music scholar Urve Lippus presented an interesting theory about Finno-Baltic rune singing in his book *Linear Music Thinking* (1995), suggesting that linear (i.e., genuinely monophonic) rune-singing was a popular variation of Latin plainsong. This corresponds to the earlier reinterpretation of the more recent type of folk song with the help of the German concept *versunkenes Kulturgut* (submerged cultural heritage).

The Church, the Court and the City

Mediaeval church singing came to Finland from both East and West. Some historians have speculated that the Orthodox Church gained a foothold in eastern Finland even before the Church of Rome established its dominance in the west. The unaccompanied Orthodox chant would thus constitute Finland's longest-lived art music tradition. The Orthodox Church is the second State church of Finland, although its current membership is only around 56,000. Monophonic Russian chant – the *znamenny* style – stemming from the Byzantine tradition influenced the Orthodox singing tradition in Karelia. The polyphonic St Petersburg style was adopted in the 18th century, but Finnish Orthodox chant has still sought to retain its links with the Byzantine *oktoechos* system. Church Slavonic was replaced by Finnish as the language of liturgy in the mid 19th century. Despite its Russian tradition, the Finnish Orthodox Church was transferred to the authority of the Patriarchate of Constantinople in 1923.

The tradition of Latin (Gregorian) chant in Finland extended officially to 1527, when King Gustavus Vasa initiated the Reformation. In practice, the musical corpus remained virtually unchanged until the early 17th century; in many cases, the words were simply adapted to the new dogma and the vernacular language. The Helsinki University Library possesses a remarkable collection of manuscripts of Latin chant, comprising some 6,300 leaves of parchment. These were preserved thanks to the 'vandalism' of the bailiffs of the Swedish Crown: they used leaves torn from liturgical books (by then useless) as covers for their account books. Most of this Finnish archive material was returned from Sweden to Finland in accordance with a provision in the 1809 peace treaty between Russia and Sweden. Although the material is fragmentary – so far, just under one thousand book fragments have been reconstituted, i.e. only some six pages per book – it contains some valuable uniques, including

English material which was destroyed in England during the Reformation. The oldest material goes back to the middle of the 10th century, and the most recent dates from the 16th century.

The daunting task of studying and ordering this corpus was undertaken by TOIVO HAAPANEN (1889–1950) in the 1920s. His doctoral thesis in 1924 dealt with the subject, but he had already begun publishing a catalogue in 1922 with the *Missalia*, followed by the *Gradualia* and *Lectionaria missae* in 1925 and the *Breviaria* in 1932. Owing to the scant resources available for the study of ancient music, a long hiatus followed, but in the 1990s ILKKA TAITTO (b. 1957) took up where Haapanen had left off, compiling the fourth volume in the series, *Antiphonaria*, which was finished in 1996. Taitto has also published an amply glossed facsimile anthology of the entire corpus, *Documenta Gregoriana* (1992).

Printed books made their appearance at the end of the 15th century. Their musical interest varies, as some show no notes at all, while others only have empty bar lines. The *Breviarium Dominicanum* (1485) and *Psalterium Latinum* (1488) were probably associated with music sung in the diocese of Turku (Åbo), as the *Missale Aboense* (1488) and *Manuale Aboense* (1522) certainly were. The liturgy is based primarily on the Parisian Dominican tradition, but also has local features, most obviously the cult of Finland's Catholic patron saint, Bishop Henry. An important document on music-making in Finland is the Latin book of school and church songs *Piae Cantiones*, the first edition of which was published in 1582. It contained 74 songs, about half of which are believed to be of Finnish origin, as they have not been found in foreign sources. The successive editions of the book reflect the development of polyphony.

At about the same time – probably in 1580 – the first Lutheran hymnal in Finnish was published in Stockholm. It consisted primarily of Swedish and German hymns, translated and

PIÆ CANTIO=

NES ECCLESIA-
STICÆ ET SCHOLA-
STICÆ VETERVM EPISCOPO-
rum, in Inclyto Regno Sueciæ paßim vsurpatæ,
nuper studio viri cuiusdam Reuer. naß: de Ecclesia
Dei & Schola Aböensi in Finlandia optime
meriti accuratè à mendis corre-
ctæ, & nunc typis com-
missæ, opera

THEODORICI PETRI
Nylandensis.

His adiecti sunt aliquot ex Psalmis recentioribus.

Imprimebatur Gryphisualdiæ,
per Augustinum Ferberum.

First edition of the Piae Cantiones, 1582.

adpated by Jacob Suomalainen (Jaakko Finno). Finnish spiritual songs, songs from the *Piae Cantiones*, and original compositions were added to later hymnals.

By the end of the 17th century, there were organs in a dozen Finnish towns in addition to Turku and Viipuri. Establishment of a liturgy for congregational singing, however, was a long-drawn-out process whose precise details are not known. Independent organ music seems to have been included at a fairly early date.

Although there were Catholic churches and monasteries in other Finnish towns as well, the centre of religious chant was the country's oldest city Turku, which is thought to have been founded in 1229. The history of the Cathedral of Turku in fact dates back to the twelfth century. The Cathedral school was established around 1270, which is also when construction of Turku Castle began. As in Sweden proper, there was music-making in the castle which culminated during royal visits. In the latter half of the 16th century – when Gustavus Vasa's younger son John was Duke of Finland – Turku Castle enjoyed a brief flowering of regular court music. Compared with the mother country, however, this remained on a modest, provincial scale.

The same observation applies to music performed in the towns. In principle, Finland had the same system of privilege as other parts of northern Europe, but as at court, it was on a more modest scale. The most recent research on Nordic, Germanic and Baltic music, represented in Finland by FABIAN DAHLSTRÖM (b. 1930), has emphasized that "town music was a Baltic phenomenon". The same goes for the teaching of singing in school. The trading routes of the mediaeval Hanseatic League ran from its principal city Lübeck to Riga in Latvia, Visby and Stockholm in Sweden, Tallinn and Narva in Estonia, and to the Finnish ports of Viipuri, Porvoo, Turku, Naantali, Rauma and Ulvila. The town musicians also moved within this sphere, often travelling from one port to another. Rather than separating towns and peoples, the Baltic Sea thus brought them together. For a long time, Finnish music was firmly rooted in Germany.

Northern Viennese Classicism

Art music as an independent Finnish institution began with the founding of the Turku Music Society in 1790. The Society maintained its own orchestra, with interruptions, until 1924; in 1927 the tradition was picked up by the Turku City Orchestra. The longest continuous orchestral tradition in Finland, however, is that of the academic chapels. The Chapel of the Academy of Turku was founded in 1747, and its successor in Helsinki still exists today.

The Turku Music Society rapidly amassed an extensive and up-to-date music library – scores of 'ancient' music were hard to come by in those days. The emphasis in the collection was on the Mannheim school and the works of Haydn, Mozart and Beethoven. Although the library and the Society's archives were saved from the fire of Turku, the lack of references has prevented any systematic survey of the works actually performed in the early years.

A more general phenomenon of which the Society's activities were part might be termed *Northern Viennese Classicism*. It produced the first Finnish composers known by name, and thus initiated the history of music composition in Finland. Their music, however, had no specifically Finnish content; like their Continental colleagues, they composed in the fashionable Viennese Classical style, which gradually began to take on features of the budding Romantic movement. Typically for the period, most of these composers were amateurs with careers in the civil service or other professions.

Moreover, only one of these composers was properly Finnish to the extent that he spent most of his life on Finnish soil. This was ERIK TULINDBERG (1761–1814), who studied at the Academy of Turku and then took up a civil service post in Oulu far up in the north, where the aforementioned Acerbi met him in 1799 (cf. p. 15). A few years before his death, he was transferred back to Turku. Tulindberg was an accomplished violinist, and also played the cello. He assembled an outstanding private music library, containing works by Haydn, Mozart, Pleyel and others. The collection certainly included Haydn's string quartets op. 9, which seem to have served as a model for Tulindberg's own six string quartets. Although Tulindberg probably never went to Stockholm, he was elected member of the Royal Academy of Music in 1797. He must have had contacts with the Academy, as he dedicated his work *Deux Concerts à Violon Principal* to the Academy's founder Patrick Alströmer. The only work by Tulindberg to be preserved in the Academy collection, however, is his First Violin Concerto in B major. Tulindberg's interest in folk music may have been a factor in his election, although his compositions show no trace of this interest.

The concerto and quartets are all composed in a flowing though somewhat bland Viennese Classical style. Soon consigned to oblivion, they were rediscovered in the 20th century. The quartets lacked the score for second violin, added most recently by Kalevi Aho in 1986.

THOMAS BYSTRÖM (1772–1839) had a much more distinctive style than Tulindberg. The son of a prominent businessman and mayor of Helsinki, Byström had an eventful career in the army which took him to the royal court of Stockholm, where he taught the piano to the crown prince, Oscar. In 1794, Byström became the first Finnish-born musician to be elected to Sweden's Royal Academy of Music. He served the Academy as teacher and expert, and was a candidate for its chairmanship. He published Vierling's treatise on thoroughbass in Swedish. In 1832, Byström was elected honorary member of the Philharmonic Society, and that same year he received the Order of the Sword.

Byström's songs were published from 1794 on in the

Musikaliskt Tidsfördrif, and his *Air Russe variée* for piano in its 1789–99 volume. His chief achievement, however, consists of a series of three violin sonatas (B flat major, G minor, E flat major), published by Breitkopf & Härtel in 1801. In terms of harmony, texture and form, the sonatas are bolder and more varied than Tulindberg's works. They are also progressive in that the violin part (although still conventionally termed *obbligato*) rises to full equality with the piano. At its best, Byström's melodic invention is expressive and distinctive. Critics have detected the influence of Beethoven in the sonatas, and even claimed that they prefigure Chopin (!). Their stylistic progressiveness, however, turned out to be their downfall: they were evidently too difficult for amateur performers. Some comments in contemporary letters state that Byström "sometimes composed almost too chromatically". Like Tulindberg's music, the sonatas were forgotten and only rediscovered in Finland in the 1930s.

The musical Lithander family comprised CARL LUDVIG (1773–1843), ERNST GABRIEL (1774–1803), GUSTAV DANIEL (1776–?), FREDRIK EMANUEL (1777–1823), CHRISTOPHYLOS (or CHRISTLIEB) SAMUEL (1778–1823), DAVID WILHELM (1780–1807) and CHARLOTTE LITHANDER-CARLBLOM (dates unknown). They were all born in Noaroots on the Estonian island of Hiiumaa, where their father, who had studied at the Academy of Turku, served as vicar. They were all amateur composers and professional teachers of music.

The family's most notable composers were Carl Ludvig and Fredrik Emanuel. Like Byström, Carl Ludvig Lithander was trained in Stockholm for an officer's career. He spent the years 1814–1818 on official leave in London, where he managed to publish several compositions and made the acquaintance of the leading musical figures of the day. He dedicated his Piano Sonata in C major to Muzio Clementi. He returned to Stockholm, but for reasons of health soon resettled in Germany, also giving concerts in the Netherlands and Denmark. He spent the remainder of his life as music director and organist at Greifswald.

Carl Ludvig Lithander (third right) playing in the string quartet of the Karlberg Military Academy in Stockholm.

The influence of Beethoven is clearest in C.L. Lithander's Second Piano Sonata in F sharp minor (published 1822). In his compositions, Lithander made use of the popular tunes of the period as well as of Swedish folk songs. In addition to his many piano pieces, he composed two Mozart-style *Singspiele*, of which *Säckpiparen* (The Bagpiper) remained unperformed. *Lantara* was performed in Stockholm in 1817, but only the overture has survived.

Fredrik Emanuel Lithander studied in Porvoo and later worked as an accountant and piano teacher in Turku. He was Crusell's accompanist at the latter's concert in Helsinki in 1801. In 1811 he moved to St Petersburg, where he gave private piano lessons and published a number of compositions, some of which were also published in Stockholm. His main piano works are *Variations on a Theme by Haydn*, *Sonata facile* and a set of variations entitled *Chanson russe*.

The most renowned of the Finnish-born composers of the

period was BERNHARD HENRIK CRUSELL (1775–1838), who also won fame as one of the foremost clarinet virtuosos of his time. Unlike the other composers discussed, he came from a humble home and opted for a career as a professional musician early on. With his patron, Major Wallenstjerna, he moved to Stockholm in 1791, at the age of 16, and spent the rest of his life there. He initially served as clarinetist and director of the band of the Queen Dowager's Guard regiment, until Abbé Vogler arranged for his appointment to the Court Chapel, where he served as clarinetist from 1793 to 1833, giving frequent concerts in Stockholm until the 1820s.

Crusell completed his studies under the renowned Franz Tausch in Berlin, and gave concerts in Berlin and Hamburg in 1798. In summer 1803 he studied composition in Paris with Henri Montan Berton and François Gossec, and became acquainted with the leading French musicians of the era. On his way home, he gave concerts in Copenhagen and various towns in Germany. On his next German tour in 1811, he made valuable contacts with local music publishers.

In the early 1820s Crusell was plagued by a nervous disorder, and he travelled to the Carlsbad baths for a cure in 1822. On the way there, he met Felix Mendelssohn and Carl Maria von Weber. The treatment seems not to have had much effect, but apparently the court chapel's commission for the opera *Den lilla slafvinnan* (The Little Slave Girl) helped him forget his illness. It has been surmised that Crusell was influenced by the example of Weber, but the work owes more to the *Singspiele* of Mozart. The premiere in 1824 in Stockholm was a success. There is some justification for the claim that Crusell's work was the first opera by a Finnish-born composer. Terminological disputes aside, the work, whose plot is based on Ali Baba and the Forty Thieves, is more in the nature of a *Singspiel*: the original version had some two hours of spoken dialogue and only one hour of music. With abridged dialogue but expanded music, the work was revived in

Turku in 1996, where the freshness of the music made a favourable impact. The main soprano aria contains an extensive virtuoso clarinet *obbligato* played on stage. Performed by the composer himself at the premiere, this part was played in Turku by Fabian Dahlström, a Crusell expert who has published critical editions of several of the composer's works.

Bernhard Henrik Crusell (1775–1838).

The main emphasis in Crusell's composition, however, is on instrumental music; his three concertos and three quartets for his own instrument are standbys of the international clarinet repertoire.

Besides Viennese Classicism, another major source for Crusell's music was French opera and instrumental music. His choral and solo songs reveal more Romantic and indigenous Swedish traits. All of Crusell's music is characterized by solid craftsmanship.

Crusell and Byström both had careers in Sweden and, unlike Tulindberg, they are considered there as Swedish composers. Of all the composers discussed above, only Crusell's music has had a permanent place in the repertoire right from the start, and is still quite frequently performed today. The other Finnish composers of the period were forgotten for over a century, and thus did not serve as the foundation for a living tradition of instrumental composition. Thus the history of Finnish music lacks three of the five major periods in art music: the Renaissance, the Baroque, and Classicism. It was only the Romantic movement, and particularly its nationalist offshoot, that wove the voice of Finland into the international polyphony of music.

'The Father of Finnish Music'

The transfer of the university from Turku to Helsinki marked a watershed in 19th-century Finnish music. As a result, the lectureship in music went to FREDRIK (FRIEDRICH) PACIUS (1809–1891), a more competent all-round musician than any of his predecessors. Although the political objective of the move was to weaken Finland's ties with Sweden, its effect with respect to music was in fact the reverse: the new music lecturer was found in Stockholm.

Born in Hamburg, Pacius was a man of many talents. He spent the years 1824–1826 in Kassel, studying the violin with the famous violinist, conductor and composer Ludwig Spohr, and theory and composition with Moritz Hauptmann. While still a student, he was able to publish some of his compositions in Germany. From 1826 to 1828, he went on an extended concert tour in Germany. Among the audience in Stralsund was G.C. Flygarson, a member of the Stockholm Philharmonic Society, who almost immediately persuaded Pacius to move to Stockholm as first violinist of the court chapel, a post he held from 1828 to 1834. Just as impulsively, he made his choice between the lectureships offered to him at Uppsala and Helsinki, a city previously unknown to him. He later recalled his dramatic sailing on an undecked postal vessel across the wintry sea in February 1835; part of the journey had to be accomplished over the ice on foot. His choice was no doubt eased by the fact that the Swedish he had learned in Stockholm would stand him in equally good stead in Finland.

On his arrival, Pacius methodically set out to organize Helsinki's music life; the university had in fact specifically requested that he extend his activities beyond closed academic circles. The highlight of that spring was a performance of Spohr's oratorio *Die letzten Dinge*, performed by an ensemble recruited by Pacius among society ladies, students, military bands, academic music-lovers and a handful of professional musicians. This concert was a landmark event and introduced a tradition of performances of major religious works at Eastertide. The climax in the series of oratorio performances conducted by Pacius came in 1839 with the performance of Handel's *Messiah*. Pacius also regularly arranged symphony concerts until 1853, when he gave up, disheartened by constant problems in assembling an orchestra. He introduced German and Italian Romantic composers into the repertoire, conducting works by Spohr, Weber, Rossini,

Fredrik Pacius (1809–91). Drawing by Karl Peter Mazer, 1836.

Bellini, Schumann and Mendelssohn. His own compositions were naturally also featured, most notably the Violin Concerto (1845), the second Finnish work in the genre after Tulindberg's concerto. The solo part bears witness to the composer's virtuosity as a violinist.

Symphonic music was not Pacius's most characteristic idiom, however. His principal composition is the opera *Kung Karls jakt* (King Charles' Hunt), whose premiere on March 24, 1852 has an aura of legend about it. This was the first opera composed in Finland, and it had a libretto based on Finnish history (the Swedish period). The author of the libretto was the composer's friend Zachris Topelius, a notable writer, influential public figure and patriot. *Kung Karls jakt* is a Romantic grand opera, modelled mainly on the precedent of Weber, Bellini, Verdi and Donizetti. Pacius handles the full operatic machinery and musical conventions with dexterity; at the same time, the work contains a great deal of genuine musical invention. The opera was successfully performed in Stockholm, and has been revived from time to time. A recording made in 1991 (conducted by Ulf Söderblom) was selected Record of the Year by the Finnish

Broadcasting Company, and also won a noted French musical award.

Pacius's second opera, *Die Loreley* (to a libretto by E. von Geibel; 1887), did not fare so well. It was branded outdated even in its own day, although the aging composer had sought to produce a Wagnerian *Gesamtkunstwerk*. Pacius evidently hoped for success for this German-language opera in his native country, but discovered on a visit that the old ties had broken. The performance of *Die Loreley* in Helsinki with amateur forces was a major effort undertaken by RICHARD FALTIN (1835–1918), Pacius's friend, countryman and successor as lecturer of music at the university. A versatile musician and a major influence on Helsinki's cultural scene, Faltin continued the oratorio tradition introduced by Pacius, and made his main musical contribution in the field of religious music, acting as organist of the present Cathedral of Helsinki from 1870 to 1913.

Pacius's and Topelius's collaboration also gave rise to the *Singspiel* – sometimes also styled an opera – *Princessan af Cypern* (The Princess of Cyprus), first performed at the inauguration of the New Theatre of Helsinki (today the Swedish Theatre) in 1860; on the same occasion, Filip von Schantz conducted his *Kullervo Overture*. Considering the patriotic tone of the inauguration, the Grecian theme of Pacius's work may seem puzzling. The subject, however, in fact came directly out of the *Kalevala*. With Lönnrot's consent, Topelius had in fact transposed Lemminkäinen, the Maidens of Saari and Kylllikki to Aphrodite's island! The mill song of Lemminkäinen's mother Helka is actually set to a *Kalevala* tune. When the work was performed on the occasion of Czar Alexander II's visit to Finland in 1876, Princess Maria was obliged to leave the imperial box on account of a fit of hysterical laughter brought on by the inadvertently comic effect produced by the marriage of Classical and Finnish myth.

In addition to opera, Pacius concentrated on the composition of choral and solo songs (cf. p. 200). In 1838, he founded the Akademiska Sångsällskapet male choir, Finland's oldest choral society never to have been disbanded (although renamed Akademiska Sångföreningen in 1846). Pacius required musical literacy from his singers, and added German Romantic songs to their repertoire. In his own songs, he made skilful use of a variety of musical textures and choral sonorities. In addition to German and English poets, he set a number of patriotic songs by J.L. Runeberg and other Finnish poets, and made arrangements of many Finnish folk songs. His best-known song is *Vårt land* (Our Country; 1848), a setting of a poem by Runeberg. It immediately gained the status of the national anthem among Swedish-speaking student circles, but owing to Finland's language controversy was slow to consolidate this position among the nation at large. A similar process occurred in Estonia, where Pacius's tune also became established as the national anthem.

Towards the end of his long life, Pacius was revered as the grand old man of Finnish music, and was sometimes styled "the Father of Finnish Music". He was also known as "the Genius" and "the Master", terms later applied to only one Finnish composer. In the 19th century, Pacius was a genius and master in his chosen home country; in the 20th century, a composer could only become a genius and master in Finland by first gaining that status abroad. Even Sibelius, however, unreservedly recognized the importance of Pacius's work: "Everything we musicians do here now is based on the life's work of Fredrik Pacius." Despite his German origin, Pacius was in fact as Finnish as a Finnish composer could be in those days. Even after his death, his Finnish-born colleagues and followers continued to seek their musical education and inspiration in Germany.

Building a Musical Infrastructure

The man who conducted the orchestra at the inauguration of the Helsinki New Theatre in 1860, FILIP VON SCHANTZ (1835–

1865), was a native Finn. When construction of the playhouse began, the farsighted decision was taken to train Finnish musicians for its orchestra. Von Schantz and six other Finnish musicians received an imperial scholarship to study at the Leipzig Conservatoire from 1857 to 1860. These musicians formed the new orchestra's domestic core, which continued to be supplemented for many years by foreign musicians and assisting amateurs. The foundation for a permanent orchestra had been laid, however, and a period of theatre orchestras began in Helsinki. Besides playing at drama performances, von Schantz's orchestra gave notable concert series presenting the music of new names such as Gade, Liszt and Wagner.

Regrettably, von Schantz's orchestra was short-lived. The New Theatre burned down in 1863, and the conductor and musicians moved to Stockholm, where their evening concerts at the fashionable restaurant Berns Salonger gained considerable popularity. At the end of each concert, the orchestra played von Schantz's arrangement of the *Porilaisten marssi*, which later became the honour march of the Finnish Army. With its unusual syncopated rhythms, this served as the basis for later arrangements, including one by Robert Kajanus. Only one year later, however, von Schantz's orchestra moved on to Gothenburg and then to Copenhagen, where it was eventually disbanded. Von Schantz was one of the foremost Finnish musical talents of the 19th century, but his career, like that of many others, was cut short by irregular habits which contributed to his untimely death at the age of 30.

The language controversy between advocates of Swedish and Finnish frequently caused serious dissent within the music world, too, but in the 1870s it resulted in an unexpected flowering of one major music form, the opera. In 1872, Kaarlo Bergbom (cf. p. 200) founded the Finnish Theatre, forerunner of the Finnish National Theatre, as a Finnish counterpart to the Swedish-language New Theatre. A music-lover and opera fan,

Bergbom founded a 'singing department' at his theatre, i.e. the Finnish Opera. In fact the theatre's main emphasis was on opera throughout its first period of operation, from 1873 to 1879 (cf. p.200).

It may seem surprising that opera, still branded an 'elite art' a hundred years later, should have been more popular among the public than spoken theatre. The reason was that Finnish-language drama was still in its infancy in terms of both actors and repertoire. It was easier for Bergbom to find excellent singers to attract audiences. His star performers included Emmy and Sofie Strömer, Ida Basilier, Alma Fohström, L.N. Achté (who also conducted the opera orchestra), Bruno Holm and the popular visiting Czech tenor Josef Navrátil. The first operatic premiere, in November 1873, was Donizetti's *Lucia di Lammermoor*. All in all, the Finnish Opera performed some 30 works in Finnish, offering the public the entire opera canon of the period with the exception of Wagner.

The language controversy, which had spawned the first flowering of Finnish opera, also proved its downfall. The New Theatre and its orchestra arranged competing opera and operetta performances in Swedish. Helsinki was a small town and lacked the population base to provide sufficient audiences for two opera companies. They foundered as a result of financial problems, and Finland had to do without a permanent opera company for many long years. The international opera houses, however, now discovered Finnish singers. L.N. Achté married his primadonna Emmy Strömer, and their two daughters Aino Ackté and Irma Tervani both made international careers in the opera.

One of Bergbom's pet projects was a new opera in the Finnish language. He wrote a synopsis for a libretto based on the 16th-century legend *Elinan surma* (The Death of Elina), and in 1870 approached ERNST FABRITIUS (1842–1899) about setting it to music. Fabritius had studied violin, piano and conducting at the Leipzig Conservatoire at the same time as von Schantz. He composed the third Finnish violin concerto (1878), and also composed a concert overture and overtures to the plays *Fiesco* and *Maria Stuart*, the latter of which was performed in 1881 but later lost. Fabritius also completed two movements of a symphony, which were performed in a concert in 1878, but the score of this work, which was never finished, was also lost. The musical idiom of Fabritius's chamber works and songs reflects the first influence of Schumann, Chopin and even Tchaikovsky in Finnish music. With his experience in composing for the stage, he might have had the makings of an opera composer, but Bergbom's plan was foiled by his inability to find a "nimble versifier" to craft a libretto in verse on the subject. The opera *Elinan surma* was eventually composed by Oskar Merikanto.

Fabritius was an accomplished violinist who had even given a concert in Stockholm, but he had to give up the idea of a solo career owing to a nervous disorder. He also relegated composition to a hobby after entering the agricultural sector; he was a pioneer of horse-breeding in Finland.

Orchestral conditions being what they were, no real tradition of orchestral composition developed in Finland in the 19th century. It was not enough for a composer to complete a score: like Pacius, he would usually have to assemble and rehearse his orchestra from the available forces, conduct the concert and perhaps even play the solo part, as Pacius and Fabritius did for their own violin concertos. There were only a handful of composers and works, and there was no genuine interaction between them. The first Finnish symphony was composed in 1847 by AXEL GABRIEL INGELIUS (1822–68), but it was no more than a historical curiosity. Although it contained a movement entitled *Scherzo finnico*, based on Kalevala meter in 5/4 time, there was nothing particularly Finnish about the music itself, and Ingelius's treatment of the orchestra was amateurish. On the other hand, he made a notable contribution as a pioneer of Finnish music criticism (in Swedish). He was filled with patriotic zeal, and set a number of Finnish poems to music, but was unable to attain even the hint of a national expression achieved by Pacius with the skilful use of local colour.

Pacius's son-in-law KARL COLLAN (1828–1871) easily surpassed Ingelius as a song composer, although he too was an amateur composer. A scholar with a broad range of interests, Collan wrote his doctoral thesis on Serbian folk poetry, and served as lecturer of German at the University of Helsinki and, until his death, as the university's librarian. He also produced the first translation of the *Kalevala* into Swedish. Besides the Swedish poems of Topelius and Runeberg, Collan set a handful of Finnish poems, but his most accomplished songs are settings of German poetry, notably that of Heinrich Heine. Collan may be said to have imported into Finland the Romantic lieder tradition of Schubert, Schumann and Mendelssohn.

KONRAD GREVE (1820–1851), like Pacius a German, was a better orchestral composer than Ingelius. He came to Turku in 1842 as a music teacher and director of the Turku Music Society orchestra, but returned to Leipzig in 1845 and again in 1846–47 to continue studying the violin (with Ferdinand David) and conducting. During his last years in Turku, he concentrated increasingly on composition. He composed several *Singspiele* to texts by the Turku author Nils-Henrik Pinello, which had popular success in both Turku and Helsinki. The well-orchestrated overture to the play *Sommarnatten* (Summer Night; 1847), Beethovenian in spirit, still holds its own in the concert repertoire.

A late 19th-century Finnish composer of exceptional promise was ERNST MIELCK, who was born in Viipuri (Vyborg) in 1877 and died in Locarno, Switzerland in 1899, two days before his 22nd birthday. Mielck was sickly even as a child, and ordinary school was out of the question for him. Considering that he was only allowed to begin learning the piano at the age of ten, his musical development was astoundingly rapid. He devoted himself heart and soul to music, taking little interest in the outside world, apart from the Dreyfus affair and a couple of pretty cousins who were the object of his boyish dreams.

Music and art were practised by all the members of Mielck's wealthy upper-middle class family. His mother Irene was the sister of Ernst Fabritius and had studied singing. In 1891, at the age of fourteen, Mielck was sent to Berlin, where the renowned Stern Conservatoire accepted him as a student. In 1895–96 and 1897–98 Mielck studied privately with Max Bruch in Berlin, and even became something of Bruch's favourite student. Before this, Mielck had made his debut as a pianist at home, playing Mendelssohn's Concerto in G minor and Tchaikovsky's Piano Trio. His real breakthrough came at a concert conducted by Robert Kajanus in 1897, at which Mielck's String Quintet and Symphony in F minor were first performed and the composer played the solo in Grieg's Piano Concerto. The symphony, as the first Finnish work of professional quality in the genre, attracted particular attention. At the time, Sibelius had yet to compose his first symphony proper, and Ingelius's effort had been long forgotten. The high point of Mielck's career came with a concert of his works in Berlin in December 1898, with Josef Rebiček conducting the Berlin Philharmonic. The programme consisted of Mielck's Symphony, the *Dramatic Overture* and the new *Konzertstück* for piano and orchestra, with the composer himself playing the solo. The concert received generally favourable reviews, and thus helped Mielck get most of his printed works published in Germany.

His long-dormant disease, lymphatic tuberculosis, broke out in spring 1899. An operation failed to improve matters, but Mielck was nevertheless sent to a convalescence home in Switzerland. There the disease spread fatally to the lungs. He was buried in Locarno on his 22nd birthday.

Virtually Mielck's entire musical oeuvre was composed in the

**Ernst Mielck
(1877–99).**

space of four years. Technically it displays sure taste and precocious maturity. Stylistically, however, his music remains firmly rooted in a rather conventional Classical-Romantic tradition. With his Classicist and rather Nordic orientation, Bruch must have been the ideal teacher for the young composer. Mielck did not live to take a stand on the musical reforms of his era or to the budding National Romantic movement, and his main stylistic models, apart from Bruch, were Beethoven, Mendelssohn, Chopin and Brahms.

Owing to his premature death, Mielck's early promise remained unfulfilled. Although there is no way of telling what he might have achieved had he lived longer, we may point out that at the same age Sibelius had not yet achieved anything comparable. Mielck has a place of honour as the first Finnish symphonist and the first Finnish composer to have had a concert of his works performed in Berlin.

"Finland can be considered to have entered its musical maturity in 1882", Toivo Haapanen writes in *Suomen säveltaide* (Finnish Music; 1940). That year saw the founding of the music institute and the first permanent symphony orchestra, the two main pillars of musical infrastructure. There was still a long wait, however, for the founding of the third pillar, the opera. On the other hand, church music had a well-established tradition in Finland.

The annals of Finnish music history never fail to cite the epochal significance of the founding in 1882 of the Helsinki Orchestra Society (known since 1914 as the Helsinki City Orchestra, or Helsinki Philharmonic) by ROBERT KAJANUS (1856–1933, cf. p. 170) and of the Helsinki Music Institute (renamed Helsinki Conservatoire in 1924 and Sibelius Academy in 1939, Finland's only tertiary institution of music education) by MARTIN WEGELIUS (1846–1906). A measure of hindsight or historical fallacy is involved here, however. At the time, no one could have known that these institutions would prove any more permanent than the many previous attempts to establish an orchestra or music school. For its first thirty years, Kajanus's orchestra was buffeted by one crisis after another, and at times the conductor himself answered for its finances. Drama performances were the principal source of income for many years; to this extent, the ensemble did not differ in any way from the earlier theatre orchestras. The Helsinki Philharmonic was the Finnish National Opera's house orchestra until 1963, when the Opera's own orchestra was founded. The Opera itself had to await construction of an opera house of international standard until 1993.

Wegelius's music institute also had a very modest beginning, and the founder himself patriarchally supervised all of its activities down to the smallest detail. Nonetheless, there is some justification for the claim that in effect the institute was a conservatoire right from the start, as Wegelius had made a close study of several well-established conservatoires on the Continent, and organized his own institute along the same lines. A reform of international significance was his introduction of systematic solfège and music analysis, which were little used in Continental schools at the time. Wegelius also wrote textbooks on solfège, music analysis, thoroughbass and harmony, and the first comprehensive history of Western music to be written in the Nordic countries (*Hufvuddragen af den västerländska musikens historia från kristna tidens början till våra dagar*, 1891–93). At the end of his history, he notes that "the history of Finnish music will have to be made before it can be written". Thus, he did not consider that Kajanus or Sibelius had made

The 'Paris orchestra' of the Helsinki Philharmonic Society in 1900, under the baton of Robert Kajanus.

Finnish music history yet, nor did he admit that there had been professional music-making in Finland, too, since the 'beginning of the Christian Era'.

For the infrastructure of Finnish music, at any rate, it was vital that the two institutions were now headed by native professionals – ever since von Schantz's time, the theatre orchestras had been directed mainly by foreigners. Thus 1882 was the year in which the foundation for a national Finnish music culture was laid.

Relations between the institutions of Wegelius and Kajanus were not always untroubled. Wegelius had planned to finance his institution by arranging orchestral and chamber music concerts, which naturally competed with Kajanus's concerts. Kajanus countered by setting up an orchestra school for his own ensemble. Both men were also composers. Although Kajanus's creative achievement was overshadowed by his conducting career, which lasted half a century (1882–1932), he may still be considered the most prominent Finnish composer before Sibelius, particularly in the field of orchestral music. While studying in Leipzig from 1877 to 1882 (with H. Scradiek, E.F. Richter, K. Reinecke and S. Jadassohn) and in Paris in 1879, Kajanus met Grieg, Sinding and Johan Svendsen; the latter was his teacher and later a personal friend. Kajanus espoused Svendsen's National Romantic aspirations, reflected particularly in the use of folk themes in his compositions. In Svendsen's spirit, Kajanus applied Finnish themes and folk tunes to the orchestral works *Kullervon kuolema* (The Death of Kullervo; 1880) and *Suomalainen rapsodia* (Finnish Rhapsody) nos. 1 (1881) and 2 (1886). His most notable work, however, was the nationalist-Wagnerian symphonic poem *Aino* (1885) for orchestra with final chorus, composed to celebrate the 50th anniversary of the *Kalevala*. This work provided the impetus for Sibelius's compositions on *Kalevala* themes. Despite their rivalry as composers, Kajanus devoted himself as a conductor to presenting Sibelius's music, which he conducted frequently both in Finland and abroad. His recordings of Sibelius's works in London 1931 are considered authentic documents of the original performance tradition.

Thus Finland had established its basic music institutions. Institutions, however, do not generate music; they merely provide a framework and a soundboard for its creation. The fact that a young man who was to be one of the greatest composers of our century entered Wegelius's institute only three years after its founding was a fortunate but unforeseeable coincidence. It was no coincidence, however, that the first continuous national tradition of creative music should arise from the institute's sphere.

Sibelius and His Contemporaries
Jean Sibelius

The Nordic countries have given the world two composers with an unchallenged position in the basic international repertoire: Norway's Edvard Grieg and Finland's Jean Sibelius. The latter's Danish contemporary Carl Nielsen was a notable symphonist, but his position has never become so widely consolidated. Some thirty recordings have been made of Sibelius's complete symphonic oeuvre, and his Violin Concerto is the most frequently recorded 20th-century work in its genre.

JEAN SIBELIUS (1865–1957) grew up in a Swedish-speaking home, but gained a solid knowledge of the Finnish language and culture at his school, Hämeenlinna Lyceum. He began studying the violin at the age of 15. He performed with his sister Linda (piano) and his brother Christian (cello), and was already composing chamber music, mostly in a Viennese Classical style, as a schoolboy. He familiarized himself with the various techniques of composition from A.B. Marx's classic German textbook, which he discovered in the school library.

Having completed his baccalaureate in 1885, Sibelius went to Helsinki to study; there, violin studies at the music institute soon got the upper hand over law studies at the university. His primary goal was to be a great violinist. The crucial influence of these years, however, was that of Ferruccio Busoni, who was the institute's piano teacher at the time. Through Busoni, Sibelius gained contacts in the international music world, and in later years Busoni was a dedicated champion of his music. In contrast, Sibelius was not particularly close to his own teacher, Martin Wegelius.

Performances of Sibelius's Suite for String Trio and String Quartet in A minor at the Institute's concert in spring 1889 attracted attention, and he received a grant for studying abroad. Paradoxically enough, the main outcome of his studies in Berlin (1889–90; Albert Becker) and Vienna (1890–91; Robert

Fuchs, Karl Goldmark) was to make Sibelius more deeply aware of the importance of his national culture and language. He immersed himself in the world of the *Kalevala*, and started work on the *Kullervo Symphony*. The premiere of this work in Helsinki on April 28, 1892 may be considered to mark the beginning of a national Finnish musical language. In June that year, Sibelius married Aino Järnefelt, the daughter of a cultivated family well-known for championing the Finnish cause. For their honey-moon, the young couple travelled to Karelia to collect folk tunes.

In Vienna, Sibelius was impressed by Bruckner, traces of whose Third Symphony can be heard in *Kullervo*. Later he was influenced by Wagner, whose principal operas he saw at Bay-reuth and Munich in 1894. He even planned to compose an opera called *Veneen luominen* (The Making of a Boat) in Wag-nerian spirit. As the spell weakened, however, he became more critical of Wagner, turning instead to the Neo-Germanic sym-phonic poem represented by Liszt. Sibelius transferred some of the material for the projected opera to the *Lemminkäinen Suite*, which was premiered at a concert of his works in 1896. As early as 1892, he had composed the Symbolist-inspired *En saga* (*Satu* in Finnish), which he revised in 1902. Prompted partly by the sharp criticisms voiced by Karl Flodin in a review of the revised version of *Lemminkäinen* in 1897, Sibelius decided to withdraw the first two movements of the suite as well as the whole *Kullervo Symphony* from public performance. The symphony became something of a legend to later generations; it was not performed again in full until after the composer's death. His orchestral ballad *Skogsrået* (The Wood Nymph; 1894) was also forgotten.

In the 1890s, Sibelius taught violin and music theory at the Music Institute and at Robert Kajanus's orchestra school, and in 1896–97 he was acting lecturer of music at the University of Helsinki, where his duties included composing and conducting

Jean Sibelius as a young student.

cantatas for coronations and academic ceremonies. The post then came up for application, and Sibelius gave a demonstration lecture which is the only surviving document from his own pen concerning his aesthetics, particularly his views on tonality and the relationship between art music and folk music. Unexpectedly, the lectureship went to Kajanus, but as a form of compensation the government awarded Sibelius an annual grant from 1898 on, later commuted into a regular pension. This provided a measure of security to the composer, but did not solve the financial problems which plagued Sibelius throughout his active years as a result of his impulsive, aristocratic lifestyle.

The incidental music to *King Christian II*, a play by Sibelius's writer friend Adolf Paul, was a popular success and aroused the interest of the German publisher Breitkopf & Härtel. A concert of Sibelius's works in 1899 featured his First Symphony and the

Song of the Athenians, an allegorical work which fired patriotic enthusiasm at a politically difficult time. At the very end of this year, Sibelius composed music for a pageant for the Finnish press celebrations. Under the name of *Finlandia*, the closing section became the leading symbol for Finland's national aspirations.

In 1900, Sibelius accompanied the Helsinki Philharmonic as second conductor on a foreign tour that culminated at the Paris World Fair and featured many of his works. Through the efforts of Baron Axel Carpelan, Sibelius received financial support which enabled him to resign his teaching post at the Music Institute in 1901 and to travel to Italy, where he started work on the Second Symphony. That summer Sibelius conducted *Tuonelan joutsen* (The Swan of Tuonela) and *Lemminkäisen kotiinpaluu* (Lemminkäinen's Return) in Germany. The Second Symphony was a resounding success at a concert of Sibelius's new works in March 1902, which was received as an event of national importance. His incidental music to Arvid Järnefelt's play *Kuolema* (Death; 1903) included the *Valse triste*, which became his best-known work along with *Finlandia*. This piece alone would have sufficed to ensure him a comfortable income if the copyright system had been what it is today.

The first performance of the Violin Concerto in Helsinki in 1904 was not a success. Again, Flodin criticized the work severely, inducing Sibelius to revise it. Even the premiere of the revised version in Berlin in 1905 under the baton of Richard Strauss failed to secure its breakthrough, and the work's true stature, like that of Beethoven's Violin Concerto, was not revealed until decades after it had been composed. Otherwise, however, Sibelius was beginning to make headway abroad. In 1905 Sibelius concluded a contract with a new German publisher, Robert Lienau, and at the end of that year he made his first concert tour of Britain. In 1906 Sibelius conducted the premiere of *Pohjolan tytär* (Pohjola's Daughter) in St Petersburg.

His music was also beginning to be performed in the United States.

In autumn 1904 the family had moved to a new house, Ainola (designed by the prominent architect Lars Sonck) in Järvenpää. Ainola became Sibelius's permanent home; after his death, it was transformed into a museum. The first major work to be composed there was the Third Symphony, first performed at a composer's concert in 1907. Sibelius also conducted the symphony in St Petersburg and Moscow, but its modernist tendencies met with mixed reviews. The work was strongly criticized after a performance in the United States in 1908, whereas a performance conducted by the composer during his second tour of Britain had a more favourable reception. In spring 1908, Sibelius underwent an operation for a throat tumour in Berlin, and he was compelled to abstain from tobacco and alcohol for many years.

During his third visit to Britain in spring 1909, Sibelius met Debussy and started work on the string quartet *Voces intimae*, which he completed in Berlin. A trip with his brother-in-law Eero Järnefelt to the Koli hills in eastern Finland that autumn provided the first impetus for the Fourth Symphony, which received its premiere at a concert of Sibelius's works in spring 1911. The public failed to appreciate the gloomy, modernistic impression made by the work. Sibelius conducted repeat performances in Helsinki in 1912, in Birmingham on his fourth tour of Britain, and in Copenhagen, but the reviews were uniformly unfavourable. At the end of the year, the Vienna Philharmonic refused to perform the symphony, which had already been announced on the programme. The audience whistled at the end of a performance conducted by Wilhelm Stenhammar in Gothenburg in 1913, and when Walter Damrosch conducted the work in New York, the critics wrote that "Sibelius had joined the Futurists".

In 1914, having been commissioned to compose *Aallottaret*

(The Oceanides; 1914) for the Norfolk Music Festival, Sibelius made his only visit to the United States. During this journey, he received an honorary doctorate from Yale University and, *in absentia*, from the University of Helsinki. An extensive American tour planned for the following year had to be cancelled on account of the war, which also hampered Sibelius's contacts with his German publishers. He received the honorary title of professor in 1916.

In the summer of 1915, however, Sibelius visited Gothenburg. His 50th birthday concert in Helsinki in December that year was a national event, featuring the premiere of his Fifth Symphony and the first Finnish performance of *Aallottaret*. Robert Kajanus made a speech at the gala dinner, giving this classic description of Sibelius's arrival on the Finnish music scene: "Barely had the barren soil begun to be tilled when a tremendous roar was heard from the virgin forests. Away with the hoes and spades! The mighty spring flood of Finnish music gushed forth. Single-handed, Jean Sibelius cleared the path." The composer himself, however, was not happy with the symphony, and conducted a revised version in Turku the following year. This version has been lost. Still dissatisfied, Sibelius continued to make revisions to the Fifth Symphony in the years that followed, while also working on his Sixth and Seventh Symphonies.

The Finnish Civil War of 1918 was a matter of strong personal concern for Sibelius, who had composed the *Jaeger March* for the ultimately victorious White side. He had to spend some of the war months in Helsinki, controlled for a time by the Reds, who also searched his home in Ainola. After the war, the death of Carpelan in 1919 was a deep shock for Sibelius, and he completed the revision of the Fifth Symphony in part as a tribute to his friend's memory. The final version was heard at a composer's concert in November that year.

The early 1920s saw little in the way of new music by

Sibelius. He made his fifth and last visit to Britain in February-March 1921. The tour comprised eight concerts in different cities; in London, he met Busoni for the last time. He followed up the tour with a visit to Oslo. The Sixth Symphony was premiered at a concert of Sibelius's works back home in February 1923, and he conducted the work on his first visit to Stockholm in March that year. He also gave a concert in Rome in March, and in April made his third and last visit to Gothenburg. The Seventh Symphony received its first performance under the composer's baton in Stockholm in March 1924, and that autumn he had five sold-out concerts in Copenhagen. No new works were heard at Sibelius's 60th birthday concert, conducted by Kajanus in Helsinki in 1925.

Sibelius did not conduct or even attend the first performances in 1926 of his last major works, the incidental music to *The Tempest*, commissioned by the Royal Theatre of Copenhagen, and *Tapiola*, commissioned by the New York Symphony Society. He gave his last concert abroad in Copenhagen that year. He completed his last numbered opuses in 1929, opp. 114–116 for violin and piano, and a work for violin and string orchestra – presumably marked as op. 117 – that was not performed until the 1990s. He had started work on his Eighth Symphony, which was impatiently awaited by the entire music world, at least by 1927, and a copyist's receipt for clean-copying the first movement, dated 1933, has been preserved. Unable to cope with the expectations, Sibelius burned the symphony and a number of other manuscript scores in the Ainola fireplace sometime in the 1940s.

The long years during which Sibelius published no new works came to be referred to as "the silence of Järvenpää". He appeared in public for the last time at a Council of State concert held in honour of his 70th birthday in 1935. His 90th birthday celebrations in 1955 have been referred to as the greatest public homage ever paid to a living composer. Sibelius died of a

Jean Sibelius at the Nordic Music Festival in Copenhagen, 1919. Left to right: Frederik Schnedler-Petersen, Robert Kajanus, Jean Sibelius, Georg Hœberg, Erkki Melartin, Wilhelm Stenhammar, Carl Nielsen, Johan Halvorsen.

cerebral hemorrhage on September 20, 1957. He was given a State funeral and buried on the south-facing slope of Ainola's garden.

Compared with many of his contemporaries, Sibelius had a dual role to fulfil. First, he invented the national language of Finnish art music. This achievement alone would have sufficed to ensure him a place in the history of Finnish and European music. In his later works, however, he also produced his own synthesis of the international trends of the age. Sibelius's Third and Fourth Symphonies were received as Modernist music. In his mature works, he was able to transcend the limitations of the National Romantic style and achieve universal stature.

Not even in his most intrinsically Finnish work, the *Kullervo Symphony*, did Sibelius use unadulterated folk melodies, but the style of his music was strongly influenced by the modality of ancient Finnish folk music, its endless reiteration of melodic motifs, its restricted ambitus, and the rhythm of *Kalevala* verse – somewhat in the same manner as primitive Russian folk music later influenced the music of Stravinsky. All these were national features, but international influences were also at work in the *Kullervo*. Sibelius wished to bring Finnish mythology to life in his music, just as Wagner had revived the Germanic myths in his gigantic dramas.

By the time of the First Symphony, Sibelius had surmounted his Wagnerian crisis – a disorder that affected almost all the musicians of the time. The stylistic impulses of this work rather seem to suggest Tchaikovsky; however, Sibelius's work has no specific programme, although it adheres to the universal Late Romantic conventions. Perhaps as a result of his contact with Italian culture, the music of Sibelius begins to reveal a Classicist tendency from the Second Symphony on. The organic relation between motivic metamorphosis and form which is so central to Sibelius's later music can already be detected in embryo in the opening movement of this work. On the other hand, the closing movement, a triumphant finale in sonata form, is still fully in accordance with the Romantic tradition.

The Third Symphony makes a clean break with all programme and, above all, National Romanticism. The public found this work – like the expressionistic Fourth Symphony, with its stylistic concentration reminiscent of chamber music – inscrutable and unapproachable. While the Third Symphony still concludes ceremoniously in C major, the disconsolate, submissive A minor chords at the close of the Fourth Symphony refuse even this concession. Thus, the audience at the composer's 50th birthday concert in 1915 was relieved to find that his Fifth Symphony, although continuing along Classicist lines, was an extroverted, radiant affirmation of life, with an almost cosmic dimension. The merging of the first two movements in the final version foreshadowed the form of the Seventh Symphony; in fact, Sibelius had already combined the scherzo and finale in the Third Symphony, thus turning his back on the formal conventions of the symphonic genre.

We may safely assert that Sibelius is the only contemporary master
who has the true Beethovenian pathos in his veins, the only one still
capable of symphonic thinking and using artistic material that is
suited to symphonic depiction. But the listener who goes to
a concert with a ready-made symphonic recipe in his pocket is
due for a disappointment, for Sibelius's symphonies have a form
of their own, one that arises from their content – as all artistic
form should do.

Thus wrote Leevi Madetoja, a former pupil of Sibelius, in conjunction with the maestro's 50th birthday. Since then, the name of Beethoven has come up time and again in discussions of Sibelius's music. This is justifiable to the extent that Sibelius, like Brahms, adhered to Beethoven's motivic-thematic treatment of the symphony, which had been overlooked by the Late Romantics. Wagner, his admirer Bruckner, and Mahler all followed the path of monumental programme music to which Beethoven's Ninth Symphony pointed the way. "A symphony should be like the world. It should comprise everything", Mahler, visiting Helsinki on a concert tour in 1907, said to Sibelius. For Sibelius, however, the essential elements of the symphony were "its severity and style and the profound logic that produces an inner bond between all melodic motifs".

In the history of the symphony, this inner logic essentially meant that Sibelius had abandoned the standard structures he still used in the early symphonies, and allowed form to build up on the terms of the thematic process. In the Seventh Symphony, this prompted him to abandon the conventional movements, merging them into a single whole. It would be a historical fallacy to consider this solution to have been Sibelius's final goal. For the composer himself, after all, not the Seventh but the Eighth was his last symphony, and the Eighth was again to have comprised several movements.

Sibelius was essentially an orchestral composer. Along with the symphony, the symphonic poem played an important part in his oeuvre. Although initially inspired by Liszt's example, he abandoned the detailed programme that was one of the conventions of the genre as developed by Liszt and Richard Strauss, being content to convey a general mood in his works. In a discussion with the folk music scholar A.O. Väisänen, Sibelius made a revealing comment on a work he was planning on the *Sampo*, the mythical source of riches in the *Kalevala*: "I'll do something on the subject yet. The most intriguing thing about the Sampo is that we don't know what it really is. Throughout the forging of the Sampo, the music must be heard pianissimo, as if at a great distance. Otherwise everything must be symphonically conceived. The composition shouldn't sound literary; the poem is only the starting point. What a fine motto is provided by the verses: 'Ennen päivän nousemista, Koijumalan koittamista!'* Koijumalan koittamista – what a wonderful colour that suggests!"*

Sibelius's early symphonic poem *Skogsrået* (The Wood Nymph; 1894, rediscovered in 1996) is still rather programmatic, being associated with the text of a melodrama of the same name by Viktor Rydberg. With its cosmic reflections, the symphonic fantasy *Pohjolan tytär* comes closest to Strauss's musical world. A related work is *Luonnotar*, a tone poem for soprano and orchestra, a nod in the direction of contemporary trends and a prototype for a new vocal-orchestral genre. The refined *Bardi* (The Bard) is associated with the world of the Fourth Symphony; *Dryadi* (The Dryad) and *Aallottaret* (The Oceanides) contain touches of Nordic Impressionism. The sym-

---

*"Now, before the day is dawnjng / Or the morning twilight glimmers." From *Kalevala. The Land of Heroes*. Transl. by A. F. Kirby, 1901.

phonic poems culminate in the almost monothematic *Tapiola*, whose simple basic motif could be taken as the ultimate refinement of rune singing. *Tapiola* is a counterpart to Debussy's *La mer*, a poetic summing-up of the essence of the forest. Sibelius's pantheistic feeling for nature is reflected by the fact that his landscape contains no human being, unlike Mahler's symphonies, which tend to be battlegrounds for an abstract hero, the composer's literary *alter ego*.

Sibelius's music for the stage, dictated by the subject of the play, has a more eclectic range, from the refined *salon* style of the *Karelia Suite* and *King Christian II* and the quasi-Orientalism of *Belshazzar's Feast* to the Impressionist premonitions of the late symphonies in *Pelléas et Melisande* and *Swanwhite* and the archaism of *Everyman*. As with the symphonic poems, Sibelius's crowning achievement in incidental music is his last work in the genre, the 35 numbers composed for *The Tempest*. For many years, until the first complete recording of the work was released in 1992, only the two orchestral suites arranged by the composer were known. Sibelius's most extensive through-composed work for the stage, the tragic pantomime *Scaramouche*, has also recently attracted notice thanks to a recording. On the stage this work suffers from the uneven quality of the libretto by the Danish author Poul Knudsen.

Chamber music was not prominent in Sibelius's oeuvre. The five-movement string quartet *Voces intimae* represents a departure from the conventions of the genre, to which the early, stylistically derivative chamber music works adhere. The numerous violin pieces by Sibelius include many gems, but also a number of rather neutral, salon-style numbers. The same goes for his compositions for piano, an instrument for which he had no particular fondness. Among them, however, the three austere sonatinas hold pride of place.

Solo songs constitute an important aspect of Sibelius's oeuvre, ranging from Nordic romances to grand, dramatic pieces. His settings of poems by Runeberg, which both open and close his song output, reflect the Swedish-Classical aspect of his personality which contrasted with the mythical Finnish aspect, that of "the apparition from the forest". The best-known Runeberg songs include *Våren flyktar hastigt* (Spring is soon gone), *Den första kyssen* (The first kiss), *Flickan kom ifrån sin älsklings möte* (The girl came from a tryst with her lover) and *Norden* (The North). The Finnish element is more central to his a cappella choral songs, which entirely transformed Finland's *Liedertafel* tradition of male quartets at the turn of the century. Sibelius used Finnish texts more frequently in the choral songs than in the solo songs. Examples include lyrical folk poetry, such as *Rakastava* (The lover), *Saarella palaa* (Fire on the island) and *Sortunut ääni* (The broken voice) from the *Kanteletar* anthology; *Terve, kuu* (Hail, Moon) and *Venematka* (Boat voyage) from the *Kalevala*; and *Metsämiehen laulu* (The forest dweller's song) and the delicate *Sydämeni laulu* (Song of my heart) by Aleksis Kivi.

Many Finnish composers have been thought to have "wilted under the shadow of the great oak tree". This was not so much Sibelius's doing as the result of the blind veneration which isolated him into a solitary aura of myth at an early date, and which made him the 'official' representative of Finnish music. Sibelius was too much of an individualist to have initiated a school of composers. Many Finnish and foreign composers who were influenced by him adopted mere superficial mannerisms from his music. A deeper influence has only made itself felt in recent years, with the discovery of the inner, structural originality of his musical thinking, independent of external style. Thus, after many Finnish composers who superficially imitated Sibelius, Joonas Kokkonen was the first who could be said to truly carry on a Sibelius tradition, expressed not in stylistic features but in symphonic structure.

Sibelius's reputation as a great composer was well-established in Britain and the United States by the 1930s, supported by several prominent conductors and critics such as Rosa Newmarch, Cecil Gray and Olin Downes. Sibelius's success in the Anglo-Saxon world is partly explained by the thinness and conservatism of its own music culture. An indigenous music culture was only beginning to emerge in the United States, which was reflected in a naive reception of Sibelius's music, overemphasizing the role of Finland's exotic nature. Britain, to be sure, had a well-established musical tradition, but no charismatic composers of its own. Sibelius offered a (relatively) safe alternative to the incomprehensible atonal and apparently superficial Neoclassical trends on the Continent.

In Germany and France, Sibelius met with a more critical reception, as his music was considered to represent a young national exoticism compared with these countries' ancient music traditions (to the Americans, this was a merit). Particularly acid were the comments of the influential philosopher and critic Theodor W. Adorno, who questioned Sibelius's very competence and thought his style outdated compared with Mahler and Schönberg. Adorno was echoed almost verbatim by René Leibowitz in a pamphlet published on the occasion of Sibelius's 90th birthday (!) and entitled *Jean Sibelius, le plus mauvais compositeur du monde*.

Sibelius's position on the Continent was problematic, as his music, which adhered to the principles of tonality, was overshadowed by what was thought of as New Music. As a symphonist, too, Sibelius suffered from the fact that composing symphonies was unfashionable both at the beginning and at the end of his career. Among more recent writers, the German scholar Carl Dahlhaus perceptively emphasized the special aesthetic position occupied by the group of composers who fell between the Late Romantics and the atonalists and Neoclassics, including Sibelius in this group of 'Moderns' mainly on the strength of his Fourth Symphony. In France, too, Sibelius has had champions (Marc Vignal, Henri-Claude Fantapié, Jacques Mercier), and a Sibelius symposium of Finnish and French scholars was held in Paris in 1993. The dimension of inner time in Sibelius's music, which is perceived as differing from that in Continental music, has attracted particular interest, surprisingly influencing both young French composers (Tristan Murail) and American Minimalists. The Danish composer Per Nørgaard began to take an interest in Sibelius as early as the 1950s. The rather static quality of Sibelius's music, once derided as "that perpetual tremolo", has turned out to have foreshadowed the concept of 'field' in contemporary music (e.g. that of György Ligeti). The range of international Sibelius research was shown by the First International Sibelius Congress, arranged by the University of Helsinki in 1990, which attracted some 30 scholars from fourteen countries (including Japan, which has a very active Sibelius Society). The Second Congress in 1995 had an even larger attendance, with a conspicuous role played by the young generation. Doctoral theses and other studies on Sibelius are published yearly in various parts of the world. The most tangible proof of the continuing interest in Sibelius's music is the proliferation of recordings of his works – including rarities, such as his early chamber music, *Skogsrået* and the first versions of the Violin Concerto, *En saga* and the Fifth Symphony. The Swedish BIS label is preparing the first recording of Sibelius's complete works.

The first analytical Sibelius studies in Finland were written in the 1940s by Eino Roiha and Ilmari Krohn. The first biography was published in 1916 by Erik Furuhjelm, and this was complemented by accounts written by Karl Ekman (1935) and the composer's long-time secretary Santeri Levas (1957/60). The turning-point came, however, with the publishing of the towering five-volume monograph (1965–88) by ERIK TAWASTSTJERNA (1916–93). Tawaststjerna was the first scholar to have access to

Sibelius's diaries and correspondence, which he supplemented with original sources from numerous collections and archives in Finland and abroad. His outstanding contribution, however, was a profound vision of the artist and the man, and his ability to place Sibelius in his proper context in European culture. A new wave of theoretical research is now rising in Finland, represented by Veijo Murtomäki's doctoral thesis (based on Schenker analysis) and many young scholars within the sphere of the Sibelius Academy. The catalogue compiled by Kari Kilpeläinen of the extensive collection of Sibelius manuscript scores in the Helsinki University Library has made a great deal of previously unknown material available for study. Fabian Dahlström, who has made a thoroughgoing study of Sibelius's oeuvre, compiled the first thematic bibliography of his works. A project of national significance is a critical edition of Sibelius's complete works, on which work began in 1996.

Contemporaries of Sibelius

Sibelius's brother-in-law ARMAS JÄRNEFELT (1869–1958) was a composer of elegant, lyrical pieces, whose composing was, however, overshadowed by his international career as a conductor (cf. p. 173). Järnefelt was chief conductor of the Royal Opera in Stockholm from 1907 to 1932 (court conductor 1911, first court conductor 1923); there he conducted, among other works, all of Wagner's operas except *Rienzi*. Already at the turn of the century he arranged notable private Wagner performances in Helsinki, where he returned in his old age to direct the National Opera and the Helsinki Philharmonic.

OSKAR MERIKANTO (1868–1924) surpassed even Sibelius in popularity. The simple, popular melodies of his songs were known throughout Finland. Merikanto himself contributed to this by frequently touring the country as pianist and accompanist, giving church concerts and inspecting organs. Merikanto's songs combined Finnish folk song features with lively, Italianate bel canto melody. Another factor in their success was that he consistently sought to set poetry written in the Finnish language. Although not really a dramatist, Merikanto was also a pioneer of Finnish opera. In fact he composed the first opera in the Finnish language, *Pohjan neiti* (The Maiden of the North; 1898, first performance in Viipuri 1908), as well as two further operas, the previously mentioned *Elinan surma* (1910) and *Regina von Emmeritz* (1920), and worked as an opera conductor. His son Aarre Merikanto was also a composer.

ILMARI KROHN (1867–1960) was a composer of esoteric religious music. Krohn is actually known better as the founder and first professor of musicology in Finland (docent at the University of Helsinki from 1900 to 1918 and professor from 1918 to 1935). Krohn developed a system for classifying folk tunes which Béla Bartók later made use of. In his textbooks on music theory, Krohn introduced into Finland the theoretical impulses of Hugo Riemann, Alfred Lorenz and Arnold Schering; as a

Oskar and Aarre Merikanto. Photo 1919.

result, a German orientation predominated in Finnish musicology for many years.

The most important Finnish composers born in the 1870s were ERKKI MELARTIN (1875–1937) and SELIM PALMGREN (1878–1951). The former, who was born and died in the same year as Maurice Ravel, made a career as director of the Helsinki Conservatoire, carrying on the work of Wegelius for a quarter of a century (1911–1936). Meanwhile, he

Erkki Melartin.
Caricature by H. Aspelin.

produced an extensive oeuvre covering nearly all the musical genres. Melartin composed his six symphonies more or less at the same time as Sibelius, but managed to remain remarkably free from his great colleague's influence. Instead, his symphonies reveal the influence of Mahler. Melartin was first in the Nordic countries to conduct Mahler's music, the Andante of the Second Symphony in Viipuri 1909. He also, however, absorbed impulses from Impressionism and even Expressionism (reflected in the Sixth Symphony and the piano sonata *Fantasia apocaliptica*). A complete recording of Melartin's symphonies in the 1990s attracted international interest. Melartin's *Marjatta Legend* for soprano and orchestra (1914) offered a rather modernist rendering of a *Kalevala* theme.

Melartin also composed a good many lighter pieces in salon style, including the first Finnish full-length ballet *Sininen helmi* (The Blue Pearl; 1930). This work and the incidental music to *Sleeping Beauty* recall Tchaikovsky's ballet music. The latter work contains one of Finland's favourite wedding marches. In contrast, Melartin's two-act opera *Aino* (1908) is one of the most consistently post-Wagnerian Finnish compositions.

Melartin travelled widely, visiting India, North Africa and

Egypt. He conducted his own works throughout the Nordic countries and in Russia and Berlin, where he gave a successful performance of his works with the local Philharmonic in 1923. Melartin's broad-ranging interests extended from literature, art history and anthroposophy to photography, the raising of exotic flowers and painting (he gave two public exhibitions of his paintings).

After Selim Palmgren had played his Second Piano Concerto at the Nordic Music Festival in Copenhagen in 1919, the critics styled him "the Crown Prince of Finnish music". He was also called, variously, the Chopin or Schumann of the North. These epithets underline the Romantic element in his piano music, but Palmgren was also said to be the composer who first brought Impressionism to Finland. This somewhat contradictory image contains one unifying factor: the piano. A brilliant pianist, Palmgren decided to make piano music his own territory, especially as Sibelius had neglected the genre somewhat. Palmgren never composed a single symphony, and few other independent orchestral works; instead, he produced five piano concertos (No. 1 in G minor 1903; No. 2, *Virta* (The River), 1913; No. 3, *Metamorfooseja* (Metamorphoses), 1916; No. 4, *Huhtikuu* (April), 1927 and No. 5 in A major, 1941) and a large number of pieces for solo piano. As the subtitles suggest, the concertos had a fantasia structure, except for the Fifth, which had a more classical, three-movement structure. The most popular of the concertos was the Second, the subtitle of which refers to the river Kokemäenjoki, which flows through Palmgren's home town, rather like the Vltava in Smetana's *Ma vlast*. One of the pianists to include this work in their repertoire was Ignaz Friedman.

Impressionist touches appear in the whole-tone scales and clavierist figuring of some of Palmgren's piano pieces, but in fact he cared little for French music – when in Paris, he composed *Chopin's Tomb*, not Debussy's. Nor does he make any reference to Debussy in his memoirs, whereas he writes extensively about the music and literary activity of Schumann.

Palmgren himself was a music critic for some twenty years. He studied in Germany, also attending Ferruccio Busoni's master classes in Italy, where he composed *24 Preludes* for piano (1907); he then focused on opera, composing *Daniel Hjort* (1910). This was something of a passing fancy, however; later on, Palmgren mainly cultivated choral and solo songs along with piano music. There were practical reasons for this: Palmgren served as director of the Helsinki University Chorus for some time, and in 1910 he married the singer Maikki Järnefelt, Armas Järnefelt's first wife. Their joint concerts and tours in Finland and abroad were highly popular. In 1919–20 they went on a tour of the United States, as a result of which Palmgren was appointed professor of composition at the Eastman School of Music in Rochester, N.Y. – a post previously offered to Sibelius, who had declined. After serving a five-year term at Eastman, Palmgren returned to Finland, where he taught piano at the Helsinki Conservatoire. When this institution was renamed the Sibelius Academy in 1939, Palmgren became its first professor of composition.

Although Swedish was Sibelius's mother tongue, his essential Finnishness was never questioned, and he rose far above all linguistic controversy. Among the composers referred to above, Järnefelt, Krohn and Merikanto were Finnish-speakers, but their impact as composers remained marginal. Thus a genuine Finnish-language music culture only arose with the following generation of composers born in the 1880s. Their champion was HEIKKI KLEMETTI (1876–1953) (see p.198), an ardent champion of the Finnish language and the leading choirmaster of the day, who translated a large number of choral works into Finnish and commissioned new works for his choirs from Finnish-speaking composers. Klemetti made several successful foreign tours with his choirs, including one to the United States.

The leading representatives of the new, Finnish-speaking generation of composers were TOIVO KUULA (1883–1918) and LEEVI MADETOJA (1887–1947), both unusual at the time in that they were 'men of the people' from modest social circumstances who had come to Helsinki from faraway, provincial Ostrobothnia. Another new feature was that although they both studied for a time in Germany, they were attracted most strongly to Paris.

Kuula spent the years 1909–10 in Paris, where the 'neo-French' school – including Debussy, Dukas, Chausson and Magnard – was a revelation to him. He wrote to his friend Madetoja that "Italy is a land of beautiful women, but a musical tomb", where one hears nothing but opera, and that the Germans made music by "counting, like our Krohn's forms, which are mathematics." In Paris, however, one "enjoys new, fresh and evocative music, which has enough reason in it, but for its reasoning calls upon new, lovely, wondrous motifs which bespeak ardent, blazing emotions. – In no other music in the world will you find anything so consummate and mature."

At a composer's concert in Helsinki in February 1911, Kuula presented the fruits of his stay in Paris. The programme included two legends for singers and orchestra, *Merenkylpijä-neidot* (The Bathers) and *Orjan poika* (The Slave's Son). This concert was acclaimed for its "total reform of old values", and the leading Finnish-speaking critic Evert Katila asserted that after this concert only one name rose above that of Kuula in Finnish music. The influence of Debussy's Impressionism is particularly strong in the symphonic legend *Impi ja Pajarin poika* (The Maiden and the Boyar's Son; 1911) for soprano and orchestra and even more so in the orchestral impressions *Metsässä sataa* (Rain in the Forest) and *Hiidet virvoja viritti* (The Goblins Lit Will-o'-the-wisps), both from 1913, the very titles of

Toivo Kuula (1883–1918)

which conjure up impressionist images.

To earn a living, Kuula worked as a conductor in Oulu (1910–11), Helsinki (1912–15) and Viipuri (1916–18). In 1914 he married the singer Alma Silventoinen, whom he had met when she was studying in Paris. Kuula composed most of his solo songs as well as the above-mentioned orchestral poems for his wife, and made concert tours with her that extended as far as St Petersburg, where he also appeared as a conductor. In addition to solo songs, Kuula also composed choral songs, the best of which have become classics of the Finnish repertoire.

Kuula's violent death in the aftermath of the Finnish Civil War in spring 1918 was a heavy blow to Finnish music. Dead at the age of 35, he had only gone through what would generally be considered a composer's first or early period. This is why the integration of Impressionist influences in his otherwise darkly Romantic musical idiom was never fully accomplished.

In his last years, Kuula worked on an extensive *Stabat mater* (Jacopone da Todi) for mixed chorus and orchestra. He never completed this work, to which his friend Madetoja put the finishing touches. The *Stabat mater* can be considered Kuula's masterpiece, and the well-known classical text should favour international performance.

Leevi Madetoja accomplished something in which his teacher Sibelius had failed: he produced a truly national Finnish opera. He was also the leading symphonist among the post-Sibelius generation. Having earned an academic degree from the University of Helsinki and completed his Finnish music studies with a composer's concert in autumn 1910, he followed in Kuula's footsteps to Paris, a city to which he would return time and again. Madetoja did not share Kuula's enthusiasm for Debussy, however; he was attracted towards the more classical style, based on the French symphonic tradition, of the Schola cantorum, whose chief representative was Vincent d'Indy. Madetoja had hoped to study with d'Indy, but their contact was restricted to one formal meeting. The musical and cultural impulses provided by the great metropolis proved all the more important, however. In 1913 Madetoja published an extensive series of articles on new French music in the *Uusi Suometar* newspaper. He was, indeed, one of the leading Finnish music writers of his time.

Like Kuula, Madetoja worked as assistant conductor in Helsinki from 1912 to 1914, then went on to become chief conductor in Viipuri (1914–16), a post in which Kuula succeeded him. Madetoja returned to Helsinki in 1916, where he taught the theory and history of music at the Music Institute, wrote reviews for the country's leading daily *Helsingin Sanomat*, and succeeded Kajanus as music lecturer at the University of Helsinki in 1926, a post he held until his death.

Madetoja's First Symphony (1916), composed in Viipuri, met with an enthusiastic reception, but his real breakthrough came with the Second Symphony in 1918. This monumental work was marked by the tragedy of war: grieved as he was by the death of Kuula, Madetoja was even more deeply shaken by the death of his brother at the hands of the Reds in spring 1918. A performance of this symphony in Copenhagen in 1919 laid the foundation for Madetoja's international reputation, and led to his first contract with the publisher Wilhelm Hansen.

In 1925 Madetoja spent six months in the small town of Houilles near Paris, composing his Third Symphony and the ballet pantomime *Okon Fuoko*, and writing a perceptive article on Maurice Ravel for *Helsingin Sanomat*. The symphony had its premiere in April 1926. Although the work was favourably received, the reviewers – comparing it with the more ambitious and demonstrative Second Symphony – failed to perceive its true significance. The Third Symphony is more Classical – although not Neoclassical – in expression, more balanced and elegant, but also containing complicated

**Leevi Madetoja
(1887–1947)**

polyrhythm and skilful counterpoint. It can hardly be called a National Romantic work; in fact, as Henri-Claude Fantapié has noted, it could well be subtitled *Sinfonia Gallica*.

Madetoja's greatest success, however, came with the opera *Pohjalaisia* (The Ostrobothnians), whose premiere at the Finnish Opera on October 25, 1925 could be compared with the reception of the Second Symphony of Sibelius. The work soon established its position as Finland's 'national opera'. In the following years, new productions were staged in Kiel, Stockholm, Copenhagen and Gothenburg, and by Radio Berlin. It has been a standby of the Finnish National Opera's repertoire ever since, both in Finland and on foreign tours.

Pohjalaiset showed Madetoja to be a born musical dramatist. He wrote his own libretto on the basis of Artturi Järviluoma's historical play, interspersing the tragic plot with lovely lyrical scenes as well as delightfully humorous elements. He skilfully wove into the music folk tunes originally collected by Kuula, with which the audience was already familiar from Järviluoma's play, and which thus made the work more readily understandable. *Pohjalaisia* was the first full-fledged Finnish opera in both the musical and the dramatic sense.

Madetoja's second opera *Juha* (1934, to a libretto already composed by Aarre Merikanto; first performed in 1935) was, if anything, even more accomplished in musical terms, although it never gained comparable popularity. Audiences may have been alienated by the symphonic overall approach. Madetoja's least successful stage project, however, was the previously mentioned ballet pantomime *Okon Fuoko* (1927, first performed in 1930), which suffers from Poul Knudsen's pseudo-artistic and confused libretto. This is a pity, for the work shows Madetoja at his boldest, approaching the style of his contemporary Modernist colleagues. Madetoja intended to produce two orchestral suites from the ballet music, but only completed the first.

In addition to operas and orchestral works, Madetoja composed a large number of choral and solo songs. International interest in Madetoja's choral works is restricted by the fact that, at Klemetti's urging, he set most of them to Finnish texts. Exceptions include a *De profundis* and Horace's classic *Integer vitae*. Madetoja composed a number of solo and choral songs to the poems of his wife L. Onerva.

The characteristic features of Madetoja's music are an uncompromising professionalism and substantiality which extends even to the most insignificant school songs and cantata commissions. His refined music may not affect the listener as directly as Kuula's extroverted, declamatory Romanticism, but a closer acquaintance with it is all the more rewarding. This no longer presents any difficulty, for Madetoja's chief works are available in relatively recent recordings.

Early Years of Independence
1920s Modernism

The First World War and the ensuing Civil War represented an upheaval after which everything in Finland had changed. In music, this was reflected in the emergence of the first generation of composers to abandon conventional tonality. Ernest Pingoud, Väinö Raitio and Aarre Merikanto formed the Modernist vanguard, although they could hardly be said to have represented a unified school. In contrast, Yrjö Kilpinen and Uuno Klami adhered to tonality – and thereby gained the greatest popular successes.

Modernism was first brought to Finland by ERNEST PINGOUD, a Russian émigré, in his first composer's concert in Helsinki in November 1918. Previous sources give his birth year as 1888, but in fact he was born in St Petersburg in 1887 – an error that he never bothered to correct. He died by his own hand in Helsinki in 1942.

Pingoud emigrated to Finland in 1918, fleeing the revolution, married, and worked for a while in Viipuri and Turku, until he was appointed superintendent of the Helsinki Philharmonic, a post he held until his death. He also intermittently ran his own and the Fazer concert agency, forming extensive international contacts in the music world.

A true cosmopolitan, Pingoud was an unusual phenomenon in Finnish cultural circles at the time. He may have been the only Finnish composer of the era who never produced a single composition inspired by the *Kalevala* or a choral song. Almost at the start, he had the audacity to announce in an article that "national art represented the infancy of all art", charged Finnish music with nationalistic self-assertion, and even cautiously criticized Sibelius himself; small wonder that his idealism was not always viewed with favour. Pingoud's music was virtually forgotten after his death, and has only come to notice again in recent years, during which he has been rehabilitated as a worthy member of the trio of Finnish Modernists.

From 1906 to 1911, Pingoud studied music, literature, philosophy and even geology at various German universities. His teachers included Hugo Riemann and, for three years, Max

Reger, who considered him to be one of his most talented pupils. While still a student, Pingoud began a notable career as a critic, sending 'musical letters' to the *St. Petersburger Zeitung* from Berlin between 1909 and 1911, and writing concert and opera reviews in St Petersburg from 1912 to 1914. A series of twelve essays entitled *Studien zur Musik der Gegenwart* (Studies on Contemporary Music) reveals that he was very well versed in the new musical trends of the era, of which he considered Richard Strauss and Scriabin to be the chief representatives, although he later took a more critical stance to them, as he did to Schönberg and Stravinsky. In Finland, Pingoud continued his writing career in Swedish – he evidently never learned Finnish well enough to publish in the language. A selection of his writings was translated into Finnish and published in 1995.

After his 1918 concert, Pingoud conducted concerts of his own works virtually every year in Helsinki until 1925, and in 1923 he also gave a successful concert in Berlin. He was essentially an orchestral composer; the backbone of his oeuvre consists of fifteen-odd symphonic poems and fantasias rather than his three symphonies and three piano concertos. The symphonic poems frequently had literary titles (*Confessions*, *La dernière aventure de Pierrot*, *Flambeaux éteints*, *Le prophète*, *Cor ardens*, *Narkissos*, *Le chant de l'espace*, *La flamme éternelle*) and sometimes even had mottos, but they were not programmatic in the sense that Strauss's works were. He was unanimously praised for his brilliant deployment of the orchestra, but reproached with going to extremes. His ballet *La face d'une grande ville* was the first work to represent urban 'machine romanticism' in Finnish music.

The native Finnish Modernists came close to sharing Pingoud's fate. Many works by both Raitio and Aarre Merikanto were either never performed during their lifetime or were performed so seldom that one can hardly speak of any reception for them at all. As a result, the 'Modern Project' recommenced afresh after the Second World War, while the pioneers of the 1920s were not revived until the '70s and '80s.

The best-known and most scandalous instance of neglect was the failure to perform AARRE MERIKANTO's opera *Juha* (1922), largely because Aino Ackté considered it too modern and passed the assignment on to Madetoja. Merikanto never heard a full performance of his opera in his lifetime, as it was first broadcast on the radio just two months after his death. The stage premiere took place in Lahti in 1963, but it was only in the late '60s and early '70s that the work's position as one of the most important operas to have been composed in the Nordic countries was established (Finnish National Opera 1967, Savonlinna Opera Festival 1970, Helsinki Festival and first recording 1972). Merikanto's vigorous and colourful score, which combines features of Expressionism and 'Finnish verismo', has been compared with the music of Janácek.

As the son of the well-loved Oskar Merikanto, it was natural, perhaps inevitable, that Aarre Merikanto (1893–1958) should adopt almost diametrically opposite stylistic ideals. Although personally averse to Modernism, Oskar Merikanto always warmly supported his son's ambitions, both intellectually and financially. He arranged for Aarre to become a student of Max Reger at the Leipzig Conservatoire in autumn 1912, at a time when he had barely started his studies in Finland. The main result of his two-year stint in Leipzig was the *Theme, 5 Variations and Fugue* for orchestra (1915; initially 9 variations), which the composer himself said was modelled on Regers' *Hiller Variations*. In the winter of 1915–16, Merikanto was a private student of Sergei Vasilenko in Moscow. As a result, heavy German polyphony gave way in his music to more colourful harmonies and orchestration, foreshadowing Merikanto's music in the 1920s, though without yet reaching maturity.

In Merikanto's case, the phrase '1920s Modernism' is unusu-

**Aarre Merikanto
(1893–1958)**

ally apt. He started work on *Juha* on January 2, 1920, and his peak creative years lasted virtually throughout the decade. Embittered by the fate of his opera, Merikanto destroyed or mutilated many of his scores, including that of his perhaps most important orchestral work, *Sinfoninen harjoitelma* (Symphonic Study; 1928). Merikanto's last student Paavo Heininen reconstructed this work in 1981. He did the same for the String Sextet, from the score of which the composer had cut out long passages. The most extraordinary fate was that of the Third Violin Concerto. The composer burned the score, which could thus no longer be reconstructed – yet Heininen accomplished even this miracle! He 'recomposed' the work, giving it the subtitle *Tuuminki* (Idea; from Merikanto's own comment: "What an idea that was!"). The premiere of Heininen's concerto took place at Merikanto's centenary concert in 1993.

Merikanto's greatest triumph during his lifetime was the *Schott Concerto* for nine instruments, which won a prize at an international competition for composition arranged by Schott & Söhne in 1924. Hermann Scherchen conducted the premiere at the Donaueschingen festival in 1925. This work represented a new genre, the chamber concerto, which the competition was specifically intended to promote. The finale contains the first twelve-tone chord in Finnish music. Even in his most radical works, however, Merikanto never went as far as to make consistent use of atonality or dodecaphony. He turned to a more conventional and traditional style from the 1930s on. The change has been explained with the incomprehension with which his music met and a general change in Finland's musical climate. One tangible impulse for Merikanto's new 'national colourism' and 'folk dance' style was undoubtedly provided by the *Kalevala* centenary in 1935, to which Merikanto contributed the orchestral work *Kyllikin ryöstö* (The Abduction of Kyllikki).

The last years of Merikanto's life were outwardly successful. He taught at the Sibelius Academy from 1936, and was appointed professor of composition in 1951. He also gained some intellectual recompense for previous neglect, and won several notable competitions. Nonetheless, his music from this period is not as unanimously acclaimed today as are the legendary works of the '20s.

A similar stylistic shift took place in the music of VÄINÖ RAITIO (1891–1945): he followed up his radical music of the '20s with a fairly conventional late period. Raitio contributed no less than two works to the *Kalevala* festivities in 1935, both based on folk tunes: *Lemminkäisen äiti* (Lemminkäinen's Mother) and *Neiet niemien nenissä* (Maidens of the Headland). In contrast to Merikanto's development, however, Raitio switched from orchestral music to opera, retaining his special stylistic characteristics. Considering that Raitio must have been aware of the fate of *Juha*, his choice seems all the more inexplicable. Nonetheless, he succeeded in getting two full-length operas based on historical themes staged, *Prinsessa Cecilia* (Princess Cecilia; 1933, first performed in Helsinki 1936) and *Kaksi kuningatarta* (Two Queens; Helsinki 1944). Friedrich Ege wrote a thoroughly approving review of the former work in the *Zeitschrift für Musik*:

Here in the remote North – a wholly different Europe, cut off from
the rest of the world – in a middle-sized city in a small country,
one can hear an utterly wonderful, a most modern and,
in the best sense of the word, a European opera!

Plans to stage the opera in Lübeck had to be shelved when war broke out. In Finland, too, both operas had very favourable reviews, but only had a handful of performances, They have never been revived since, and are thus virtually unknown to present-day listeners.

In some other respects, too, Raitio was the most enigmatic personality among the Finnish Modernists. Little is known about his life, apart from what he revealed shortly before his death in an autobiographical survey for the book *Suomen säveltäjiä* (Finland's Composers; 1945), edited by the composer and music writer SULHO RANTA (1906–60). After studying in Finland, Raitio, like Merikanto, went to Moscow, where the concerts of Serge Koussevitzky's orchestra seem to have inspired him more than his studies (with A. Ilyinski). The Muscovite influence can be detected in the works performed at the second and third concerts dedicated to Raitio's music in Helsinki in 1920 and 1921, including the orchestral poems *Joutsenet* (The Swans), *Nocturno* and *Fantasia estatica*. While the first two works contain Impressionist elements, the *Fantasia estatica* indubitably enters the world of Expressionism, thus heralding his most powerful works in the 1920s. Raitio may have received further impulses during a stay in Berlin from 1920 to 1921, but it is noteworthy that his principal Modernist works were all composed before his third foreign trip, to Paris in 1925–26. After this, Raitio settled in Viipuri to teach music. In 1933 he returned to Helsinki, and worked as a freelance composer for the rest of his life.

The main works of Raitio's Expressionist period include *Antigone* (1922), a 'colour poem in three movements'; *Kuutamo Jupiterissa* (Moonlight on Jupiter; 1922); *Fantasia poetica* (1923), a companion piece to the *Fantasia estatica*; and *Puistokuja* (Avenue in the Park; 1926, based on a poem by Elina Vaara) for soprano and orchestra, unperformed during Raitio's lifetime. The pungently Neoclassical miniature ballet *Vesipatsas*

(1929) is in an entirely different style. Raitio used to say: "Music is colour"; yet he denied having been "very greatly influenced by contemporary French music". Thus his style has proved hard to pin down. As a generalization, one might say that Raitio created his own, independent brand of Expressionism, for which it is difficult to show direct influences, whether German, Russian or French. A recording of some of Raitio's principal orchestral works was released in 1992.

Väinö Raitio (1891–1945)

The most unusual composer of the period, in stylistic terms, was YRJÖ KILPINEN (1892–1959), who concentrated almost exclusively on lieder. His reputation assumed downright heroic proportions in the 1930s, particularly in Germany but also in Britain; in his home country, he was made an honorary professor in 1942 and a member of the Academy of Finland in 1948. Kilpinen composed a gigantic oeuvre comprising some 800 lieder, and characterized by extensive cycles, each consisting of a single poet's texts. Indeed, it has been said that Kilpinen set poets rather than poetry to music.

Kilpinen's career was given a decisive boost by recitals dedicated to his music given by a number of renowned performers, including Helge Lindberg, a Finn (Vienna 1927), Gerhard Hüsch, a German (Cologne 1931, Berlin 1934) and the English singer Astra Desmond (London 1933). Kilpinen's German friends and champions also included the composers Paul Graener and Emil von Reznicek and the cellist Paul Grümmer.

From his earliest songs in Finnish, Kilpinen adhered to the

Yrjö Kilpinen
(1892–1959)

German lieder tradition, which bears a closer affinity to chamber music than to the solo song with accompaniment. On the other hand, these songs already reveal the composer's predilection for ostinato in the piano score, a feature hardly compatible with the 'symphonic sweep' some critics claim to detect in Kilpinen's song cycles.

From 1922 to 1926, Kilpinen had a period of Swedish poetry, during which his style crystallized. Witty and humorous elements are accompanied here by philosophical contemplation, expressed in tritone-based dissonances in the *Reflexer* (Reflexes) cycle to poems by Pär Lagerkvist.

The *Tunturilaulut* (Fell Songs) to poems by V.E. Törmären (12 songs in 1926 and a further 15 in 1928) display Kilpinen's distinctive style – comprising pedal points, open fourths, fifths and octaves and a thin, spare piano texture – at its freshest, as it does his genuine melodic inventiveness. The crucial work of his German period consists of the theosophic-mystical Morgenstern cycles (a total of 75 songs), which also reflect the influence of Mussorgsky. In the *Lieder um eine kleine Stadt* to texts by the dilettante poet Berta Huber (1942), Kilpinen returned to an idyllic style reminiscent of the early Schubert. His three Hesse cycles are austere and enterprising. In his last years, Kilpinen returned to Finnish poetry. The Expressionism of his Katri Vala cycle (1946) gives way to archaic stylization in the monumental *Kanteletar* cycle (64 songs op. 100, 1948–50). There has been some speculation that Kilpinen turned to the texts of the left-wing poet Vala after the war in order to dispel his wartime image as an admirer of National Socialism.

Stylistically, Kilpinen's music remained an isolated phenomenon, far removed from the topical Modernism of the era, but with its Neoclassical echoes not directly in the National Romantic mainstream either, even though Kilpinen himself considered that "to achieve international stature in art is possible only from a national foundation". He was completely averse to Impressionism, while the Expressionist tendencies of his music naturally had no connection with the aspirations of the Second Viennese School, branded in Germany as decadent art, *entartete Kunst*. Apart from ideological considerations, Kilpinen's success in Germany is explained in part by his revival of the German lieder tradition, which many had already given up for dead.

A Finnish Sacre

UUNO KLAMI (1900–1961) followed Kilpinen as a member of the Academy of Finland in 1959, but that is about the only link between the two composers. Klami may well have been the most brilliant orchestrator of all Finnish composers – including Sibelius – and he certainly had the strongest French orientation among them. Ravel and Stravinsky's Russian period were his greatest sources of inspiration, and his *Kalevala Suite* ranks as 'the Finnish *Sacre*'.

Like Madetoja, Klami came from a modest social background in the remote provinces. Both were 'born orchestral composers', and mastered the tricks of the trade without apparent effort. They ranked with Sibelius among Finland's 'fatherless' composers, who lost their fathers in infancy. When Klami's mother also died, he was left alone in the world at the age of 16. Immediately upon completing elementary school in 1915, Klami successfully applied for admission to the Helsinki Music Institute. His early chamber music works at the Institute's concerts from 1921 to 1924 aroused interest on account of their modernity and French orientation, also reflected in the titles of the movements. How Klami came to be captivated by French music is not known, but that being the case it was natural for him to make his first study trip abroad to Paris (1924–25), where he met Ravel and received instruction from Florent Schmitt. His formal studies there seem to have been minimal, however; more important was the rapt absorption of influences, particularly in the field of orchestral music. Stravinsky's *Sacre du printemps* and Prokofiev's *Scythian Suite* "shook him to the bone", as did de Falla's new Spanish style and Ravel's *Rhapsodie espagnole*, in Klami's words "the world's loveliest score". While in Paris, Klami composed his First Piano Concerto, which earned the trendy subtitle *Night at Montmartre* for its jazz touches. The greatest stir at the first concert of Klami's music in Helsinki in 1928, however, was created by the *Karjalainen rapsodia* (Karelian Rhapsody; 1927), which became one of his most popular works. His affirmative, lively, carefree use of folk music themes was completely at odds with the National Romantic tradition, and marked a decisive break with the influence of Sibelius.

Klami made his next study trip to Vienna in 1928–29. Paradoxically enough, the strongest influence on him there, too, was Ravel. Klami had already heard the composer conduct *La Valse* in Paris; it was again on the programme on Ravel's visit to Vienna. This work obviously served as a model for *Opernredoute*, which Klami composed in Vienna. Ravel's influence is also unmistakable in Klami's orchestral suite *Merikuvia* (Sea Pictures).

The detailed history of the *Kalevala Suite*, long considered Klami's chief work, only came to light quite recently. Klami originally planned it as an oratorio, then as a full-length stage work; at the 1933 premiere of the first, four-movement version, it was still called 'Choreographic Images from the Kalevala'. It

Uuno Klami (1900–61)

was not until ten years later that the final revised version, in five movements, was first performed. Later on, two later compositions have also been elevated to the status of 'chief works'. The oratorio *Psalmus* for soloists, choir, orchestra and organ ad lib, set to an old Finnish hymn text by Juhana Cajanus, suffered from the partial failure of the premiere in 1937, and was forgotten for decades, until revivals in the early 1960s and thereafter awakened critics to its significance as one of the greatest achievements in Finnish music. In this work, Klami broke free from his early allegiance to Ravel and Stravinsky. The same is true of his late, unfinished ballet *Pyörteitä* (Whirls), which is loosely based on the *Sampo* motif in the *Kalevala*. The piano score for the first act was unexpectedly discovered in 1985; until then, only Klami's orchestration of the second act had been known, and even that had never received a full concert performance. The first act, orchestrated by Kalevi Aho, was performed in 1988, and proved a picturesque masterpiece bursting with rhythm and colour, without precedent either in Klami's previous work or, indeed, in any Finnish music.

Klami's two symphonies (1938 and 1945) are somewhat rhapsodic in their treatment of form, and the composer himself admitted that symphonies were not his forte. The Violin Concerto (1943, revised version 1954) is more obviously linked with the Classical heritage. The ostensibly modest, Neoclassical Second Piano Concerto for piano and string orchestra (1950) has aroused deserved interest in recent years. Other notable orchestral works include the splendidly colourful overtures *Suo-*

menlinna (1940) and *King Lear* (1946), and *Nummisuutarit* (The Heath Cobblers; 1936), one of the wittiest works in Finnish music.

Among the 1920s Modernists, Klami gained the most prominent status and the widest popularity, owing to the colour and freshness of his music and his avoidance of theoretical debate. Even at its most sharply dissonant, his music never entered the realm of atonality or twelve-tone technique, and thus always remained approachable.

KALEVI AHO

FINNISH MUSIC IN THE POSTWAR YEARS

The Second World War: A Watershed

The Second World War marked a prolonged hiatus in Finnish art music. For Finland, the war fell into two main phases, the Winter War (November 30, 1939 – March 13, 1940), in which the Soviet Union attacked Finland, and the Continuation War (June 1941 – August 1944), during which Finland, allied with Germany, sought to reconquer the territory lost in the Winter War. At the an end of the war in 1944 Finland had to cede a large portion of Karelia and the Petsamo region in Lapland to the Soviet Union. The peace treaty also entailed ousting German troops stationed in Lapland from Finnish territory, leading to the 'Lapland War' against the retreating Germans from autumn 1944 to April 1945.

Few concerts were held during the war years, as the musicians and composers were serving in various duties, some of them entertaining troops at the front. Only few composers actually saw frontline service – although one who did was Einar Englund, who fought during the Continuation War in battles on the lighthouse island of Bengtskär, in eastern Karelia, and finally near the city of Viipuri.

The war years shook the very foundations of Finnish society. Although the atmosphere of that period is reflected directly in the works of only a handful of composers (including Englund), the war experience gradually led Finnish music away from national romanticism, and enabled Finnish composers to emerge from the shadow of Sibelius. After the war, many Finnish composers were impatient to catch up with the Continent's lead in new musical ideas. New trends followed one another in Finnish music in such rapid succession that several styles were always simultaneously present, and the general image of Finnish music has been pluralistic ever since the war. Some composers, such as Einojuhani Rautavaara, veered sharply from one stylistic ideal to another.

Main Trends in Postwar Finnish Music

The development of Finnish art music since World War II can be divided into three main periods. The first unified phase lasted from 1940 to around 1965. Its main gist was a progression from late romanticism (Tauno Pylkkänen, Ahti Sonninen) via neoclassical influences (Einar Englund, Joonas Kokkonen, Usko Meriläinen) to twelve-tone music (Erik Bergman, Paavo Heininen and others) and the avantgarde experiments of the early 1960s (the young Erkki Salmenhaara).

The second main phase, which began in the mid 1960s, followed a similar pattern. After a short-lived avantgarde and modernist period, composers again began to take an interest in tonality and stylistic pluralism, in some cases also in transcending the conventions of genre and in non-European musical cultures (Einojuhani Rautavaara, Aulis Sallinen, Pehr Henrik Nordgren, Kalevi Aho and the avantgarde composers of the early '60s). Stylistic liberation also fuelled the sudden rise to international prominence of Finnish opera. The key year in the 'Finnish opera boom' was 1975, which saw the successive premieres of Aulis Sallinen's *Ratsumies* (The Horseman) and Joonas Kokkonen's *Viimeiset kiusaukset* (The Last Temptations). The 1980s were marked by the 'second coming' of the modernist movement (Jukka Tiensuu, Eero Hämeenniemi, Kaija Saariaho, Jouni Kaipainen, Magnus Lindberg). This time, modernism held sway a good deal longer than before, and modernist aesthetics gained an almost institutionalized hold on Finnish composition.

The third phase in Finnish art music appears to have set in during the early 1990s, when many of the leading modernists of the '80s began to seek a new link with tradition; they can in fact no longer be classified unquestionably as modernists. A new, more permissive pluralism generally seems to have gained ground in the '90s, and composers again seem to be more concerned than they were in the '80s with their audiences and the reception of their music, and also with musical genres outside the realm of art music proper, such as light music, jazz and exotic cultures (e.g. Hämeenniemi, Juhani Nuorvala).

Stylistic Classification of Contemporary Finnish Composers

Since contrasting stylistic aspirations have existed side by side in Finnish music throughout the postwar period, the composers are divided below into no less than six main categories. The *traditionalists* are composers whose music is based primarily on motivic-thematic thinking. Their musical dramaturgy is also dynamic; in other words, their music always appears to be going somewhere, being based on the principle of establishing and building up tension, then releasing it. Among the technical discoveries of this century, the traditionalists have primarily confined themselves to methods of composition that were developed before the Second World War, have a well-established position in contemporary music, and have thus become part of our musical heritage. This classification therefore includes not only late romantics and neoclassics, but also many composers employing twelve-tone technique (dodecaphony).

The *modernists* are composers who have made use of the most recent techniques of composition developed after the war. Focusing on timbre rather than melody, they have sought to extend the dimension of sonority in their music. To achieve this, they may obscure the sense of progression in their music,

The Finnish Composers' Association was 50 years old in 1995. Participants at the gala dinner included Olli Kortekangas, Timo-Juhani Kyllönen, Eero Erkkilä, Kaija Saariaho, Harri Suilamo, Kalevi Aho, Markus Fagerudd, Jovanka Trbojević and Patrik Vidjeskog (front row, left to right); Pentti Raitio (standing behind Kortekangas); Magnus Lindberg, Einari Marvia, Einar Englund, Joonas Kokkonen, Usko Meriläinen, Erik Bergman and Mikko Heiniö (standing, first row). Tapio Louhensalo and Tapani Länsiö are standing behind Kokkonen, and Jarmo Sermilä peers out from behind Heiniö.

employ static dramaturgy (i.e., there is no musical progression at all), or combine static and dynamic dramaturgy. This group includes all those who use serial, aleatory and field techniques as well as composers specializing in electroacoustic music and those who use computer software as an aid to composition.

The *pluralists* occupy the middle ground between traditionalism and modernism; their music contains features of both groups. They may seek a broad stylistic synthesis in their works, and also sometimes make use of allusions or stylistic hints. They do not always seek an aesthetically pure, clearly defined style, but may base their music on 'the aesthetic of the impure'.

In contrast to the previously described groups, the *neo-traditionalists*, *neoexpressionists* and *neo-neoclassics* take modernist aesthetics as their starting point, from which they then return towards traditionalism, expressionism or neoclassicism. We will come back to these terms in connection with the individual presentations.

From Late Romanticism to Neoclassicism (1940–1960)

In the Footsteps of the Late Romantic Tradition

The 1930s Generation

Among the composers who produced most of their work in the postwar years, Helvi Leiviskä, Olavi Pesonen and Kalervo Tuukkanen made their debut just before the war, in the late 1930s.

HELVI LEIVISKÄ (1902–1982), the most prominent Finnish woman composer during the middle years of this century, studied under Erkki Melartin and later continued her studies in Vienna. Her principal works include three symphonies (1947, 1954 and 1971) and the *Sinfonia brevis* (1962). Her style is emphatically contrapuntal; the Third Symphony even abandons tonality. Strict mastery of form was her overriding concern. For a while Leiviskä's work fell into oblivion, but interest in her music has revived in the 1990s.

The bulk of the oeuvre of OLAVI PESONEN (1909–1993) consists of small-scale choral and solo songs, often in a late romantic style. In his principal works, two symphonies (1949, 1953) and the orchestral fugue *Fuga fantastica* (1948), Pesonen makes much use of polyphony, also weaving more modern, highly chromatic elements into his style. For many years, he was a leading maker of Finnish music policy – he was employed as chief inspector for music education at the National Board of

Kalervo Tuukkanen was a prime mover of the Finnish Composers' Association in its early days.

Education, and served two terms as chairman of the Finnish Composers' Association.

Pesonen's teacher of composition was Leevi Madetoja, who also taught KALERVO TUUKKANEN (1909–1979). Primarily an orchestral composer, Tuukkanen produced six symphonies (1944–78) and numerous works for choir and orchestra; among the latter, *Karhunpyynti* (The Bear Hunt) won a silver medal in the arts contests at the Olympic Games in London in 1948. He also composed two violin concertos, one cello concerto and the one-act opera *Indumati* (1962). Tuukkanen built upon the style of his teacher Madetoja, seasoning it with driving neoclassical rhythms reminiscent of Klami. Tuukkanen also applied the morphological theories of his second teacher Ilmari Krohn in a highly original manner, frequently seeking to call forth extra-musical associations with his music. In his sixth and last symphony (1978), he experimented with pure free tonality, employing a more contemporary idiom than in his previous works.

Like Pesonen, Tuukkanen was an influential public figure in his day: it was on his and Erik Bergman's initiative that the Finnish Composers' Association was founded, and Tuukkanen served for many years as its secretary. In the 1950s, he organized the first extensive recordings of contemporary Finnish music, the Fennica series. From 1967 to 1969 he was visiting professor of music in Hong Kong.

Postwar Traditionalists

The first major new composer to emerge after the war was TAUNO PYLKKÄNEN (1918–1980). A precocious talent, Pylkkänen concentrated on opera, composing his first opera *Bathseba Saarenmaalla* (Bathsheba of Saaremaa; 1940) at the age of 22, although he revised the work in 1960. This opera was based on a historical-mythical Estonian subject by Aino Kallas, as was the notable *Mare ja hänen poikansa* (Mare and Her Son; 1942–43) and the radio opera *Sudenmorsian* (The Wolf's Bride; 1950), which won third prize in the Prix Italia competition in 1950 and was broadcast in several European countries. The heroine of the latter work is Aalo, the wife of a forester, who leads a double life, spending her nights among the wolves and her days with her husband. Aalo is obliged to run away from home, but one night she returns to nurse her baby and see her husband; the poor, tormented man, egged on by the villagers, shoots her. In 1996 a stage version of this powerful one-act opera was performed at the Joensuu Festival in an arrangement for chamber orchestra by Hannu Bister. *Simo Hurtta* (1948), an opera in four acts, based on a historical theme from a work by Finland's most famous poet, Eino Leino. Pylkkänen's chamber opera *Varjo* (The Shadow; 1952) has been compared with the works of Giancarlo Menotti. The more populistic *Opri ja Oleksi* (1958) aroused widespread interest on account of its theme, the fate of the Karelian population evacuated to Finland after the war. The music legend *Ikaros* (Icarus; 1960) was followed by the notable TV opera *Vangit* (The Prisoners; 1965). Pylkkänen served as artistic director of the Finnish National Opera from 1960 to 1969.

Pylkkänen's music is characterized by a natural sense for operatic drama and easy, flowing melodies. He was sometimes called the 'verist' of Finnish opera. Many of his works have proved their mettle in recent revivals. Thus Pylkkänen helped pave the way for the Finnish opera boom that began in the

Several of Tauno Pylkkänen's nine operas have been revived successfully.

'70s. He composed several notable song cycles, including *Kuoleman joutsen* (The Swan of Death; 1943), *Kuunsilta* (Moonbridge; 1953) and *Visioner* (Visions; 1958), and also produced a great deal of orchestral, chamber, incidental and film music and the ballet *Kaarina Maununtytär* (1961). From the 1950s on, as new winds began to blow in Finnish music, Pylkkänen came in for harsh criticism from young critics for his adherence to the national romantic style. After his ninth and last opera, *Tuntematon sotilas* (The Unknown Soldier, 1967; with a libretto based on Väinö Linna's celebrated war novel), he stopped composing, perhaps in part because he felt that the times were alien to his musical ideals.

ERKKI AALTONEN (1910–1990) studied composition with Selim Palmgren in the 1930s, but his musical development was hampered by the war. Among his five symphonies (1947–64), the second, or *Hiroshima Symphony* (1949), inspired by the horror of the bomb, was an international success, and was performed in Hiroshima itself and several East European countries in the 1950s. The most important work of Aaltonen's later period is his Violin Concerto (1966), in which he abandoned tonality and experimented with twelve-tone technique.

AHTI SONNINEN (1914–1984) produced a large, varied and somewhat contradictory oeuvre, combining high patriotism and archaic features with more topical international trends.

After studies with Selim Palmgren, Sulho Ranta and Aarre Merikanto, Sonninen made his breakthrough immediately after the war with a Piano Concerto (1944–45) and the orchestral work *Sinfonisia tuokioita* (Symphonic Moments; 1946–47), the latter was in a bold modernist style unmatched in the works of other Finnish composers of the '40s. From the very beginning, Sonninen thought it his duty to bring out national values in his music. Many of his works are based on the *Kalevala*, ancient folk poetry and folk music, a case in point being the important cantata, *Lyökäme käsi kätehen* (Let Us Join Hands; 1948–49), with a text from the *Kalevala*. Among his finest works to be based on folk tunes is *Taivahan takoja* (Heaven's Forger; 1957), a pungent cycle of songs accompanied by instrumental ensemble. When the avantgarde arrived in Finland in the 1960s, Sonninen retreated into the past, composing a number of 'neoprimitive' works based on Finnish mythology, including the ritual opera *Karhunpeijaiset* (The Bear Feast; 1968).

Sonninen achieved his greatest success with the three-act ballet *Pessi ja Illusia* (1951–52), based on a fairytale by Yrjö Kokko, which had a run of some 150 performances at the Finnish National Opera and was also produced independently by the Royal Swedish Opera in Stockholm. Many individual numbers from the ballet score have survived as independent pieces. Sonninen's first opera, *Merenkunin-kaan tytär* (The Sea King's Daughter; 1949), enjoys the distinction of being the first Finnish opera to be composed for radio; it represented Finland in the Prix Italia competition. His neoclassical Spanish-style song cycle *El amor pasa* (1953) was another international success. Sonninen experimented with new techniques of composition (including dodecaphony), but his modernist works have perhaps not borne the test of time quite as well as his more 'national' music. In his chief work, *Suomalainen messiadi* (A Finnish Messiad; 1959–1972), Sonninen combined archaic and contemporary elements in a musical and national credo;

the text was based on *Kirjokansi*, a selection of folk poetry edited by Martti Haavio. Sonninen also composed a large quantity of pedagogic works and film music.

Three further composers who followed the late romantic tradition deserve to be mentioned. SULO SALONEN (1899–1976) matured late as a composer, but produced a distinguished oeuvre in religious music, ranging from functional liturgical music scored in traditional style to a twelve-tone *Toccata* (1955) for organ and a free tonal *Missa a cappella* (1957), a new departure in Finnish church music. Salonen's widely-acclaimed *Requiem* (1963) was the first Finnish work in the genre. Chromatic polyphony dominates the choral work *De profundis* (1972). Salonen's Quintet for Winds (1963) approaches the style of Hindemith.

The main works of LAURI SAIKKOLA (1906–1995), a national romantic composer with neoclassical leanings, include ten symphonies (1938–1988). His parodic orchestral poem *1500 m* won third prize in the 1947 'Finnish Games', a national arts and sports event; the radio opera *Taivaaseen menijät* (Going to Heaven; 1950) won third prize in the Prix Italia; the Fifth Symphony (1958) won a prize in the Helsinki Philharmonic competition in 1958, and the opera *Ristin* (1957–58) won the Wihuri Foundation's competition for new operas.

SEPPO NUMMI (1932–1981) specialized in vocal music, carrying on the lieder tradition of Yrjö Kilpinen. Nummi was also an influential music critic and a resourceful organizer of music festivals; he was the originator of the now highly popular series of Finnish summer festivals (cf. p. 204). From 1962 to 1968 Nummi was managing director of the Jyväskylä Arts Festival, and from 1969 to 1977 of the Helsinki Festival.

Finnish Neoclassicism of the '40s and '50s

EINAR ENGLUND (b. 1916) made his sensational debut just after Pylkkänen and Sonninen. Englund is a typical instrumental composer who has composed little vocal music of note. Whereas in the 1940s and '50s the music of Sonninen showed the influence of Prokofiev, Englund was one of the first Finnish composers to be influenced by Shostakovich; he wrote a brief study of the Russian composer as early as 1946. Englund's comic orchestral suite *Kiinan muuri* (The Great Wall of China; 1949) even contains a *March à la Shostakovich*, which is a parody of the Nazi march *Horst Wessel*. Incidentally, the influence of Shostakovich (and Bartók) can also be felt in the small but refreshing neoclassical oeuvre of MATTI RAUTIO (1922–1986), which culminated in a Piano Concerto (1971).

The premieres of Einar Englund's first two symphonies in the late 1940s were momentous events in Finnish music; their impact at the time is reflected in Joonas Kokkonen's comment: "After them we were all Englundians." These neoclassical works broke free from the symphonic precedent of Sibelius, although the great master's indirect influence can still be detected in them. Englund himself later stated that all of his symphonies are really war symphonies. The First Symphony (1946) was actually subtitled *Sotasinfonia* (War Symphony); memories of war surface repeatedly in the form of march themes. One of the seminal experiences for the Second Symphony, or *Mustarastassinfonia* (Blackbird Symphony) (1947), was Englund's wartime memory of a violent artillery barrage followed by a silence, which was broken by a blackbird's song.

Englund's compositions are musicianly in the best sense of the word – the composer himself is an accomplished pianist with a legendary talent for improvisation. Englund's work in the 1950s contains features reminiscent of the late Bartók, particularly apparent in the orchestral suite *Neljä tanssi-impressiota* (Four Dance Impressions; 1954), an arrangement of the miniature ballet *Sinuhe* (1953); in the rather undemonstrative, austere Cello Concerto (1954); and in the First Piano Concerto (1955), his most frequently played concerto.

Einar Englund admiring a painting by Lars Gunnar Nordström. Englund liberated the Finnish symphony from the shackles of the Sibelius tradition.

After the one-act ballet *Odysseus* (1959), Englund composed virtually no art music at all for the next ten years, for he felt that the response to his own, tradition-bound style was not adequately appreciated, as the latest avantgarde fashions swept onto the scene in the early 1960s. During these years, Englund concentrated on composing light music for the Radio Pops Orchestra under the *nom de plume* of Marcus Eje, and on producing hundreds of arrangements for pedagogic purposes. He also composed the music to seventeen films between 1952 and 1962, the most renowned being *Valkoinen peura* (The White Reindeer; 1952), which he reworked into an orchestral suite two years later.

Among other postwar neoclassics, two major public figures in the Finnish music world were NILS-ERIC RINGBOM (1907–1989), the composer of several song cycles and five symphonies (1939–70), and NILS-ERIC FOUGSTEDT (1910–1961), who composed some rather frequently performed choral songs as well as orchestral music. Ringbom served as superintendent of the Helsinki Philharmonic from 1942 to 1970, while Fougstedt was chief conductor of the Radio Symphony Orchestra from 1951 to 1960. Fougstedt's oeuvre includes *Angoscia* (1954), the first Finnish twelve-tone work for orchestra, *Trittico sinfonico* (1958), which attracted considerable attention in its time, and his chief work, the philosophical *Aurea dicta* (1959) for choir and orchestra.

Among the prominent neoclassics of the 1940s and '50s, the names of JOONAS KOKKONEN (1921–1996) and USKO MERILÄINEN (b. 1930) stand out. Kokkonen was largely a self-taught composer whose main stylistic precursor was Bartók. From about 1959, Kokkonen began to apply the twelve-tone technique to his music. The chief work of his neoclassical period is the fine four-movement chamber symphony *Musiikkia jousille* (Music for Strings; 1956–57), one of the standbys in the Finnish string repertoire. The chamber music of Kokkonen's first period, including a Piano Trio (1948), Piano Quintet (1953) and Duo for Violin and Piano (1955), is severely linear, and treats the instruments more ascetically than the string symphony.

Usko Meriläinen studied with Aarre Merikanto, but his main stylistic model was the music of Igor Stravinsky. Particularly Stravinskyan works include the *Partita 12* for twelve brass instruments, the First Piano Concerto (1955) and the *Concerto for Orchestra* (1956). Meriläinen's neoclassical period, dominated by rhythmic motoricity, was short-lived, as indeed was his twelve-tone period, though remote echoes of both styles can still be heard in his more recent works.

From Twelve-Tone Music
to Avantgarde Experiments (c. 1954–1965)
The Twelve-Tone Period in Finnish Music

After Merikanto, Raitio and Pingoud, the next generation of Finnish composers with a modernist outlook did not appear until the 1950s. The emergence in Finland of new musical trends was greatly facilitated by the founding in 1949 of

Nykymusiikki, or 'Society of Contemporary Music', which arranged concerts of avantgarde music, lectures and panel discussions, and invited well-known foreign composers and performing musicians to Finland. The society was admitted as the Finnish member organization to the ISCM in 1951.

One of the active members of the new society was the leading Finnish modernist of the 1950s and '60s, ERIK BERGMAN (b. 1911). After early studies in Finland, Bergman studied with Heinz Tiessen in Berlin in 1937–39 and 1942–43. The decisive turning-point in his career came in 1954, however, when he went to Ascona, Switzerland to study with Wladimir Vogel. There he became familiar with both the twelve-tone technique and the potential of the *Sprechchor* (speaking chorus) – neither was known other than theoretically in Finland in the early 1950s. In Bergman's footsteps, a few other Finnish composers (Tauno Marttinen, Einojuhani Rautavaara and Usko Meriläinen) set off in the '50s to study the elements of dodecaphony with Vogel. By the end of the decade, the twelve-tone technique had become firmly entrenched in Finnish music.

From the start, Bergman took a special interest in the potential of the human voice, employing the choirs he directed – the male choir Muntra Musikanter, and the mixed choir Akademiska Sångföreningen – as his musical laboratories. Many of Bergman's major compositions are in fact choral works.

Bergman's early works were still tied to the late romantic tradition. The orchestral scherzo *Burla* (1948) opened a period of searching, which culminated with his first truly notable work, the cantata *Rubaiyat* (1953) to the poems of Omar Khayyám, which first revealed Bergman's interest in non-European, often ancient cultures.

The predominance of dodecaphony in Bergman's music lasted from 1954 until the composition in 1962 of *Sela* for baritone, choir and chamber orchestra. Other major works of this period include *Aton* (1959), a cantata set to the *Hymn to the Sun* of Pharaoh Ekhnaton; the orchestral works *Aubade* (1958) and *Simbolo* (1960), which approach total serialism; and many choral works, including the much-performed, humorous Sprechchor cycles to poems by Christian Morgenstern, *Drei Galgenlieder* (1959) and *Vier Galgenlieder* (1960). The fine choral works *Svanbild* (Swan Picture; 1958) for baritone, solo quartet and male choir, and *Fåglarna* (The Birds; 1962) for baritone, 5 solo voices, percussion, celesta and chorus, are settings of poetry by his wife Solveig von Schoultz, as indeed are many of Bergman's other vocal works.

Bergman's twelve-tone period did not last much longer than that of most other Finnish composers who adopted the technique. They either reverted to a simpler, free tonal idiom (e.g. Kokkonen, Marttinen, Aulis Sallinen) or began to employ tone fields and/or aleatory rhythm (Bergman, Meriläinen and others).

Joonas Kokkonen's first twelve-tone work was the First String Quartet (1958-59), followed immediately by the beautiful orchestral song cycle *Lintujen Tuonela* (Underworld of the Birds; 1959). The crucial difference between Kokkonen's twelve-tone technique and that of Bergman is that while the latter strives for non-thematic, rhythmic complexity, Kokkonen pursues a thematic, rhythmically fairly straightforward dodecaphony. Unlike Bergman, Kokkonen also provides a distinct chordal resolution for his twelve-tone works, the most important instance being the E major chord met in the *religioso* climaxes of many of his works. Even during his dodecaphonic period, Kokkonen – unlike Bergman – remained a traditionalist at heart.

The music of Kokkonen's middle period (1958–67) is more intellectual and abstract in construction than his earlier and later works. His new formal thinking was modelled on Sibelius – particularly the third movement of Sibelius's Fourth

Symphony. This movement contained an entirely new structural element, based on building up a single theme towards its final form in swelling waves, as it were. The principle has been called *wave form* in Finland. Kokkonen's most important twelve-tone compositions were the Symphonies Nos. 1–3 (1958–60; 1961; 1967), all characterized by solidity of form and complete unity of material. The First Symphony moves towards an increasingly complex and dissonant musical world, until the conflicts are resolved in a transfigured music of atonement. The Second Symphony is more subjective and pessimistic; a tragic undercurrent is always present, and the work ends uncharacteristically on an unresolved twelve-tone chord. The succinct Third Symphony, which won Kokkonen the Nordic Music Prize in 1968, is already a more colourful and classicist transitional work which no longer applies the twelve-tone technique throughout. Other key works of this phase include the *Sinfonia da camera* (1962) for twelve strings and the Second String Quartet (1964–66).

In the 1960s Kokkonen became the most influential figure in Finnish music. He worked as a music critic for various newspapers and journals between 1946 and 1963, and served as professor of composition at the Sibelius Academy from 1959 to 1963. Kokkonen continued to teach composition privately until the 1970s following his appointment in 1963 to the Academy of Finland, when Erik Bergman succeeded him as professor at the Sibelius Academy. Bergman was made an academician in 1982.

During his active years at the Academy, Kokkonen consistently sought to further Finnish music policy. He held a record number of chairmanships in various associations; perhaps the most important of these were in the Finnish Composers' International Copyright Bureau TEOSTO (1968–88), the Finnish Cultural Foundation's Board of Trustees, and the Wihuri Foundation.

TAUNO MARTTINEN (b. 1912) began his career as a romantic composer, but the critics slated his early works mercilessly. Marttinen found a twofold solution to his stylistic problems – in a combination of the twelve-tone technique, which he studied with Vogel in Ascona in 1958, and of Finnish mythology, particularly the *Kalevala*.

In 1956 Marttinen composed *Kokko, ilman lintu* (Eagle, Bird of the Air) for mezzo-soprano and orchestra to a text from the Finnish epic. In this work, he abandoned tonality and disowned his entire previous output, giving *Kokko* the opus number 1. The First Symphony (1958) opened a brief dodecaphonic period proper in his work, the most important compositions of which were the orchestral work *Linnunrata* (The Milky Way; 1961) and the Violin Concerto (1962). In the early 1960s Marttinen made a name for himself as an experimental modernist (with music like *Loitsu* (Incantation; 1963) for three percussionists, a work of primitive force, and *Alfa* (1963) for flute and seven cymbals). He ventured into new territory with the comic opera *Päällysviitta* (The Overcoat; 1963), in which each of the principal characters is assigned a specific twelve-tone row, but which is no longer dodecaphonic throughout. His two subsequent operas abandoned the twelve-tone technique in favour of free tonality; both works, *Kihlaus* (The Betrothal; 1964) and *Tulitikkuja lainaamassa* (Borrowing Matches; 1967) rank with *Päällysviitta* among the foremost Finnish comic operas.

EINOJUHANI RAUTAVAARA (b. 1928) studied composition with Aarre Merikanto. On Sibelius's recommendation, he received a scholarship in 1955 from the Koussevitzky Foundation to study in New York and Tanglewood (with Aaron Copland, Vincent Persichetti and Roger Sessions). He completed his studies in 1957–58 in Ascona (with Vogel) and Cologne (with Rudolf Petzold). He later worked as lecturer of composition at the Sibelius Academy (1966–71), received a five-year 'professorship in the arts' from the Finnish government (1971–75), and was professor of composition at the Sibelius Academy from 1976 to 1988.

Three main strands run through Rautavaara's highly varied oeuvre: his personae have always included the traditionalist, as in the popular piano suite *Pelimannit* (The Country Fiddlers; 1962); the modernist and constructivist, represented by *Kolme symmetristä preludia* (Three Symmetrical Preludes; 1950) for piano; and the romantic and mystic, as in the piano suite *Ikonit* (Icons; 1955) and the song cycle *Fünf Sonette an Orpheus* (1954). The big hit of his early years was *A Requiem in Our Time* for wind orchestra (1953), which won the Thor Johnson competition in the United States, and is still one of his most frequently played works.

Rautavaara's development has never been consistent or straightforward; he has jumped straight from one extreme to another. Thus, his First Symphony (1956/88), still associated with the national tradition, was followed by the aphoristic Second Symphony (1957/84), in which he sought to achieve complete chromaticism. The latter work was in fact a free orchestral arrangement of the *Seitsemän preludia* (Seven Preludes; 1957) for piano. Dodecaphony was only a short step away.

Rautavaara's twelve-tone works show up the complexity of his aims particularly clearly. On the one hand, in his Fourth Symphony, *Arabescata* (1962), he was the first Finnish composer to apply strict constructivism and total serialism, combining these with partially aleatory form. On the other hand, his Second String Quartet (1958) was overtly romantic in spirit for all its dodecaphony, as was the Third Symphony (1961), one of the high points in Rautavaara's symphonic oeuvre, which employs a tonal twelve-tone technique and has a distinctly 'Brucknerian' character. Rautavaara also used tonal dodecaphony in the lovely song cycle *Die Liebenden* (1958). The twelve-tone opera *Kaivos* (The Mine; 1957–60/62) was inspired by the Hungarian uprising. Its first performance did not take place on stage but on television, making this the first Finnish TV opera. Two works for string orchestra, *Canto I* (1960/72) and *Canto II* (1960) were direct spin-offs of the opera.

The twelve-tone period of USKO MERILÄINEN was limited to the early 1960s. The ballet *Arius* (1958–60) was still based on freely used chords of 5–6 notes, without tonal associations. The First Piano Sonata (1960); *Riviravi* (1962), a work for young pianists; and the First String Quartet (1965), one of Meriläinen's best compositions from the early '60s, were all strictly dodecaphonic. Already two years before composing the quartet, however, Meriläinen had taken a freer approach to his musical material in the orchestral work *Epyllion* (1963), "a musical painting on the fringes of dodecaphony, with colourism as its essential feature". The rhythmically free *Impression* (1965) for chamber ensemble prefigured the treatment of rhythm in Meriläinen's later works.

GOTTFRID GRÄSBECK (b. 1927) first created a stir in the 1960s as an avantgardist with a Concerto for Two Tape Recorders and Orchestra (1964) and the 'stage cantata' *Stämmor ur elementen* (Voices from the Elements; 1966) for large male choir, male vocal quartet, tape, six projectors and dancers. In the late 1960s, a clear shift towards traditionalism occurred in Gräsbeck's work. Some of his most recent works are highly archaic and modal. Like Gräsbeck, who lives in Turku, SAKARI MONONEN (b. 1928) of Kuopio has remained something of an outsider among Finnish composers. Mononen also experimented with various new techniques of composition before settling for his present free tonal style, but even in the 1960s his radicalism did not extend to formal construction, in which one frequently encounters traditional structures.

OSMO LINDEMAN (1929–1987) started out as a modernist instrumental composer, experimenting with field technique and aleatory counterpoint in his two symphonies (1959, 1964) and two piano concertos (1963, 1965). The failed performance of one of his instrumental works, together with a study trip to Poland in 1968, provided the impetus for him to abandon instrumental music entirely for electroacoustic music, in which the composer can achieve total control of the performance. Lindeman's restricted electroacoustic output was created entirely in the home studio he built for the purpose; his best-known compositions are the tape works *Ritual* (1972) and *Spectacle* (1974).

PENTTI RAITIO (b. 1930), who studied with Kokkonen and Bergman, worked for a while as a primary school teacher, then from 1967 to 1992 as principal of the Hyvinkää Music Institute. Most of his relatively limited oeuvre is vocal music, the outstanding works being perhaps the rhythmically rich *Kuun tietä* (Road to the Moon; 1965) for soprano and chamber ensemble, and the exceptionally dramatic and powerful *Lemminkäinen kuokkavieraana Pohjolassa* (Lemminkäinen as an Uninvited Guest in Pohjola; 1978) for male choir. His instrumental music is largely dodecaphonic – the most important works in this category include a Wind Quintet (1975), *Canzo d'autonno* for strings and percussion (1982), a Flute Concerto (1983) and a Cello Concerto (1993).

After studies with Merikanto and Kokkonen, PAAVO HEININEN (b. 1938) went to Cologne to study with Rudolf Petzold and Bernd Alois Zimmermann, and followed this up by studying with Vincent Persichetti in New York. From his very first works in the '50s, Heininen has been a consistent twelve-tone composer and an unswerving modernist. He remained faithful to these principles even when many of his Finnish colleagues turned from modernist ideals towards stylistic pluralism and free tonality.

Heininen's first publicly performed compositions, including the Piano Sonatina (1957) and First Symphony (1958), testified to his precocious mastery as a composer. Although the premiere of the symphony was a disaster – owing to insufficient rehearsal time, only the first and last movements were played – Heininen continued to compose for orchestra (*Tripartita*; 1959 and *Concerto for String Orchestra*; 1959). The problem with the reception of these works was that "on the one hand, [Heininen] sought conventional formal solutions; on the other hand, in his dodecaphony he shirked all reference to tonality". He was thus "caught, as it were, between two generations" (Mikko Heiniö), belonging neither to the traditionalist camp nor to the youngest generation of avantgarde composers. Heininen was aware of the difficulties that audiences experienced with his music, and in the '60s he composed several purportedly simpler, more classical works (e.g. the Second Symphony, *Petite symphonie joyeuse*; 1962). Since he still steadfastly refused to violate the critical musical taboos of twelve-tone music (such as the absolute ban on triads), the difference between his 'easy' and 'difficult' works in the '60s remained obscure to listeners. Indeed, it was one of the 'difficult' orchestral works, *Soggetto* (1963), that gained Heininen his first significant critical success. He continued along the same lines with the sextet *Musique d'été* (1963/67) and one of his very finest compositions, *Adagio... concerto per orchestra in forma di variazioni* (1963/67). His other major works of the '60s included the First and Second Piano Concertos (1964, 1966).

In 1966 Heininen was appointed lecturer in composition and music theory at the Sibelius Academy, launching him on a brilliant teaching career (cf. pp. 123–124).

The Young Avantgarde of the '60s

The *Finnish Musical Youth* was established in 1957 on the initiative of Matti Rautio and Seppo Nummi. Modelled on the international Jeunesses Musicales, the society's active period lasted only until 1965, but between 1961 and 1964, when the composers Kaj Chydenius and Erkki Salmenhaara and the critic Seppo Heikinheimo took turns in its chair, it provided a forum for the young generation of avantgarde composers and critics in Finland.

The Finnish Musical Youth sought to make the most recent Continental music known in Finland, using much the same methods as the older Society of Contemporary Music, i.e. concerts of recorded music, lectures and live concerts proper. Many of the members (including Salmenhaara and Chydenius) were also prolific writers. As a result, the Finnish music public first encountered the music of Webern, Stockhausen, Boulez, Cage, Ligeti and the Polish avantgardists. Of the composers themselves, Stockhausen visited Finland three times in these years, Nono twice and Cage and Ligeti both once. The Musical Youth soon turned its back on twelve-tone technique and total serialism. The latter never really became established in Finnish music; already in 1961, Kaj Chydenius announced that the time of serial music was past. The young generation also declared that dodecaphony was *passé*, at a time when Finland had only just become acquainted with the technique. The new focus was on field technique, graphic notation, improvisation and musical happenings. Soon collage, allusions and stylistic hints entered the picture, deriving their sources from tonal music on the one hand, and from popular music and jazz on the other. This paved the way for the pluralist period of the late '60s in Finnish art music.

Besides Salmenhaara and Chydenius, the leading composers of the Musical Youth were KARI RYDMAN (b. 1936) and HENRIK OTTO DONNER (b. 1939). Rydman is a self-taught composer whose most experimental period lasted from 1962 to 1964, when he composed *Sonata I–VI*, a series of works for varying ensembles ranging from two to seven players. Stylistic loans and allusions begin to appear in the one-movement String Quartets II–IV (1963–64). The works *Khoros I* and *II* (1964,

Kari Rydman's career as a composer led from avantgarde music to popular ballads.

1966) make open use of loans from light music. In 1965 Rydman released a record of popular ballads, abandoning the musical avantgarde for good. The *Symphony of Modern Worlds* (1968) merges a variety of styles, whereas the orchestral poem *DNA* (1970) approaches impressionism. Among Rydman's later compositions, the finest include many sensitive ballads, which avoid the clichés of popular music, and a few 'more serious' works, such as the Viola Sonata (1979) and the nostalgic *Inventions for String Orchestra* (1982).

Henrik Otto Donner is a more 'hard-boiled' composer than the romantic Rydman. While studying composition with Nils-Eric Fougstedt and Joonas Kokkonen, Donner started his musical career as a jazz trumpeter, and performed in a number of different bands during the 1960s. In his art music in the early '60s, he initially approached total serialism, but had abandoned it by the time he composed the *Cantata profana* (1962), which contains a taped section at the end. *Ideogramme I* and *II* (1962, 1963) are among his most experimental compositions; the former features a background of noise furnished by a group of twelve transistor radios, while the latter is a work of 'spatial music' composed for the Helsinki Art Hall; the audience was expected to move from one gallery to the next during the performance. Among Donner's happenings proper, the most controversial were *Street Piece Helsinki* (1963) and *For Emmy 2* (1963), the main feature of the Finnish Musical Youth's 'sabotage concert', at the end of which the saxophonist and bass player stayed behind for an extended jam session. Donner used the collage technique throughout the work *Moonspring, or Aufforderung zum. . . or Symphony I (Hommage à Charles Ives)* (1964) for string orchestra and Hammond organ. Elements of jazz could be heard in *XC* (1969), one of Donner's chief works, which was selected for performance at the ISCM festival in Baden in 1970. From the late 1960s, Donner gradually abandoned art music almost entirely, returning to jazz and also composing a large number of popular ballads and choral pieces, many of them for the left-wing *New Song* movement. Donner has also become known as an energetic and influential maker of cultural policy; he has held many official posts, including chairman of the National Committee for Music (1974–79), the Guild of Light Music Composers and Authors of Finland ELVIS (1987–94) and the Finnish Composers' International Copyright Bureau TEOSTO (1994–).

KAJ CHYDENIUS (b. 1939) composed but little art music in the 1960s, concentrating instead on serving as a spokesman for happenings, instrumental theatre and aleatory music. In 1965–66 he composed the music for Arvo Salo's political musical drama *Lapualaisooppera* (The Lapua Opera), which caused an uproar throughout Finland. With this work, Chydenius abandoned the high aesthetic of art music once and for all. Seeking a direct, concrete, immediate contact with a larger audience, he discovered the channel for doing so in social protest. Many of his political cabaret songs have become Finnish classics in their category. Chydenius has also composed a great deal of music for the theatre, especially the left-wing KOM Theatre, which he has directed on several occasions.

ERKKI SALMENHAARA (b. 1941) studied composition with Joonas Kokkonen and then with Ligeti in Vienna in 1963. He obtained a PhD in music in 1970 with a thesis on musical material and its treatment in Ligeti's *Apparitions*, *Atmosphères*, *Aventures* and *Requiem*. From 1963 to 1971 Salmenhaara worked as music critic for the largest Finnish daily, *Helsingin Sanomat*.

As a composer, Salmenhaara passed from early tonal works directly to avantgardism. The choral work *Kuun kasvot* (Face of the Moon; 1960/64) was already highly chromatic. During the next five years, he proceeded via experimentation (*Suoni successivi* for two pianists, 1962; *Pan ja Ekho* for four cymbals, tam-tam and amplifier, 1963; Concerto for two electric violins, 1963) to field technique (First Symphony, *Crescendi*, 1962/63; Second Symphony, 1963/66; *Elegia I* and *II* for different chamber ensembles, both 1963), then on to a freely chromatic motive technique (Third Symphony, 1963/64, serious in tone) and a field technique based on triads (the crucial orchestral work *Le Bateau ivre*, 1965/66). The Second Symphony, the revised version of which won the Finnish Broadcasting Company's music award, is one of the most 'Ligetian' works in contemporary Finnish music. The darkly sensuous *Le Bateau ivre* marked a turning-point in Salmenhaara's music, from which he progressed towards an increasingly pronounced tonality.

With its happenings, the Finnish Musical Youth succeeded in arousing an impassioned debate and infuriating the more conservative critics. Thus, Nils-Eric Ringbom sneered that the society's first concert in 1962 was mere unbridled nursery noise, without rhyme or reason. His review led to the Musical Youth's events being branded "nursery chamber concerts". Although few of the works performed at them ever reappeared in the repertoire, this was a vital phase in Finnish music history, as it brought Finland right up to the pulse of the times. By fuelling a lively debate, the "nursery chamber composers" brought a breath of fresh air into the Finnish music world, and indicated possible ways out of the dead end at which the avantgarde had arrived (new awareness of tradition, return to tonality, ballads, jazz, political music).

From the Restoration to the Second Coming of Modernism (c. 1965–1992)

Traditionalism of the '70s and '80s, and the 'Finnish Opera Boom'

Following the first postwar wave of modernism (from around 1955 to 1965), the Finnish music climate again became more diversified. Since modernism had discovered no permanent solution to the problems of new music, composers inclined to traditionalism were given, as it were, a new opportunity. Meanwhile, the concept of traditionalism had expanded, as many of the composition techniques that had remained untried in Finland until the mid 1950s had now truly become part of a living tradition. The pluralistic tendencies that rose to the fore in the late 1960s also paved the way for the rise of Finnish opera. Among the traditionalists, a distinct group consisted of composers who had 'converted' from modernism or avant-gardism; these composers (Gräsbeck, Rydman, Salmenhaara) could be styled 'neotraditionalists' to distinguish them from those who had always followed the traditionalist banner. Even the Finnish neotraditionalists actually fall into two groups; the first generation, cited above, turned from the avantgardism of the '60s to tradition, while the second generation traded the modernism of the '80s for a more traditional idiom.

The return of Einar Englund to the art music scene took place in 1971 with the first performance of his Third Symphony (1969–71), one of his finest works. The work was originally subtitled "Cholecystitis" (a reference to the gall bladder infection that plagued him during its composition), but in the 1990s Englund renamed it *Barbarossa*, considering it to be his 'true' war symphony. The aggressive music of the second movement, for example, clearly evokes associations with war. A statement by Englund in 1976 gave expression to the liberating effect the new pluralism of the late 1960s had on him:

Composers no longer fence themselves within strict systems, nor are they as susceptible as before to the temptations of short-lived fads. The time has come to choose between all the new things, good and bad, that modern music has brought forth.

The 'new' Englund did not differ significantly from the 'old': his music continued to be based on motivic-thematic work, often with distinct tonal pivots. In terms of formal construction, his music is also firmly rooted in tradition; sonata form, passacaglia, fugue, etc. can be found in many of his works. Englund dedicated his Fourth Symphony, subtitled *Nostalginen* (Nostalgic, 1976) and scored for strings and percussion only, "to the memory of a great composer", i.e. Shostakovich; nonetheless, this retrospective work is primarily a reflection on Englund's own life. The Fifth Symphony, *Fennica* (1977) is in a single movement, whereas the Sixth, *Aforismeja* (Aphorisms, 1984) is a six-movement choral symphony – a new departure for Englund – with a text consisting of Pentti Saarikoski's Finnish translations of the aphorisms of Heraclitus. Englund's Seventh Symphony, or *Tamperelainen sinfonia* (Tampere Symphony, 1989), was his contribution to an invitational competition celebrating the completion of the Tampere Concert Hall in 1990.

Englund has also produced a series of concertos during his 'second period', following up the Second Piano Concerto (1974) with concertos for violin (1981), flute (1985) and clarinet (1991), and – perhaps the most successful of all – a Concerto for 12 Cellos (1981) in five movements, with a dance-like vigour and drive. Among his later chamber music, the much-performed Piano Sonata (1978), Violin Sonata (1979), Cello Sonata (1982), Piano Trio (1982) and String Quartet (1985) deserve mention. Englund discusses his role in the

Finnish music world in his caustic memoirs, *I skuggan av Sibelius* (In the Shadow of Sibelius; 1997).

Joonas Kokkonen's third stylistic phase can be said to have begun in 1968 with the classicist orchestral work *Sinfonisia luonnoksia* (Symphonic Sketches). In the music of this period, Kokkonen abandoned strict twelve-tone technique for freer motive work, while building up with increasing consistency on a foundation of pure triads – particularly major chords. The much-performed Cello Concerto (1969) contains his most melodic and songful music. The three-movement Fourth Symphony (1971) has as its key structural element the triad series C – A flat – E(e). The whole symphony is framed by a bright pedal point in E.

The most important composition of Kokkonen's third period and, indeed, his masterpiece on any count, is the two-act opera *Viimeiset kiusaukset* (Last Temptations; 1973–75) to a libretto by Lauri Kokkonen, the composer's cousin. The hero is the revivalist preacher Paavo Ruotsalainen, who lies on his deathbed, reliving his life and the most painful decisions he had to make in flashback. The opera's success outdid even that of Madetoja's *Pohjalaisia* – it remained in the Finnish National Opera's repertoire for seven years running, was also staged in Kuopio and Oulu, and was revived in a new National Opera production in Helsinki's new opera house in 1994. The National Opera also performed the work on tour in Stockholm and Oslo (1976), London (1979), Wiesbaden and Zürich (1981), and New York and East Berlin (1983). The total number of performances approaches 250. The work has a very solid formal structure: the duration of its units follows the Fibonacci sequence (3,5,8,13 etc.), and the ratio between the durations of the two acts is the golden section. *Viimeiset kiusaukset* gives full expression to Kokkonen's religious beliefs, which also find vent in the chorale-like, transfigured climaxes of many of his other works.

Other notable works of Kokkonen's third period include the Third String Quartet (1976), his most significant work in the genre; . . . *durch einen Spiegel. . .* for strings and harpsichord (1976) and the luminous *Requiem* (1979–81), dedicated to the memory of the composer's second wife.

After *Viimeiset kiusaukset*, Kokkonen's creative urge began to ebb. In contrast, AULIS SALLINEN (b. 1935) has gradually assumed a position as one of Finland's internationally best-known composers since the mid 1970s. Sallinen studied with Aarre Merikanto, and had a brief modernist period which culminated with *Mauermusik* (1962), composed in memory of a young man shot dead at the Berlin Wall. After this work, he developed a simpler but highly personal style with strong emotional appeal, which explains the popularity his works have attained. Working with very simple resources, Sallinen is able to project moods convincingly, and to achieve powerful effects. Many of his works are monothematic, and his motivic method of composition owes a great deal to the technique of Sibelius. Sallinen's best-known work from the late '60s is the Third String Quartet, *Aspekteja Peltoniemen Hintrikin suru-marssista* (Aspects from the Funeral March of Hintrikki Peltoniemi; 1969), based on variations on a well-known Ostrobothnian fiddler's tune. The dark, melancholy First Symphony (1971) in one movement is built up primarily on the F sharp minor chord. The short Second Symphony (1972) contains a solo part for percussion. The colourfully orchestrated Third (1975) and Fourth (1979) Symphonies are more 'symphonic' in character. Sallinen's conception of the symphony does not, however, entail a 'symphonic' progression towards some final destination (e.g. a theme working towards its final form, as in Kokkonen's wave-form works). He presents his musical material in relatively finished form, and then either obstinately repeats it or varies on it in different ways. The more fragmentary Fifth Symphony (1985) is subtitled *Washington Mosaics*, and the programmatic Sixth Symphony, *From a New Zealand Diary* (1990), describes the sights and sounds of New Zealand. The one-movement Seventh Symphony, *The Dreams of Gandalf* (1995–96), takes its subtitle from the fantasy world of J.R.R. Tolkien.

Among Sallinen's other instrumental works, *Chamber Music I–III* deserves special mention; the much-played No. 3, *Donjuanquijoten yölliset tanssit* (Nocturnal Dances of Donjuanquixote) is scored for cello and string orchestra. Highly impressive in its simplicity is the Fourth String Quartet, *Hiljaisia lauluja* (Quiet Songs; 1971). The Fifth Quartet, *Mosaiikin paloja* (Fragments of Mosaic; 1983), consists – as the title suggests – of several brief, aphoristic sections. The notable *Dies Irae* (1978) for male choir and orchestra is a vision of the world after a nuclear war. *Elämän ja kuoleman lauluja* (Songs of Life and Death; 1994) is based on poems by Lassi Nummi on the subject of death. Sallinen has also composed a Violin Concerto (1968), a Cello Concerto (1976) and a Flute Concerto, *Harlekiini* (The Harlequin; 1994).

Sallinen's chief works, however, are his operas, which along with Kokkonen's *Viimeiset kiusaukset* had a crucial role in the rise of Finnish opera in the 1970s. Sallinen rose to international fame almost overnight with *Ratsumies* (The Horseman; 1974), premiered at the Savonlinna Opera Festival in 1975 and staged later by the Kiel Opera (1980) and Tallinn's Estonia Theatre. The libretto by Paavo Haavikko, Finland's best-known living poet, combines Finnish history and mythology. The musical idiom is traditional yet highly individual, unmistakably Sallinen's own. The tonal style of his second opera, *Punainen viiva* (The Red Line; 1976–78; Sallinen himself wrote the libretto based on a novel by the classic Finnish realist author, Ilmari Kianto) sounds at times like 'modern *verismo*'. This work also became very popular in Finland, and was performed by the National Opera on many foreign tours (London 1979,

Aulis Sallinen and Joonas Kokkonen were the leading figures in the 'Finnish opera boom' that began in the 1970s.

Stockholm 1980, Wiesbaden and Zürich 1981, Moscow, Leningrad and Tallinn 1982, New York 1983). New productions were staged in Savonlinna 1982–83, Osnabrück 1985 and Dortmund 1985. Like *Ratsumies*, Sallinen's third opera *Kuningas lähtee Ranskaan* (The King Goes Forth to France; 1983) is based on a libretto by Paavo Haavikko. This piece contains parody and comedy, and has a broader and more varied stylistic range than any other work of Sallinen's. Commissioned jointly by the Savonlinna Opera Festival and the Covent Garden Opera, it was staged as a new production in London in 1987 and before that, in 1986, in Kiel and at the Santa Fé Opera Festival in New Mexico.

In his fourth opera, *Kullervo* (1986–88), Sallinen returned to national mythology – the composer's own libretto is based on the Kullervo episode in the *Kalevala* and on Aleksis Kivi's play of the same name. It is Sallinen's darkest and most tragic opera. The work was commissioned for the Finnish National Opera's opening performance at the new opera house in Helsinki (in November 1993); the same ensemble, however, had already performed the work at the Los Angeles Opera on February 25, 1992, an event which attracted enormous interest in the international music world. The work was also produced at the Nantes Opera in December 1995. Sallinen's fifth opera, *Palatsi* (The Palace; 1992–93) is on a smaller scale, a satirical tale about the corruption of political power; the ruler in the libretto by Irene Dische and Hans-Magnus Enzensberger is modelled on Haile Selassie, the former Emperor of Ethiopia, and the Romanian dictator Nicolae Ceauşescu. In *Palatsi*, Sallinen works with very familiar-sounding musical material, which the listener continually associates with the archetypal rhetoric of opera. Premiered in Savonlinna in summer 1995, the work will also be staged in Nantes during the 1996–97 season.

Some of the classics of new Finnish choral music came from the pen of BENGT JOHANSSON (1914–1989), who included tone fields and polytonal elements in his works. Johansson worked his way to a style of his own in his major choral works of the '60s and '70s. Johansson himself used the term "antique style" for his choral music, expressing his efforts to combine something of the quality of the madrigal with impulses from contemporary field technique. This style was heralded by *The Tomb at Akr Çaar* (1964) to a poem by Ezra Pound. The text of Johansson's choral *Triptych* (1965) is from the Bible, and he also used Latin texts for some of his works (such as *Requiem*, 1966). The opera *Linna* (The Castle; 1974; libretto by Aarni Krohn) reverts to a more traditional idiom. From 1952 to 1975, Johansson was employed as a sound engineer at the Finnish Broadcasting Company, and he drew on his experience in the field by composing the first Finnish tape music, *Kolme elektronista etydiä* (Three Electronic Etudes; 1960).

As previously mentioned, TAUNO MARTTINEN shifted away from the twelve-tone technique when he composed his comic operas, arriving at a free tonal style, almost improvisatory in effect, with a loose web of motivic links, and transitions scored with rhythmic precision juxtaposed with acoustic surfaces produced by means of aleatory counterpoint. In the 1960s, Marttinen pursued his series of operas with *Lea* (1967), based on Aleksis Kivi's play on a Biblical theme; then came what was perhaps the composer's most important opera, *Poltettu oranssi* (Burnt Orange; 1968) to a libretto by Eeva-Liisa Manner. The tragic events of this work centre on the sessions of the young, mentally unbalanced Marina with her psychiatrist, and Marina's problematic relationship with her parents.

Marttinen's ultra-rapid, spontaneous composition technique has resulted in a remarkably extensive oeuvre, currently comprising over 300 opus numbers, including fifteen operas and ten symphonies. Many of the operas are one-act works for small ensemble – these include *Mestari Patelin* (Master Patelin; 1974), *Psykiatri* (The Psychiatrist, 1974), *Meedio* (The Medium, 1976), *Häät* (The Wedding, 1984) and *Minna Graucher* (1984). More serious in tone are his larger-scale operas, such as *Laestadiuksen saarna* (The Sermon of Laestadius), also known as *Noitarumpu* (The Witch's Drum); 1976), *Jaarlin sisar* (The Earl's Sister; 1977), *Faaraon kirje* (The Pharaoh's Letter; 1982), *Suuren joen laulu* (Song of the Great River; 1982–84) and *Seitsemän veljestä* (The Seven Brothers; 1989). Apart from opera, Marttinen's most important compositions are based on themes from the *Kalevala*. The Finnish epic has a special universal significance for the composer, as he has discovered in it similarities with the ancient myths of the East. His major *Kalevala* works include the ballet *Päivänpäästö* (Release of the Sun; 1975–77/83), the four-movement *Lemminkäinen* for three solo singers, choir and orchestra (1966–68/74), *The Väinämöinen Trilogy* (1981–82) and *Panu, tulen jumala* (Panu, God of Fire; 1966).

The self-taught composer EERO SIPILÄ (1918–1972) was trained as an organist and earned a living as lecturer of music at the Kajaani teacher training institute. His interest in old music is evident throughout his oeuvre. He composed his most notable choral works in the 1960s, combining a variety of old and new techniques. In the motet *Super flumina Babylonis* (1963), Sipilä experimented with a new, Polish-influenced choral technique with clusters and glissandoes. Static cluster harmonies and second shifts in melody also characterize the choral work *Fot mot jord* (Foot Against the Ground; 1969). Sipilä's chief work is the cantata-like *Te Deum laudamus* (1969) for choir and orchestra. The song cycles *Schein und Sein* (1966) and *Tiitiäisen satupuusta* (Tiitiäinen's Storytree; 1971) contain a quirky, sardonic humour contrasting with the general high seriousness of his choral music.

LEONID BASHMAKOV (b. 1927) studied with Aarre Merikanto in the 1950s, but his real breakthrough as a composer came in the '60s. His music bears a stylistic affinity to the neoclassicism of Arthur Honegger, although Bashmakov's idiom is more modern. Bashmakov is primarily an instrumental composer, although his most important work is an extensive *Requiem* (1988) to a text by Lassi Nummi. He has composed six symphonies (1963, 1965, 1971, 1977, 1979, 1982) and the noteworthy ballet *Tumma* (1976). Among his concertos, especially the Cello Concerto (1972) and Second Violin Concerto (1983) rank among the finest Finnish works in the genre. He has also composed concertos for more unusual solo instruments, including the organ (1975), piccolo trumpet and strings (1992), horn, percussion and strings (1992) and bassoon and chamber orchestra (1994). He has produced a sizable chamber music oeuvre, much of it for unusual combinations of instruments.

Unlike Bashmakov, ILKKA KUUSISTO (b. 1933) has focused primarily on opera and vocal music. He is one of the leading humorists in Finnish music, as the song cycles *Aviollinen sarja* (Bridal Suite; 1966) and *Suomalainen vieraanvara* (Finnish Hospitality; 1970) testify. A great deal of musical amusement is also provided by the *Muumiooppera* (Moomin Opera; 1974), based on Tove Jansson's world-famous fantasy characters, and *Miehen kylkiluu* (Man's Rib; 1977), based on a classic Finnish play by Maria Jotuni. Kuusisto's most ambitious opera is *Sota valosta* (War over Light, 1980) to a libretto based on a play by Eino Leino, combining two ancient *Kalevala* themes, the release of the sun and the Marjatta legend, with topical national, social and political allegory. Kuusisto followed up this work with the operas *Jääkäri Ståhl* (Jaeger Ståhl; 1982), *Pierrot ja yön salaisuudet* (Pierrot and the Secrets of the Night; 1991), *Postineiti* (The Postmistress; 1992), *Fröken Julie* (Miss Julie; 1993) and *Isänmaan tyttäret* (Daughters of the Fatherland; 1995–96). Kuusisto was director of the Finnish National Opera from 1984 to 1992.

Two noted Finnish conductors, JORMA PANULA (b. 1930) and ATSO ALMILA (b. 1953) have also made a name as composers, chiefly of popular opera. Panula's breakthrough as a composer came with the musical *Ruma Elsa* (Ugly Elsa; 1958). He composed the operas *Jaakko Ilkka* (1978), *Jokiooppera* (The River Opera; 1982) and *Peltomiehen rukous* (The Ploughman's Prayer; 1984) for the Ilmajoki Music Festival, and the opera *Lalli ja pyhä Henrikki* (Lalli and St. Henry; 1987) for the Tampere Opera. Almila has composed several concertos as well as two operas for the Ilmajoki festival, *Kolmekymmentä hopearahaa* (Thirty Pieces of Silver; 1987) and *Ameriikka* (America; 1991).

JOUKO LINJAMA (b. 1934), whose teachers included Merikanto, Kokkonen and B.A. Zimmermann, has been most successful in his organ compositions and in oratorio-like works such as *Missa de Angelis*, 1969; *Millaista on* (What's It Like;

1964/68); *Kunnianosoitus Aleksis Kivelle* (Homage to Aleksis Kivi; 1970–76) and choral works (including the *Kalevala Suite*, 1981). Together with Sulo Salonen, Linjama is one of Finland's foremost contemporary composers of church music. His best-known organ works include *Concerto per organo* (1971), *Missa cum jubilo* (1977) and a Concerto for organ, marimba, vibraphone and two wind quartets (1981). Linjama combines polyphoric, Renaissance-inspired features with triadic material and field technique.

Two composers who have concentrated on *Gebrauchsmusik* are PEKKA KOSTIAINEN (b. 1944), who has produced an extensive body of choral works, and HARRI WESSMAN (b. 1949), a prolific composer of small-scale, elegantly scored instrumental and pedagogic music. Kostiainen has sought inspiration in ancient Finnish mythology and shamanism; together with Ahti Sonninen, Tauno Marttinen and the 'ethno-jazz' composer SEPPO PAAKKUNAINEN (b. 1943; cf. p. 218), Kostiainen is one of the foremost modern reinterpreters of the *Kalevala* and Finnish folk poetry. Among his works based on the Finnish epic, perhaps the most notable is *Tuli on tuima tie'ettävä* (Fire's a Fearful Thing to Know; 1984) for tape, mixed choir and symphony orchestra. Kostiainen is a great admirer of the choral style of the Estonian composer Veljo Tormis, who has sought inspiration in the distinctive features of the archaic folk music of the Baltic-Finnic peoples. Kostiainen has composed many of his main choral works for the Musica choir, which he directs in his hometown Jyväskylä; the best-known and most-performed among these is the shamanistic *Pakkasen luku* (Frost Spell; 1983).

Harri Wessman has sought inspiration in the doctrine of affections and Baroque rhetoric; he is one of the leading Finnish experts on the music theories of the Baroque period. Wessman's own music is no neo-Baroque, however; it is highly personal free tonal music based on melodic and harmonic

Harri Wessman has made a study of the Baroque doctrine of affections, which he has applied to his own chamber music and compositions for children.

tensions, although the affective and rhetorical gestures of the Baroque do appear in it from time to time. From the beginning, Wessman has questioned the modernist fascination with technology, quasi-scientific theories and faith in progress. In his own music, his main aim is persuasiveness and communication.

The bulk of Wessman's oeuvre consists of chamber music for a variety of ensembles. He has also produced a large amount of valuable music for teaching purposes. Some of Wessman's pedagogic concertos feature a solo part composed to match a specific child's level of attainment at the time.

TIMO-JUHANI KYLLÖNEN (b. 1955), who studied at the Gnesin Institute and the Tchaikovsky Conservatoire in Moscow, has followed a similar path. Kyllönen's free tonal style has a Slavic feel and suggests the influence of the great Russian masters Shostakovich and Prokofiev. This can be heard in Kyllönen's First Symphony (1985–86), premiered in Novosibirsk in 1986. In his later works he has also employed newer elements, such as clusters and improvisatory sequences (*Elegia "Quasi una sonata"* for violin and piano; 1987). Kyllönen has produced a sizable oeuvre for choir and children's choir. Many of these works have an almost Southern beat. Their Latin American feel is partly explained by the fact that they are settings of the

Spanish poetry of Kyllönen's Peruvian first wife Maritza Núñez and her mother Carmen Luz Bejarano. His chief work thus far is *Passio secularis* (1988–89) for soprano, male choir and orchestra. Kyllönen has had several concerts dedicated to his music abroad.

JUKKA LINKOLA (b. 1955) is a crossover composer, whose *Crossings* (1983) for tenor saxophone and orchestra presents an idiosyncratic blend of jazz and art music. His chief works for stage include the ballet *Ronja Ryövärintytär* (Ronia, the Robber's Daughter; 1989), the opera *Elina* (1990), and the TV opera *Angelica* (1992), which won first prize in the Paris Opera Screen competition in 1993 and the Midem award in Cannes in 1994. Linkola has composed several much-performed works for brass ensembles, chamber music, vocal works (e.g. *Between Two Stages*; 1988), a great deal of incidental music and film music (including the music to the film *The Snow Queen*; 1987) and the musicals *Kairatut sydämet* (Drilled Hearts; 1992) and *Antti Puuhaara* (Antti Treebranch; 1994). He composed his First Trumpet Concerto in 1988, a Tuba Concerto in 1992 and the Second Trumpet Concerto in 1993; he has a standing commission from the Lieksa Brass Week for concertos for all of the other brass instruments as well. One of Finland's leading jazz composers, Linkola has also produced an extensive oeuvre in this field (cf. p. 219).

**"Composer in no-man's land".
Jukka Linkola is a composer of
jazz as well as of operas,
concertos and chamber music.**

He performs regularly as a jazz pianist and conductor, and set up his own octet in 1976, his main jazz workshop along with the UMO big band.

PEKKA JALKANEN (b. 1945) has brought a fresh, unconventional approach to combining folk music with contemporary musical expression. He studied musicology at the University of Helsinki and wrote his ethnomusicological doctoral thesis in 1989 on the Finnish jazz scene in the 1920s. He studied composition privately with Erkki Salmenhaara. His speciality is the cultural heritage of the Finnic peoples, which he has applied in various ways to his own works, such as *Viron orja* (The Serf of Viro; 1980) for string orchestra; *Vägehens otetut neidizet* (The Abduction; 1982) for female choir; and *Piika pikkarainen* (The Little Lass; 1985) for children's choir, reciter, kantele and bells. For the kantele, the Finnish national instrument, he has composed some of the most important works in the contemporary repertoire, including the Septet for kantele, flute, harpsichord and string quartet (1986); *Orjankukka* (Wild Rose; 1989) for one 5-string kantele and two with 36 strings; and *Siemen* (The Seed; 1993) for two concert kanteles. Jalkanen has also composed a great deal of music for children, including the opera *Tirlittan* (1986) and the musical fairytale *Oi ihana Panama* (The Trip to Panama*, Janosch, 1989).

The principal works of KARI TIKKA (b. 1946) consist of religious music, such as the oratorio *Tuhlaajapoika* (The Prodigal Son; 1984) and the opera *Frieda* (1994), a story of missionaries. Tikka has been employed as a conductor at the Finnish National Opera since 1976.

FRIDRICH BRUK (b. 1937) was born in the Ukraine, emigrated to the United States and then moved to Finland. His music follows the Russian tradition of Shostakovich and Prokofiev. His most successful works are musical vignettes, such as the piano suite *Lyyrillisiä kuvia* (Lyrical Pictures; 1974). Bruk has composed several pedagogic works, as has the Joensuu composer LASSE

EEROLA (b. 1945), who is chiefly known as a composer of skilfully scored chamber music. The Turku-born LASSE JALAVA (b. 1951) is a self-taught composer. The first performance in 1995 of his Third Symphony (1990) was received very favourably by the critics; another significant work is Jalava's partly autobiographical Fourth Symphony (1994–95). The principal compositions of LARS KARLSSON (b. 1953), who studied with Einojuhani Rautavaara, include a concerto for organ and wind ensemble, an intensely melodic, virtuoso Violin Concerto (1991/93) and the extensive cantata *Ludus latruncolorum* (1994–96).

RALF GOTHONI (b. 1946) and OLLI MUSTONEN (b. 1967) Finland's two internationally best-known pianists, are both also composers. Gothoni has concentrated on vocal music, including song cycles in a style reminiscent of Seppo Nummi's lieder, the chamber opera *Ihmeellinen viesti toiselta tähdeltä* (A Marvellous Message from Another Star; 1984), the TV opera *Hund* (Dog; 1994–95) and the Zen Buddhist cantata *Härkä ja hänen paimenensa* (The Ox and His Oxherd; 1992). Mustonen's relatively few works consist mainly of piano pieces and chamber music; some of them are meditative and almost minimalistic (*Fantasia* for piano and strings; 1985), while others contain pianistic bravura and rhythmic gusto (*Toccata* for piano and string quintet; 1989). The 1996 Helsinki Festival featured a concert of Mustonen's works.

First-Generation Neotraditionalists

As we have seen, the Finnish neotraditionalists can readily be divided into a first and second generation. The former category consists of composers who went through a brief avantgarde phase during the first onslaught of modernism in the 1960s, then became guardians of tradition (Gottfrid Gräsbeck, Sakari Mononen, Kari Rydman, Erkki Salmenhaara), while the composers of the second group built upon the foundation of 1980s modernism, but began to shift in a traditionalist direction in the late 1980s. The latter group have been in a position to produce a synthesis of modernism (which by the 1980s was already part of the Finnish music tradition) and traditionalism proper. Their most recent works also reveal a respect for conventional musical craftsmanship.

Among the first-generation neotraditionalists, Gräsbeck, Mononen and Rydman were discussed in conjunction with their modernist period. ERKKI SALMENHAARA turned away from modernism for good in *Le Bateau ivre* (1965), one of his best orchestral compositions, in which he used triads as elements of his tone fields for the first time. After this work, he turned first to a polytonality reminiscent of Milhaud; later on, a kind of extremely reduced neotonality increasingly came to dominate his style, which the composer himself has characterized as postmodern *neue Schönheit*.

A wry, nostalgic-ironic humour also appears from time to time in Salmenhaara's works from the late 1960s, as in the 'asymphonic poem' *Suomi–Finland* (1967) and the orchestral poem *La Fille en mini-jupe* (1967), peppered with stylistic loans and allusions. From about 1970, his music took on a more serious tone. The cornerstones of his neotonal period include the *Requiem profanum* (1969) to secular texts, the Fourth Symphony *Keskipäivän sinfonia*, (Noon Symphony; 1972), the lyrical opera *Portugalin nainen* (The Portuguese Woman; 1972) to a libretto based on a short story by Robert Musil, the strange, near-minimalist Fourth Piano Sonata (1980) and the Fifth Symphony, *Lintukoto* (Isle of Bliss; 1989) for choir and orchestra.

In his quiet way, Salmenhaara questions the goals of modernism, and challenges the listener to be receptive to simplicity and beauty. His new style has not been much appreciated in Finland, and as a composer he has gradually become something of an outsider. Just recently, however, there has been a revival of interest in his music.

Erkki Salmenhaara turned in the mid '60s from avantgarde music to tonality and a new simplicity.

As a musicologist and essayist, however, Salmenhaara's merit is unreservedly recognized. He was lecturer of musicology at the University of Helsinki from 1966 to 1974, and was appointed associate professor in 1975. In the volume of published writings, Salmenhaara has outdone all other Finnish composers. In addition to his doctoral thesis on Ligeti, he has published books on harmony, the history of modern music, the symphonies of Brahms, and various aspects of Finnish music; the latter include a study of Sibelius's *Tapiola*, biographies of Madetoja and Sibelius, parts I–III of an extensive four-volume history of Finnish music (part I together with Fabian Dahlström), and *Säveltäjänä Suomessa* (To Be a Composer in Finland), a history of the Finnish Composers' Association. He has also held a variety of organizational posts. Salmenhaara is thus undoubtedly one of the most influential figures in the Finnish music world.

Successors to '60s Modernism

Althought the first onslaught of the avantgarde on Finnish music receded relatively soon, the modernist ideas survived in the work of certain composers after the 1960s. ERIK BERGMAN did not turn from the twelve-tone technique to either total serialism or a more traditional style, but continued to pursue an atonal style devoid of triads, progressing gradually towards freer rhythm. In the orchestral work *Colori ed improvvisazzioni*

(1973), he finally abandoned bar lines entirely for durational notation. He has continued to cultivate a lively interest in temporally and geographically remote music cultures.

Bergman's 'exotic' works include some of his finest music. The *Hathor Suite* for soprano, baritone, mixed choir and instrumental ensemble consists of German translations of ancient Egyptian texts. *Bardo Thödol* (1974), a 'cantata of death', is one of Bergman's key works. The words, from the Tibetan Book of Death, depict the process of preparing a dead man for rebirth. *Noa* (1976) for baritone and orchestra (composed for Matti Lehtinen, the singer of all of Bergman's many great baritone solos) is a kind of virtuoso vocal concerto, with individual Hebrew words in lieu of a text. The important a cappella choral work *Lapponia* (1975) makes use of the distinctive stylistic and structural features of the music of the Sámi (the indigenous Lapp people). *Lemminkäinen* (1984), Bergman's longest, almost operatic work for a cappella choir, has a musical idiom based on ancient Finnish dirges and the mythology of the *Kalevala*, from which the text is taken.

In contrast to Pehr Henrik Nordgren, who has also sought to incorporate elements of archaic or alien musical worlds in his music, Bergman hardly ever resorts to direct quotation in his quest for synthesis. By using modes of expression derived from folk music, he seeks instead to establish a musical atmosphere which alludes to either past or distant musical cultures and, at the same time, lends his compositions a new musical dimension. Like Nordgren, however, Bergman sometimes emphasizes the latter element by adding exotic instruments to his ensembles.

Sonority has been increasingly crucial to Bergman's late period, during which he has extended his compass by composing his first concertos – a concerto for cello, *Dualis* (1978); a concerto for flute, *Birds in the Morning* (1979), a Piano Concerto (1981) and a Violin Concerto (1982) – and a fair amount

Erik Bergman, the grand old man of Finnish postwar modernism, has delved into Oriental and ancient music cultures.

of chamber music (including *Silence and Eruptions* (1979) for chamber orchestra). Meanwhile, he has continued to add to his large choral oeuvre, with works such as the humorous *Bim Bam Bum* (1976) for reciter, tenor, male choir and instrumental ensemble.

The two-act fairytale opera *Det sjungande trädet* (The Singing Tree; 1986–88) constitutes the grand synthesis of Bergman's career, and contains some of his most expressive vocal music. The work is based on an old Swedish folk tale from Småland, which is in fact a version of the myth of Amor and Psyche as told by Apuleius. It is an allegorical tale of good and evil, light and darkness, egotism and selflessness, and the ultimate triumph of love. The work was originally commissioned by the Finnish National Opera for the 1993–94 season, but had to await its premiere until September 3, 1995. Bergman's creative energy is still intact – by summer 1996, his opus list had reached no. 135.

USKO MERILÄINEN also progressed from his twelve-tone period towards greater rhythmic freedom, giving an important role to controlled aleatorics. Meriläinen's recent works have been increasingly inward-looking: although lacking in superficial theatrics, his music has a rich inner life of its own. In his Second Piano Sonata (1966), Meriläinen developed what he calls a 'character technique', in which precise motivic relationships are not as important as the more general, perceptual similarities and differences between musical 'characters'. The sonata has three basic characters: the point (which may develop into repetition of tones), the line (motives and melodies) and the field (clusters, cascades of sound). The Fourth Piano Sonata (1974) is characterized by a juxtaposition of two different, realistic and unrealistic musical worlds: 'this side' (played from the keyboard) and 'the other side' (plucked inside the piano or damped). Meriläinen's Third and Fourth Piano Concertos, *Dialogeja* (Dialogues; 1981) and *Kineettinen runo* (Kinetic Poem; 1981), emphasize a 'kineticism' developed from his early, Stravinskyan style; this is usually expressed by rapidly-moving figures that rise against a background of prolonged notes and "push each other into motion".

Whereas the Second Piano Concerto (1969) contains a passionate expressiveness and the Third Symphony (1971) can be read, according to the composer himself, as the individual's comment on an increasingly violent world, his later works seem to view the world from a greater distance. In the Second Concerto for Orchestra, *Aikaviiva* (Timeline; 1989), the stubbornly repetitive ticking of notes seems to symbolize the inexorable advance of time and old age. The Third String Quartet (1991) follows up a violent opening with a long tailing-off, in which the advance of musical time seems to have come to a complete standstill, until only a musical horizon stretching out into eternity remains. Meriläinen's other works include the electronic ballet *Alasin* (The Anvil; 1975), which the composer also listed as his Fourth Symphony; the ballets *Psykhe* (1973) and *Ku-gu-ku* (9179); five symphonies (1953–55, 1964, 1971, [1975], 1976); a Cello Concerto (1975); *Visions and Whispers* (1985), an instrumentally rewarding concerto for flute; a Guitar Concerto (1991); the orchestral work *Kehrä* (The Spindle; 1996) and a large quantity of elegant chamber music and works for solo instrument, notably flute or piano (five piano sonatas). Meriläinen was chairman of the Finnish Composers' Association from 1980 to 1992.

Throughout his career, PAAVO HEININEN has remained faithful to the ideals of his youth, perhaps more uncompromisingly than any other Finnish composer. Heininen's reputation as a 'difficult' composer has not been alleviated by the fact that in defending the abundance of detail per unit of time in his music he has not made his works easy to assimilate at a first hearing. In an essay entitled "Freedom and Conformity to Laws in Music" (1983), Heininen explains his aesthetic principles thus:

> . . . the composer is just as free as the visual artist to place his stimuli in the order of his choice, as the recipient will, in any case, learn the course of the work by heart and thus experience every part as simultaneously present. The value of events is therefore not based on their predictability, indispensability or surprise effect, but on their being perceived as exactly as good as they are once they have been assimilated.

The Third Symphony (1969/77), one of Heininen's principal works, suffered the same fate as the First; only half of the work was played at the premiere, while the full work, entirely rewritten, was only performed a decade later. In contrast to this work, the partially aleatory Fourth Symphony (1971) is scored for a smaller ensemble, and even employs sonata form. Heininen's important opus 32 contains four compositions: the 40-minute grand piano sonata *Poesia squillante ed incandescente* (1974), a string quartet (1974) and two shorter piano pieces; the unifying factor is that all four works are formed on the basis of the same row.

Heininen's two operas are among his most ambitious works. They were preceded by his most important vocal composition, *Reality* for soprano and 10 instruments (1978), in which parts of the text are broken down into their phonetic constituents.

The one-act opera *Silkkirumpu* (The Damask Drum; 1983) is based on an old Japanese legend. The two-act *Veitsi* (The Knife; 1985–88), based on a libretto by Veijo Meri, has a more complex dramaturgy and is thus 'more difficult' for audiences. This work won the Savonlinna Opera Festival's competition in 1988 and was premiered as the jubilee work of the 350th anniversary of the city of Savonlinna. In some of his recent works, such as *Dicta* (1983) for 9+14 instruments, Heininen has explored the potential of the computer as an aid to composition.

Heininen's other later works include the orchestral compositions *Tritopos* (1977), *Dia* (1979) and *Two Essays* (1996); the Third Piano Concerto (1981), concertos for saxophone (1983) and cello (1985); chamber music, including *Jeu I* for flute and piano (1980); *Jeu II* for violin and piano (1980); choral works, such as *Poetiikka* (Poetics; 1990) for male choir; and the electroacoustic work *Maiandros* (1977). Heininen is also a concert pianist and the author of penetrating analytical essays on Bergman, Kokkonen, Englund, Meriläinen and others. His contribution as a teacher has been even more important: he was lecturer or part-time teacher at the Sibelius Academy from 1966 to 1992, and in 1993 became the Academy's professor of composition. In the early 1980s, Heininen's modernist style was emulated by Finnish students of composi-

Paavo Heininen has remained uncompromisingly faithful to the modernist ideals he adopted in his youth; he also passed on these ideals as the teacher of the generation of young composers who emerged in the 1980s.

tion; many of the most gifted among them (including Tiensuu, Hämeenniemi, Saariaho, Kaipainen and Lindberg) sought his instruction.

Pluralism and Neoexpressionism

Although most Finnish composers, including those who experimented with modernism in the 1960s, eventually abandoned the pure modernist aesthetic, many of the new techniques of composition survived as one alternative among many, including more traditional ones. As we have seen, this 'impure' approach to style was already found in the works of the 'nursery chamber composers' at the time when they were experimenting with collage and other techniques as an intermediate phase in the transition from avantgardism.

Particularly abrupt stylistic and aesthetic shifts in the quest for an individual style can be seen in the works of EINOJUHANI RAUTAVAARA. He followed up an avantgarde phase in the early '60s with a leap from strict constructivism to outright intuitism and headlong romanticism (First Piano Concerto, 1969). This new style was already incipient in the *Itsenäisyyskantaatti* (Independence Cantata; 1967) and Cello Concerto (1968). The romantic, mystical aspect of Rautavaara's personality is reflected in the titles of many of his compositions, such as the piano sonata *Tulisaarna* (The Fire Sermon; 1970) and the unusual *True & False Unicorn* (1971) for choir and chamber orchestra, the orchestral work *Angels and Visitations* (1978), the organ concerto *Annunciations* (1977) and the concerto for double bass *Angel of Dusk* (1980), while the extensive, two-part *Vigilia* (1971–72) interprets Orthodox mysticism in a highly personal and impressive manner.

In his most recent music (since the 1980s), Rautavaara has arrived at a postmodern idiom of sorts, combining modern and more traditional elements. His music also appears to have irrational features, as it were, giving his best, most complex works an added dimension. An excellent example is his most famous piece *Cantus arcticus* (1972), a concerto for birds and orchestra, with a simple enough orchestral background counterpointed against the taped song of arctic birds.

Opera is the central genre in Rautavaara's oeuvre. The early *Kaivos* was followed by *Apollon contra Marsyas* (1970), a comic 'operatic musical', in which the composer made use of elements from jazz and pop music. The mystery play *Marjatta matala neiti* (Marjatta, the Lowly Maiden; 1975) is a lovely Christmas story based on the *Kalevala* and scored for soprano, flute and children's choir. Its more masculine counterpart is *Sammon ryöstö (Runo 42)* (Theft of the Sampo (Rune 42); 1974/81), for male choir. *Thomas* (1984–85) depicts the collision of civilizations, as the ancient pagan world of the *Kalevala* gives way to Christianity. For the 350th anniversary competition of Savonlinna, Rautavaara composed *Vincent* (1986–87), a paraphrase of the life of Vincent van Gogh. The protagonists in *Auringon talo* (House of the Sun; 1990) are two sisters who emigrated to Finland after the Russian Revolution, and seek to continue their isolated, aristocratic way of life as if there never had been any revolution, although times change and their fortune dwindles away. *Tietäjien lahja* (The Gift of the Magi; 1994) is a beautiful, delicate Christmas story about love and of giving and receiving gifts. In his most recent opera *Aleksis Kivi* (1995–96), Rautavaara returns to the tragic

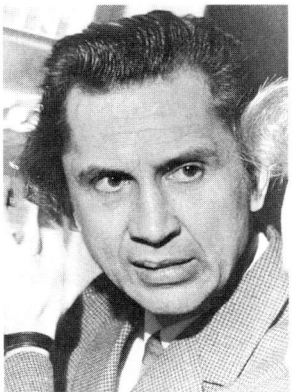

Einojuhani Rautavaara's career has been no smooth progression, but a series of radical shifts from one extreme to another.

fate of the artist (in this case a Finnish writer); the premiere will take place in Punkaharju's Retretti caverns in conjunction with the Savonlinna Opera Festival in 1997.

The other main genres that Rautavaara has focused on are the symphony (cf. p. 94) and the concerto. The opening of the one-movement Fifth Symphony (1985–86) contains some of his most 'cosmic' music. The Sixth Symphony, *Vincentiana* (1992) is based on his earlier opera; in a rather similar manner, Kalevi Aho – a former pupil of Rautavaara's – composed his Seventh Symphony (*Insect Symphony*) from the material of his opera *Hyönteiselämää* (Insect Life). Another key work by Rautavaara is the four-movement Seventh Symphony, *Angel of Light* (1994), a recording of which was a commercial hit on the international market. The flute concerto *Dances with the Winds* (1973) requires the soloist to play all four members of the flute family. The Violin Concerto (1977) is a songful piece rewarding for the performer, as is the Second Piano Concerto (1988–89).

Rautavaara has also composed a wealth of orchestral and chamber music as well as numerous often-performed choral and vocal works (including the well-known *Lorca Suite* for mixed choir; 1973). In some compositions, he has experimented with electronics.

Rautavaara was professor of composition at the Sibelius Academy from 1976 to 1988, a post in which he succeeded Erik Bergman. His students included Kalevi Aho, Olli Korte-kangas, Magnus Lindberg and Esa-Pekka Salonen. Rautavaara's international reputation has been growing rapidly in the 1990s; his first five symphonies were recorded in Leipzig, and *Vincent* was simultaneously in the repertoire of two German opera houses, Kiel and Hagen, in 1991. The operas *Thomas* and *Auringon talo* have also been performed in Germany. In spring 1996, some of the world's leading record journals fea-tured long interviews and cover stories on him. At the same time, the Ondine record label started preparing the formidable project of recording Rautavaara's complete works.

The best works of PEHR HENRIK NORDGREN (b. 1944) also contain a fascinating element of the irrational, primarily arising from the powerful stylistic contrasts he employs. Born on the island of Åland, Nordgren settled in Kaustinen in central Ostrobothnia in 1973. He studied composition privately with Joonas Kokkonen. In his first period, he produced expressive, angst-filled orchestral works featuring a highly personal combination of twelve-tone technique and Ligetian field technique (*Euphonie II* (1967) and the 'pollution oratorio' *Agnus Dei* (1970)). Nordgren's encounter with Finnish folk music and his studies in Japan under Yoshio Hasegawa (1970–73) greatly modified his musical idiom. In *Neljä kuolemankuvaa* (Four Images of Death; 1968) for chamber orchestra, he uses folk tunes as building blocks for tone clusters. The Concerto for clarinet, three folk instruments and orchestra (1970) juxtaposes quotations from Finnish folk music and instruments with a modern, dodecaphonic idiom. One of his best works is the *Autumnal Concerto* for four Japanese instruments and orchestra (1974), which pairs elements and impulses from traditional Japanese music with the entirely different European tradition.

Nordgren's idiom has simplified and clarified greatly since the mid 1970s. His most important work in the '80s was the cantata *Taivaanvalot* (Heaven's Lights; 1985), an arresting blend of the past (represented by ancient Finnish folk instruments and rune-singing tunes) and the musical present (modern instruments and musical idiom). An important strand in his oeuvre consists of fifteen works for string orchestra, composed for the Central Ostrobothnian Chamber Orchestra, a Kokkola ensemble conducted by Juha Kangas. Nordgren's collaboration with this ensemble began with *Pelimannimuoto-kuvia* (Fiddlers' Portraits; 1976), in which the musical material consists of local fiddlers' tunes. The peak achievements in this

Pehr Henrik Nordgren, who lives in Kaustinen, combines elements of Finnish and Japanese folk music in a highly original way in some of his compositions.

series are the *Symphony for Strings* (1978), the highly original *Transe–Choral* (1985) and *Cronaca* (1991). *Beaivi, áhčážan* (The Sun, My Father; 1990) is a setting of a Sámi text by Nils-Aslak Valkeapää. Nordgren has also composed the chamber opera *Den svarta munken* (The Black Monk; 1981) with a libretto based on a Chekhov story, and the TV opera *Alex*. His extensive oeuvre includes four violin concertos, four cello concertos, two viola concertos, a saxophone concerto, a trumpet concerto, three symphonies and an abundance of chamber music (including seven string quartets). Nordgren's great spiritual (but not stylistic) hero is Shostakovich; he has also written a study on the Russian composer's instrumentation.

The Austrian-born HERMAN RECHBERGER (b. 1947) settled in Finland in 1970 and studied composition with Aulis Sallinen. Before coming to Finland, he had graduated as a graphic artist and had studied classical guitar in Linz, Zürich and Brussels. He has composed several concertante works for guitar (including the *Concierto floral* for guitar and orchestra; 1993). Rechberger also plays the recorder, and in 1989 compiled the new ways to play the instrument that he had invented into a book, *Die Blockflöte in der zeitgenössischen Musik*.

While also producing perfectly normal instrumental and vocal works, Rechberger has focused on areas that other Finn-

Herman Rechberger at the Tampere Biennale, 1996.

ish composers have either neglected or overlooked entirely. Thus, *Pekka Mikkosen nousu* (The Rise of Jonathan Smith; 1978) and *Magnus Cordius* (1985) are humorous radiophonic works reminiscent of radio plays. He has also composed works scored with graphic notation, music theatre and happenings. Rechberger himself has said that the decisive impetus for his present style came from Alfred Schnittke and Mauricio Kagel; like Schnittke, Rechberger tends to combine different musical styles and periods. He takes a particular interest in the music of the Renaissance, cultivating musical loans within an otherwise contemporary idiom in the *Consort Music I–V* (1974–1986), the operas *Die Nonnen* (1988/1994–95) and *Laurentius* (1991), and his most important, imaginative and scintillating orchestral work *Venezia* (1985), which includes music theatre as well. Rechberger is not particularly interested in motivic work or strict consistency of form, but makes up for this with the fantastic richness of sound.

Other works that illustrate Rechberger's style of composition well include *Himojen puutarha* (The Garden of Delights; 1977; after the painting by Hieronymus Bosch); the lush orchestral poem *La Tentation de Saint Antoine* (1995); the *Cantiones eroticae* (1974) for choir and Renaissance instruments, which ends in laughter and confusion; the tape work *Naród* (1978), which contains elements from the folklore of seventeen different Soviet nations; and *Lemmennosto* (Raising Love; 1984) for male choir, based on ancient spells to boost sexual potency. Rechberger has also composed music for children and written a guide to composing contemporary music for children's choir, *Laula ja luo* (Sing and Create; 1975). His most recent works show the influence of minimalism.

TEPPC HAUTA-AHO (b. 1941) is a self-taught composer. His main instrument is the double bass, and he has played that instrument in the orchestra of the Finnish National Opera since 1975. He is also one of Finland's best-known jazz bassists. Hauta-aho combines instrumental experimentation with a more traditional, musicianly idiom, and his humorous works sometimes include elements of music theatre. He has composed music of various degrees of difficulty for children. Many of Hauta-aho's works exploring the potential of the double bass have found their way into the international repertoire. He won the 1986 Queen Maria Jose competition in Geneva with *Fantasia* (1986), a concerto for piccolo trumpet. He is also a jazz composer.

MIKKO HEINIÖ (b. 1948) began studying composition with Joonas Kokkonen, and later studied with Witold Szalonek in West Berlin. His music stems from his own experiences as a musician: he played pop music as a youngster; in the 1970s he was a lieder pianist and conducted his own music. His principal compos tions are concertante orchestral and vocal works. He followed up a somewhat neoclassically inspired *Concerto grosso* (1975) with a series of more constructivist works, including *Tredicia* (1976), which applied the Fibonacci number sequence to form and harmony. His two early piano concertos (1971, ´973) were followed by concertos for bassoon (1977) and horn (1978). The dodecaphonic Third Piano Concerto (1981) was more distinctive than the earlier ones, and his Fourth Piano Concerto (1986), subtitled *Genom kvällen*

(Through the Evening) was a new departure in the genre, being scored for piano, choir and chamber orchestra. The Fifth Piano Concerto is also a notable work (1989). Heiniö's Sixth Piano Concerto, *Hermes* (1994), is a dance work for choreography, piano and string orchestra; this blend of genres was premiered at the Turku Music Festival in 1995. A concertante approach also characterizes many of Heiniö's orchestral works proper, such as the *Concerto for Orchestra* (1982).

In his vocal works, Heiniö likes to set texts that are characterized either by depth of experience (as in his two settings of the poetry of Edith Södergran, *Landet som icke är* (The Land That Is Not) and *Framtidens skugga* (The Shadow of the Future); both 1980) or a humanitarian message (*Vuelo de alambre* (1983), a notable orchestral song cycle composed to texts by Chilean political prisoners). Heiniö's most extensive vocal work is *Mannerkantaatti* (Continent Cantata; 1985) for choir and orchestra, set to a text by Lassi Nummi; the most personal and moving, however, is *Tuulenkuvia* (Wind Pictures; 1991) for choir and orchestra. In *Possible Worlds* (1987), his symphonic magnum opus, Heiniö employs the musical aesthetic of multiple possibility all but programmatically. Some of his chamber music is humorous in intent – a case in point is *Champignons à l'herméneutique* for flute and guitar (1979), dedicated to various species of poisonous mushrooms. His other main chamber music works include a 'swinging' Piano Trio (1988) and Piano Quintet (1993); in the midst of the latter piece, the players recite verses from *Alice in Wonderland*. He has also composed pure choral works, such as *Kolme kansanlaulua* (Three Folksongs; 1977) and *Non-Stop* (1995).

A highly respected musicologist, Heiniö has made a special study of postwar Finnish music, and examined the arrival and reception in Finland of new musical trends in the 20th century. In his highly-acclaimed doctoral thesis *Tradition ja innovaation idea* (The Idea of Tradition and Innovation; 1984), he studied the attitudes of Finnish composers to modernism and traditionalism in the light of their writings. He wrote the contemporary section, or Part IV, of the aforementioned history of Finnish music, which was published in 1995. His writings on contemporary Finnish music are among the pioneering studies on the subject. In 1986, Heiniö was appointed professor of musicology at the University of Turku. He has held official positions in many Finnish music organizations, and has served as chairman of the Finnish Composers' Association since 1992.

KALEVI AHO (b. 1949) studied composition with Einojuhani Rautavaara at the Sibelius Academy, then with Boris Blacher in West Berlin. The backbone of his oeuvre consists of orchestral works, including ten symphonies (1969, 1970, 1971–73, 1972–73, 1975–76, 1979–80, 1988, 1993, 1994, 1996), concertos for violin (1981), cello (1983–84) and piano (1989), *Pergamon* for 4 orchestral groups, 4 reciters and (electric) organ (1990), *Syvien vesien juhla* (Deep Waters Rejoice; 1995) for orchestra, and three chamber symphonies for string orchestra (1976, 1992, 1995–96). Some of his symphonies have a concertante character with solo parts; thus, the Third Symphony is scored for violin and orchestra, the monumental Eighth Symphony features the organ as a solo instrument, the Ninth Symphony a trombone and the Third Chamber Symphony an alto saxophone. Aho has also composed extensively for chamber ensembles (quintets, quartets, sonatas, solo pieces). His operatic monologue *Avain* (The Key; 1978; libretto by Juha Mannerkorpi) was an international success, and was performed in the 1982 and 1984 seasons at the Hamburg State Opera. His second opera, the satirical morality play *Hyönteiselämää* (Insect Life; 1985–87) is based on the play of the same name by the Czech brothers Josef and Karel Čapek. The work was premiered at the Finnish National Opera on September 27, 1996. Pluralist tendencies were already present in Aho's first major work, the First Symphony (1969), and are most conspicuous in the Bassoon Quintet (1977) and the Symphonies No. 7 (1988) and No. 9 (1994) – thus, all six movements in the Seventh Symphony are in different styles, and each new movement forms an antithesis to the one that went before. The oboe figures prominently in Aho's chamber music output (Quintet for oboe and string quartet (1973); Oboe Sonata (1985)). Perhaps his outstanding chamber music composition is the extensive Quintet for alto saxophone, bassoon, viola, cello and double bass (1994). The most prominent of his numerous orchestral arrangements are the orchestration of Modest Mussorgsky's *Songs and Dances of Death* (1984), the instrumentation to Act I of Uuno Klami's ballet *Pyörteitä* (Whirls; 1988) and the lost second violin part to Erik Tulindberg's six string quartets (1995).

In his writings, Aho has stressed the importance of communication in music, and characterized his own aesthetic as that of opposition and questioning – he feels that music should arouse the listeners, enhancing their awareness of life and the world. From 1974 to 1988 he was lecturer of musicology at the University of Helsinki, and from 1988 to 1993 acting professor of composition at the Sibelius Academy. In 1992 he was nominated 'house composer' of the Lahti Symphony Orchestra; he has dedicated all of his works for

Kalevi Aho and his characteristic smile.

symphony orchestra since 1992 to this outstanding ensemble. Aho has written widely about music: he has had columns in several newspapers in the 1990s and has published the studies *Suomalainen musiikki ja Kalevala* (Finnish Music and the *Kalevala*), *Einojuhani Rautavaara sinfonikkona* (E.R. as Symphonist) and the essay collection *Taiteilijan tehtävät postmodernissa yhteiskunnassa* (The Tasks of the Artist in Postmodern Society). Aho has been involved in many organizational duties; he is a founding member and long-time chairman of the Society for the Publication of New Finnish Music (Edition Pan).

Aho has won numerous international awards: he received the Danish Leonie Sonning Prize in 1974, the arts grant "Auswärtige Künstler zu Gast in Hamburg" from Land Hamburg in 1982; the Henrik Steffens Prize in Germany in 1990, and the Polish Flisaka '96 Award for his entire oeuvre to date in 1996. *

'Here and Now' Expressionism

LEIF SEGERSTAM (b. 1944) is a maverick composer, far removed from the mainstream. He started composing as a post-expressionist with the miniature ballet *Pandora* (1967) and the orchestral song cycle *Sju röda stunder* (Seven Red Moments; 1967). In his Fifth String Quartet, the *Sopulikvartetto* (Lemming Quartet), he developed an idiosyncratic, "free pulsative" composition technique which he still adheres to.This technology enables him to compose very fast; during performances, the conductor has the opportunity, as it were, to re-compose the work, as the rhythmic freedom accorded by the score permits considerable variation in the overall dramaturgy and the relative duration of passages.

Segerstam's basic attitude to composing is that of a roman-

---

* The section on Aho was written by Erkki Salmenhaara.

tic, and his music is characterized by an almost over-expressive, churning pathos. He stresses the 'here and now' in creating and performing music, seeking, as it were, to extend it to the utmost and thereby lend it the greatest possible intensity. Even though he is a renowned conductor who regularly tours the great music centres of the world, Segerstam has managed to produce a substantial oeuvre (including twenty-one symphonies, twenty-eight string quartets, some twenty works for solo instrument and orchestra, etc.). Segerstam's 'own' orchestra at present (1996) is the Helsinki Philharmonic, and he is also chief conductor of the Royal Swedish Opera in Stockholm.

Young Modernism in the '70s
The New Moderns

The musical philosophy of JARMO SERMILÄ (b. 1939) is rooted in the ideas of Edgar Varèse; he is also well-versed in recent Czechoslovakian music, as he followed up his initial studies with Joonas Kokkonen by studying in Prague. Sermilä has served in some of the leading posts in Finnish music organizations (he was executive director of the Finnish Music Information Centre from 1971 to 1976, artistic director of the YLE experimental studio from 1972 to 1979, and has served since 1987 as artistic director of the Viitasaari Time of Music, a festival of contemporary music). He has been managing director of Jasemusiikki Oy, a publisher of sheet music and records, since 1976.

Sermilä's started his composing career at a relatively late age in the 1970s. In his chief work of the '70s, *Aikakone* (Time Machine; 1978) for large brass and percussion ensemble, he combined conventional bar notation with fields built up by means of aleatory counterpoint, prolonged, floating sounds and dotted notes expressed with space-time notation. In the percussion quintet *Myyttinen mies* (The Mythical Man; 1982) Sermilä approaches minimalism. His second work on a *Kalevala*

Usko Meriläinen, longtime chairman of the Finnish Composers' Association, and the cigar-smoking Jarmo Sermilä, its vice-chairman.

subject, *Hiiet hirveä rakenti* (The Demons Made an Elk; 1984) for two trombones, two percussionists and tape, contains free improvisation as well as repetitive elements. Sermilä's other works include tape music, chamber music (primarily for winds) and a number of orchestral works, the most important of which is probably *Quattro rilievi* for chamber orchestra (1988–89). His principal works of the '90s include *Matkalla – muuan aikamme konsertto* (On the Road – a Concerto for Our Time; 1993) for trumpet, percussion and chorus; *Un asserzione di una signora* (1994) for horn and strings (1994) and *But I Didn't Know It Was Spring* for trumpet and tape (1995). Sermilä has performed as a jazz musician (flugelhorn and trumpet), frequently playing experimental jazz with Teppo Hauta-aho and others.

Like Sermilä and Tauno Marttinen, ERKKI JOKINEN (b. 1941) lives in Hämeenlinna. Jokinen, who studied with Erik Bergman, has produced a rather small but excellent oeuvre. Bergman's influence, however, can hardly be detected in his work, which seems closer to the post-serialist school of Paavo Heininen. Jokinen has concentrated chiefly on chamber music and works for chamber orchestra. His most frequently performed works are accordion pieces, which were originally composed for Matti Rantanen and are now finding their way into the basic Finnish accordion repertoire (*Alone* for solo accordion (1979); *Reflections* for two accordions (1983)). The most important of Jokinen's accordion works, and one of his very best compositions overall, is the Concerto for accordion and chamber orchestra (1987). His other main works include four string quartets (1972, 1976, 1988, 1993); *Face* (1983) for flute, harp, harpsichord and string trio; the violin concerto *Voyage I* (1990); and *Voyage II* (1991), a concerto for chamber orchestra. Jokinen was appointed lecturer at the Sibelius Academy in 1985.

Electroacoustic Music in the '70s

A new group of composers specializing in electroacoustic music arose in Finnland in the 1970s, partly through the influence of Osmo Lindeman. The development of electroacoustic music was given a strong boost by construction of the YLE experimental studio in 1972. Its first artistic director was Jarmo Sermilä, and its sound engineers were PEKKA SIRÉN (b. 1946) and, since 1982, JUHANI LIIMATAINEN (b. 1952). Liimatainen, in particular, has been an invaluable resource for young composers who have worked for the national broadcasting company. The third sound engineer to have had a major impact on the development of Finnish tape music is ANTERO HONKANEN (b. 1941), head of the radio sound effects department.

Another studio was set up in the '70s at the University of Helsinki music department. This was the domain of JUKKA RUOHOMÄKI (b. 1947), who sought to specialize in tape music from the start. Ruohomäki's tape works are lyrical, softly sonorous. One of his best works from the '70s was the delightful 'laughing piece' *NRUT I* (1978). He took a long break from composing in the '80s, but returned to the fray in 1995 with *Viiltoja* (Slashes), for which he used sounds produced by sheet metal. This work won first prize at the Bourges festival of electronic music in 1996.

Besides composing electroacoustic music, OTTO ROMANOWSKI (b. 1952) has made a special study of the most recent computer technology in music; he may well be the leading Finnish expert in the field. Romanowski works in his own well-equipped sound studio. Among his most entertaining works is *Vocalise* (1976), in which a piano accompanies a soundtrack of growly singing. The third Finnish composer to concentrate on electroacoustic music and computers is PATRICK KOSK (b. 1951), a largely self-taught composer who started working on tape music in the University of Helsinki studio at the urging of Ruohomäki. Kosk has won several international awards for his tape works, which make use of concrete sound material. In addition to 'pure' tape music, he has made electronic music for radio and stage plays and cross-cultural events, and composed radiophonies such as *Trance Dance* (1981) and *Panoptikon* (1984).

In the late 1980s, the Sibelius Academy established its own studio, which currently represents the leading edge among public electroacoustic music studios in Finland. Composers who started their studies in the 1980s and '90s have produced most of their tape music at the Academy studio.

The 'Ears Open' Generation:
'80s Modernism and After

The late '70s and early '80s were a turbulent period in Finnish music, as modernism returned to the scene with a vengeance. The young modernist composers gathered under the banner of the *Korvat auki -yhdistys* (Ears Open Society) founded in 1977. The society's first chairman and chief ideologue was Eero

Hämeenniemi, and other active members in the early years were the composers Kaija Saariaho, Tapani Länsiö, Olli Kortekangas, Jouni Kaipainen, Esa-Pekka Salonen and Magnus Lindberg. Another pivotal figure in the 'second coming' of modernism was Jukka Tiensuu, who revived the Finnish Society of Contemporary Music, which had been disbanded in the '60s, and served as its chairman from 1979 to 1983. Tiensuu also established the *Helsinki Biennale*, dedicated to contemporary music, and was its artistic director from 1979 to 1983, then went on to set up the Viitasaari *Time of Music* summer festival, which he directed from 1981 to 1987. The *Tampere Biennale* of contemporary Finnish music was founded in 1986 by Usko Meriläinen, who is still its artistic director.

The new modernist breakthrough could not have happened without a decisive improvement in the standard of young musicians, as a result of the growth of a network of music institutes throughout Finland in the 1960s and '70s. Performances of new music had previously been largely up to the national broadcasting company and its symphony orchestra, new music ensemble and chamber choir. From the composers' point of view, the problem was the difficulty in getting their works scored for small chamber orchestra performed, as even the new music ensemble, made up of members of the Radio Symphony Orchestra, gave concerts only irregularly. A new ensemble called *Miksi ei* (Why Not) was established in the latter half of the 1970s, but proved short-lived. However, the *Avanti!* chamber orchestra, established on the initiative of Esa-Pekka Salonen and the conductor-cum-violinist JUKKA-PEKKA SARASTE, attained a highly conspicuous role by concentrating particularly on making modernist Finnish works known. The musicians of Avanti! arranged the first *Summer Sounds* festival in Porvoo in 1986, which also initially focused on the music of the young modernists of the '80s and of older modernist classics. The *Toimii!* (It Works!) ensemble, which originally included the composers Esa-Pekka Salonen, Magnus Lindberg and Otto Romanowski, the cellist Anssi Karttunen and the clarinetist Kari Kriikku, was founded in 1980. Lindberg composed *Kraft* for Toimii! and orchestra, and the ensemble generally served as a laboratory for its members' experiments with live electronics and improvisation.

The "Ears Open" composers, with the exception of Rautavaara's pupils Kortekangas and Salonen, all studied with Paavo Heininen at one time or another. Indeed, they came to be called the "Heininen school", as the older composer's influence on their aesthetics was so palpable. What united them was not so much similarity of style or personality as a *post-serialist* aesthetic – they studiously avoided any association with neoromantic or free tonal tendencies. Their aesthetics owed a great deal to twelve-tone and serial techniques. Although they did not necessarily employ these techniques systematically, their compositions shared an atonal language of intervals, melodic-rhythmic differentiation and complex polyphony, often reflected in highly complicated notation. Essential ingredients of the Ears Open ideology also included a critique of "national self-sufficiency" and demands to keep up with "international developments". The young modernists rejected the Finnish opera boom of the '70s out of hand – thus, Jouni Kaipainen coined the derisive term "fur cap operas" for the successful works of Sallinen and Kokkonen. They also turned their back on the Finnish symphonic tradition. The only members of the older generation of Finnish composers deemed worthy of performance at their new festivals of contemporary music were Bergman, Meriläinen and Heininen; Englund, Kokkonen, Rautavaara and Sallinen – viewed as the Finnish music establishment – were left out, and so were many of their younger colleagues, including Nordgren, Heiniö and Aho. Later on in the '80s, post-serialist aesthetics became virtually institutionalized as the official ideology of contemporary music by many Finnish music organizations; this attitude was firmly rooted in the Finnish music world by the end of the decade. Thus, the works representing YLE in the Prix Italia competition and the international composers' rostrum of UNESCO were regularly selected from among the modernist circle. In all fairness, these works had considerable success – Finland won numerous awards at both events. Another 'official' aesthetics continued to be represented by the operas performed by the Finnish National Opera on its foreign tours and produced for the Savonlinna Opera Festival. Contemporary Finnish opera in general has enjoyed unusually detailed coverage in the international press. As the '80s wore on, the Ears Open group began to diverge, either towards traditionalism (Hämeenniemi), neo-classicism (Tiensuu, Kaipainen, Lindberg), a new simplicity (Kortekangas) or colourism (Saariaho). Meanwhile, modernism became an established part of the music tradition, and the Ears Open composers themselves turned into the new musical establishment.

The Second Neotraditionalist Generation

EERO HÄMEENNIEMI (b. 1951), the 'chief ideologue' of the early Ears Open years, was the first to turn away from the post-serialist ideals of the years around 1980. Hämeenniemi studied at the Sibelius Academy with Paavo Heininen, and rounded off his musical education with Bogusław Schaeffer in Poland, Franco Donatoni in Italy and Joseph Schwantner in the United States. In his diploma composition, the Symphony for Strings (1977), Hämeenniemi still applied twelve-tone technique in a fairly classic, linear manner. He then began to experiment with various modernist approaches (as in the chamber music work *Dedicato* (1978), based on various musical 'gestures'), until returning in the First Symphony (1983) to a simpler but more expressive musical idiom, reminiscent at times of the twelve-tone period of Joonas Kokkonen. The expressive Clarinet So-

Olavi Pesonen, legendary for his impromptu speeches, talking with Eero Hämeenniemi at the Finnish Composers' International Copyright Bureau TEOSTO annual meeting in 1993.

nata (1984), with its melodies based on wide intervals, continued along this path. In 1984 he also completed the orchestral work *Soitto* (The Playing), which seeks to abstract the essence of the description of the hero Väinämöinen's music-making in the *Kalevala*. Other representative examples of Hämeenniemi's neotraditionalist musical idiom include the Second Symphony (1988), one of his finest works; the ballet *Loviisa* (1985–86), based on a theme by the playwright Hella Wuolijoki; the Violin Concerto (1990–91); and *Leonardo* (1991–92), also a narrative ballet, depicting the life of the Renaissance artist.

Hämeenniemi takes a lively interest in non-European civilizations. He is particularly well-versed in Indian culture, the influence of which is strongest in *Nattuvanar* (1993) for male choir, a work which won Hämeenniemi first prize at the UNESCO international composers' rostrum, in *Lintu ja tuuli* (The Bird and the Wind; 1993–94) for string orchestra, soprano and two

Indian temple dancers, and in the orchestral work *Karnatika* (1995). In seeking a way out of the impasse at which contemporary Western art music has arrived, Hämeenniemi has resorted to jazz as well as to Indian music. In the 1990s, he has played piano in Nada, a jazz ensemble he founded together with saxophonist Pentti Lahti. Hämeenniemi composed an extensive jazz work called *The Nada Project* for this ensemble in 1994; in 1993, he had already composed the multi-movement jazz works *From a Book I Haven't Read* and *From Navarasa (The Nine Moods)* for UMO, Finland's only professional big band. The latter work is built up on the moods of Indian music, which serve as the basis for improvisation.

From 1982 to 1992, Hämeenniemi was lecturer of composition at the Sibelius Academy, where he still teaches part-time, although he received a 15-year government grant in 1993. In *Tekopalmun alla* (Under the Artificial Palm Tree; 1993), a collection of polemical essays, he discusses his own musical aesthetics and critically analyses the current state of contemporary music.

For TAPANI LÄNSIÖ (b. 1953), the modernist phase in the late '70s and early '80s was not very productive. His work as director of the Polytechnic Choir since the late '80s has opened up new perspectives on composition to him. His best works are in fact scored for male or mixed choir; his choral works particularly aim at conveying the meaning of the text clearly. Most of his choral works are short and aphoristic; many – e.g. *Puut* (Trees) for chamber choir (1992) – are settings of the poetry of Paavo Haavikko. Quiet cluster surfaces and glass-like tape sounds dominate *Traum(a)* for male choir and tape (1988). Länsiö is a music critic and lecturer for 20th-century music at the Sibelius Academy since 1993.

The Ukrainian-born VLADIMIR AGOPOV (b. 1953) studied at the Tchaikovsky Conservatoire in Moscow with Aram Khatchaturian and Edison Denisov, and then, after emigrating to Finland in 1978, at the Sibelius Academy with Paavo Heininen. The Finnish composer's influence is clear in Agopov's first compositions of note, the Clarinet Sonata (1981) and First String Quartet (1982). The most important work in his small oeuvre is the cello concerto *Tres viae* (1984), with a highly expressive melody line and dramatic narrative form.

HARRI AHMAS (b. 1957) has concentrated on chamber music, much of it scored with great artistry and rewarding for the musicians. His strangest composition is *Becket* (1993), a kind of melodrama for mezzo-soprano, cello and piano. Ahmas's main work thus far is the Concerto for tuba, string orchestra, piano and percussion (1995). Ahmas is one of Finland's leading bassoon players – he is currently the Lahti Symphony Orchestra's solo bassoonist.

OLIVER KOHLENBERG (b. 1957) was born in Aachen, Germany and initially studied composition with Diether de la Motte and Klaus Huber. After settling in Finland in 1980, he continued his studies with Einojuhani Rautavaara. Kohlenberg has remained something of a peripheral composer in Finland, no doubt because he has lived in Kajaani and Oulu in northern Finland, far from the Helsinki circles which dominate the Finnish music world. Kohlenberg's works are unusual and often very extensive. The theme for the opera *Sina ja kookospuu* (Sina and the Coconut Tree; 1987) derived from his stay in Western Samoa in 1986–87. There is also a dose of exoticism in the fifty-minute Second Piano Sonata, *Umanak* (1982–83) and the First Symphony, *Pimentola* (The Place of Darkness; 1979). The Trumpet Concerto (1985) bears a stylistic affinity to the music of Berg and Henze, while *Siljan kesä* (Silja's Summer; 1988) for string orchestra is somewhat reminiscent of Pehr Henrik Nordgren's music for strings. Kohlenberg's other major compositions include a *Grande sonate* for violin and piano (1982–84); the Second Symphony, *Da camera* (1985); *Hymnus* for 16 trombones (1991–92), *Sonata flautologica* for 16 flutes (1992); a

Chamber Concerto for tuba, vibraphone and strings (1993–94) and the trio *Blue Gleam of Arctic Hystery* (1995) for baritone, percussion and piano. His chief work to date is the three-hour, three-act opera *Sipirjan lapsi* (Child of Sipirja; 1992–96) to a theme by Timo K. Mukka.

Modern Colourism

Among the Ears Open group, KAIJA SAARIAHO (b. 1952) and Magnus Lindberg had the greatest international success in the 1980s. Saariaho has remained true to the musical principles she arrived at in the early '80s. Continuing her studies in Freiburg (with Klaus Huber and Brian Ferneyhough), Saariaho became fascinated with the potential offered by electronics and computers, and in 1982 she went to work at the IRCAM studio in Paris, where she still lives. Her husband Jean-Baptiste Barrière is head of IRCAM's education department.

Saariaho's earliest works were associated with Finnish post-serialism. Her distinctive qualities began to show in *…sah den Vögeln* for soprano, instrumental ensemble and tape (1981), were more clearly in evidence in the computer-aided tape work *Vers le blanc* (1982), and finally came into their own in her first orchestral work, *Verblendungen* (1982–84). This work has an extreme clarity: the big bang in the first few bars is followed by an uninterrupted diminuendo, initially dominated by the orchestra and at the close by tape music. Here and in her later works, Saariaho pays particular attention to sonority. Her compositions often have a dreamlike atmosphere and static dramaturgy. Textures and sounds tend to glide into one another, without clear boundaries.

Working with a computer particularly helped Saariaho in her aim to control all factors of composition – both details and form – from the same set of premises. This tendency is particularly pronounced in *Jardin Secret I* for tape (1984–85) and its companion piece, *Jardin Secret II* for harpsichord and tape

Mikko Heiniö and Kaija Saariaho at the Nordic Music Days in Copenhagen, 1994.

(1984–86). The shimmering *Lichtbogen* (1985–86) for live electronics and instrumental ensemble is one of Saariaho's finest pieces. *Io* for chamber ensemble, tape and live electronics (1986–87) was composed for the tenth anniversary of the Centre Pompidou. The composition is based on a computer analysis of the sounds of instruments. *Nymphea* for string quartet and live electronics (1987) is a static piece, with alternating 'smooth' and 'rough' – jagged or granular – surfaces. Another very static work is *Maa* (Earth; 1991), a ballet in seven scenes, scored for eight instruments and electronics.

The radiophonic work *Stilleben* (1987–88) is a seminal composition, and one of Saariaho's finest. The text consists of Kafka's letters, and the idea is the theme of travel; the acoustic backdrop was provided by mixing the sounds produced by a choir, chamber orchestra and reciter with concrete and electronic sounds. This radiophony won the Prix Italia in 1988.

Other notable works by Saariaho include a pair of orchestral works called *Du cristal* (1989–90) and . . . *à la Fumée* (for amplified alto flute and cello with orchestra; 1990); *Amers* for cello, ensemble and live electronics (1992); *Solar* for chamber ensemble and synthesizer (1993); *Près* for cello and electronics (1992–94); *Graal théâtre* (1994), a violin concerto composed for Gidon Kremer; and *Trois rivières* (1993–94) for four percussionists, with an energy and drive adding a new element to Saariaho's image. One of her principal vocal works is *Château de l'âme* for soprano, eight female voices and orchestra (1995); its premiere at the Salzburg Festival in August 1996 was a resounding success. Saariaho is today one of the very best-known women composers in the world.

Although some of the younger generation of Finnish composers have responded favourably to Saariaho's music, her highly individual colourism has not been imitated. Only two composers among the generation that came to the limelight in the 1980s have cultivated a certain neoimpressionism. OLLI KOSKELIN (b. 1955) studied composition privately with Jukka Tiensuu and Eero Hämeenniemi. His public début was the expressive, post-serialist *Music for String Quartet* (1981). *Exalté* (1985) for solo clarinet consists of one steadily accelerating buildup. Broad acoustic surfaces prevail in *Tutte le corde* (1988) for guitar and tape; this work is also characterized by a repetitiveness bordering on minimalism. Koskelin's neo-impressionist tendencies, particularly evident in the piano work *Courbures* (1989), are also to the fore in . . . *kuin planeetta hiljaa hengittävä* (. . .like a planet silently breathing; 1993) for chamber orchestra and in the Clarinet Concerto (1995–96).

JYRKI LINJAMA (b. 1962) studied with Einojuhani Rautavaara, then in Budapest with Zsolt Durko and in Berlin with Witold Szalonek. Linjama is essentially a lyrical composer, whose works contain romantic gestures (*Aufschwung* for cello and piano (1985); *Elegie für Streicher* (1987)) and an inclination for 'romantic colourism'; the latter tendency is clearest in

Linjama's most important works, his two violin concertos (1989, 1991).

New Simplicity, Complexity and Vitalism

OLLI KORTEKANGAS (b. 1955) was one of Rautavaara's composition students. From his almost minimalist early works, which took turns parodying contemporary music (*Fingerprints*; 1980) and tonal music (Organ Sonata; 1979), he moved towards a more modernist idiom, the most notable outcome of which was a pair of orchestral works, *Ökologie I* and *II* (1983, 1986–87). Post-serialism did not, however, exercise the same fascination for him as for other members of his generation, and right from the start Kortekangas sought a 'modern simplicity' which set him apart from the complexity pursued by many of his colleagues. This tendency is clear in works such as the evocative *Lumen valo* (The Glow of Snow; 1984) for male choir. A significant strand in his music is represented by two spare, static works composed for the Tapiola Children's Choir, *MAA* (1984–85) and *A* (1988); the latter includes elements of music theatre. Kortekangas won first prize at the international TV opera festival in Salzburg in 1989 for his surrealist TV opera *Grand Hotel* (1984–85) and a special award in the 1989 Prix Italia for his radiophonic work *Memoria* (1988–89). The *Konzertstück* for clarinet and chamber orchestra (1992–93) is static, simple music of silence; the same goes for much of the biblical opera *Joonan kirja* (The Book of Jonah; 1994), which received its premiere on the small stage of the Finnish National Opera in October 1995. Kortekangas has been active in many Finnish music organizations, and has been employed as part-time teacher of composition and music theory at the Sibelius Academy since 1984.

The most important works by HARRI VIITANEN (b. 1954) are organ compositions. After completing his studies with Rautavaara and Tristan Murail, Viitanen has in fact worked as a

Magnus Lindberg and Olli Kortekangas were active in the early days of the Ears Open Society, founded in 1977.

church organist and taught organ improvisation at the Sibelius Academy. His chief work is the organ concerto *Firmamentum* (1988), containing the earlier toccata *Ekliptika* (1986) embedded as a cadenza. Many of Viitanen's most recent tape and organ compositions, such as *Images d'oiseau* for organ (1992) are based on adaptations of distinctive features of birdsong; for this purpose, he has also produced computer analyses of the structure of the song of various bird species.

Whereas Viitanen's works tend to be rather static, HARRI VUORI (b. 1957) is a more dynamic composer, who works out his details with great care. Vuori studied composition with Rautavaara, Hämeenniemi and Heininen. His orchestral work *Kri* (1988) received second prize in a Nordic competition in Gothenburg in 1989, and his *Š-wüt* (1992) won the competition for orchestral compositions held to celebrate Finland's 75 years of independence in 1992. Vuori's third major orchestral work is *Mandelbrotin kaiut* (The Echoes of Mandelbrot; 1995), which approaches French spectral music in sound. The experimental opera *Kuin linnun jalanjäljet taivaalla* (Like a Bird's Footprint in the Sky; 1983) is based on a Zen Buddhist story. *Mysticae metamorphoses nocturnae* for chamber ensemble (1982/90) has a highly involved structure. The *Unen ja kuoleman laulut* (Songs of Sleep and Death; 1990) for soprano and cello pose a rewarding challenge to the singer.

TAPIO NEVANLINNA (b. 1954) and HARRI SUILAMO (b. 1954) were both students of Heininen. Nevanlinna's emphasis ranges from sustained expressiveness, as in *Jousipiirros* (String Drawing; 1983) for string orchestra, to counterpoint and polyrhythmics of extreme complexity, as in the orchestral work *Lumikannel* (Snow Kantele; 1989). Rhythmic and melodic complexity also characterize Suilamo's music, particularly his early works. In the 1990s, his music has taken on a softer, more sensual dimension, as in the orchestral work *Aiva* (1991), which has a chamber music quality.

ESA-PEKKA SALONEN (b. 1958) was one of Rautavaara's most talented pupils, but his conducting career has left him little time for composing since his international breakthrough in 1983. Currently one of the stars of the younger-middle generation on the international circuit, he has served as chief conductor of the Swedish Radio Symphony Orchestra (1982–95) and the Los Angeles Philharmonic (since 1992) and as first visiting conductor of the Philharmonia London (since 1985), has guested with the world's leading orchestras, and has made numerous recordings. Salonen has given a boost to the international reputation of some of the Finnish composers of his own generation (notably Lindberg, Saariaho and Kaipainen) by conducting the premieres of most of their orchestral works as well as performances of these works abroad, and by recording their music.

From his neoromantic early works, Salonen switched to a

complex, fast-moving modernism in *Giro* (1981) for orchestra, then went on to a more transparent, classicist method of composition. Salonen's most important works include the Saxophone Concerto (1981/83); the radiophony *Baalal* (1982); *Floof* for soprano and chamber ensemble (1988), a work of absurd humour; and the 'vitalistic' *Mimo* (1992) for oboe and chamber orchestra. Salonen was artistic director of the Helsinki Festival from 1994 to 1996.

From Modernism to Neo-neoclassicism

Neo-neoclassicism here means a new style of composition that arose in Finland in the 1980s, as composers who first made a name for themselves as modernists began to turn towards classical ideals. The new attitude was expressed bluntly by Jouni Kaipainen, who declared in an interview with the *Rondo* music journal in 1991: "I am a classic." This new classicism may be modelled on the neoclassicism of the 1920s and '30s (particularly that of Stravinsky and Ravel), as is the case with Magnus Lindberg's Piano Concerto (1991): the work's godfather was Ravel, and its orchestral apparatus is the same as in Ravel's G major Piano Concerto. The crucial aesthetic model for Kaipainen's clarinet concerto *Carpe diem!* (1990) was provided by Haydn; the first movement of this work is even based on the classical structural principle, sonata form. Jukka Tiensuu's clarinet concerto *Puro* (1989) features a cadenza to be improvised by the soloist in accordance with Viennese Classical precedent, and the ensemble called for is the small, classical orchestra. In the harpsichord concerto *M* (1980) and in *Arsenic and Old Lace* (1990) for string quartet and harpsichord, Tiensuu employs tuning systems used in Renaissance and Baroque music.

These composers tend to favour fairly small, economical ensembles in their music, which is also increasingly characterized by a striving for dramatic clarity. Harmonic development and latent tonal pivots determine the structure of Lindberg's most recent works, in particular, while Kaipainen has even reverted to a characteristic melodic expression. The orchestral texture in Lindberg's Piano Concerto is reduced to homophony, as is that of Tiensuu's *Lume* (1991). All three composers have also simplified their rhythms compared with the early 1980s. Finnish neo-neoclassicism differs substantially from the Continental neoclassicism of the 1920s and '30s, being an outgrowth of the post-serialist Finnish modernism of the '80s rather than a reaction against expressionism and late romanticism. Moreover, the representatives of the new trend (especially Tiensuu and Lindberg) are seeking a synthesis of modernist and classicist stylistic ideals.

JUKKA TIENSUU (b. 1948) studied with Heininen, then in Freiburg with Klaus Huber and Brian Ferneyhough. He worked for a while at the IRCAM studio in Paris, investigating the use of electronics and computers in composition. Tiensuu is a well-rounded musician, a performing harpsichordist and pianist, and an organizer of many musical events (cf. p. 139). He began his career as an uncompromising modernist, varying his approach to composition virtually from one work to the next. Among his early works, those that have survived the test of time best include the aleatory *Rubato* (1975) for ad lib ensemble and *Sinistro* (1977) for guitar and accordion. The two octets *Yang I* and *II* (1979) are constructed in strict serialist fashion. Tiensuu composed *P=Pinocchio?* (1982) for soprano, chamber ensemble, tape and computer, using software developed by himself. The harpsichord concerto *M* (1980) has an intriguing world of microintervals produced by tuning one of the manuals of the harpsichord on the basis of pure fifths and the other of pure thirds.

During the 1980s, Tiensuu increasingly adopted the aesthetic principles of classicism. In the tango parody *Fantango* (1984) for harpsichord, the second manual of the harpsichord is tuned 1/5 of a whole tone lower than the other. *Tango*

Jukka Tiensuu with the pianist Kalle Randalu; besides being a composer, Tiensuu has also made a name for himself as a harpsichordist and pianist.

lunaire (1985), a version of *Fantango* for chamber orchestra, has become one of Tiensuu's popular hits. Another effective little piece is *,mutta* (1987) for three accordions. The excellent *Tokko* (1987) for male choir and tape won first prize at the UNESCO composers' rostrum in 1988. The sonorities and harmonies of the beautiful clarinet concerto *Puro* (1989), the most-performed Finnish wind instrument concerto in the '90s, are rooted in the acoustic spectra of the various instruments. Tiensuu's third concertante work is *Plus V* (1994) for accordion and string orchestra. In the orchestral work *Lume* (1991), Tiensuu concentrates what he has to say to the very essence. His next orchestral work *Halo* (1994) is scored for the classical symphony orchestra. His most important work in the '90s thus far is the dreamlike *Alma I (Himo)* (1995) for tape and orchestra. Tiensuu also likes to explore the potential of unusual instruments and ensembles, as in the 'ghost sonata' *Manaus* for kantele (1988) and *Vento* for clarinet orchestra (1995). Tiensuu received the Koussevitzky Award in 1973 and the Leonie Sonning Prize in 1978.

JOUNI KAIPAINEN (b. 1956) started his composition studies with Aulis Sallinen, and later had Heininen as his teacher. The moods of his music range from delicate lyricism to emotional pathos and driving energy. His first major work was *Ladders to Fire* for two pianos (1979), with a title borrowed from a novel by Anaïs Nin. In *Trois morceaux de l'aube* for cello and piano (1981), which won the UNESCO rostrum for young composers in 1981, Kaipainen made veiled allusions to Mahler and Wagner. *Cinq poèmes de René Char* for soprano and orchestra (1978–80) is a vocally rewarding work based on traditional twelve-tone technique. Many of Kaipainen's finest works are in fact vocal music, including *Stjärnenatten* (Starry Night; 1989) for soprano and instrumental ensemble and *Glühende Blumen des Leichtsinns* for soprano and string quartet (1995).

Kaipainen's principal orchestral works are his two symphonies

Jouni Kaipainen turned away from pure modernism towards classical ideals before the 1980s were over.

(1980–85; 1993); especially the premiere of the Second Symphony at the Tampere Biennale in 1994 attracted considerable public attention. The orchestral poem *Sisyfoksen uni* (The Dream of Sisyphus; 1994) represents Kaipainen at the height of tonal simplicity. The important concerto for chamber orchestra *Accende lumen sensibus* (1995–96) is an energetic neoclassical work; neoclassical tendencies were already very much to the fore in the clarinet concerto *Carpe diem!* (1990) and the melodically more restrained Oboe Concerto (1994). His most recent work is *Vernal Concerto, from Equinox to Solstice* for saxophone quartet and orchestra (1996). Kaipainen has composed choral works and a fair amount of chamber music, notably three trios for various ensembles and four string quartets. He is also known as a prolific music writer and critic, acting as spokesman for the composers who emerged around 1980 and writing essays on many of the Finnish composers of his generation.

Compared with Kaipainen, MAGNUS LINDBERG (b. 1958) is more of a constructivist and a 'harder' type of composer. Lindberg started his studies at the Sibelius Academy with Rautavaara and completed them in Heininen's class. He has spent long periods abroad, and worked for a time at the IRCAM studio in Paris. Lindberg started out with a sustained exploration of the potential of serial technique – among Finnish composers, only Rautavaara and Tiensuu had systematically done so before him. Lindberg also takes an interest in the opportunities opened up for the composer by the computer; thus, the rhythmic progression of *Kraft* (1985) for five soloists and orchestra, his chief work from the 1980s, was based on computer calculations. This forceful composition brought Lindberg the Nordic Music Prize in 1987 and the Koussevitzky Award in 1988.

Many of Lindberg's early works, such as the orchestral composition *Sculpture II*, have an extremely complex score. In *Drama* (1981) for orchestra, he combines open form with a strict organization of pitches. Over the years, his musical idiom has become freer and more expressive. The dense orchestral work *Kinetics* (1988–89) is based on the computer programme developed for *Ur* (1986) for five musicians and live electronics. In *Kinetics*, Lindberg sought to achieve a specific acoustic effect with a quieter 'background harmony'. The harmonic development is based on a series of chords repeated in the manner of a chaconne. Lindberg employed a similar method in the chamber orchestra works *Marea* (1989–90) and *Joy* (1989–90). In the Piano Concerto and the orchestral work *Corrente II* (1992), in particular, the composer resorted to a both rhythmically and harmonically simpler musical idiom, approaching neoclassicism. His chief compositions in the 1990s to date are the orchestral works *Aura* (1993–94) and *Arena* (1994–95); the former is Lindberg's longest composition, and the richest in both orchestral texture and emotional content. The energetic *Arena* was commissioned as the required work in the international Jean Sibelius conductors' competition in 1995.

Lindberg's oeuvre also includes music for chamber orchestra: the succinct *Ritratto* (1979–83); *Tendenza* (1982); the complex *Zona* for cello and chamber orchestra (1983); *Duo concertante* for clarinet, cello and chamber orchestra (1992); the neoclassical *Coyote Blues* (1993); *Engine* (1996); and chamber music, sometimes involving musical electronics (. . . *de Tartuffe, je crois* for piano quintet (1981); *Action–situation–signification* for five musicians (1982); *Metal Work* for accordion and percussion instruments (1984); Clarinet Quintet (1992)). His radiophonic work *Faust* (1985–86) won the Prix Italia in 1987.

Lindberg is one of the best-known contemporary Finnish composers internationally; his works have been performed at festivals of new music around the world, and the premieres of his works are regularly major events in Finland. Lindberg has been a member of the artistic committee of the Helsinki Festival since autumn 1994. In 1996 he was appointed professor of composition at the Stockholm Music Academy.

Another composer who can be counted a neoclassic in his practical and economical use of musical material and ensembles is TAPIO TUOMELA (b. 1958), who differs from the other composers in this group in that he began his composing career as a traditionalist (Piano Concerto, 1981) before turning towards modernism and neoclassicism. Tuomela's first composition teacher was Einar Englund; he subsequently studied with Eero Hämeenniemi and Paavo Heininen, and rounded off his studies in New York (with Joseph Schwantner) and Berlin (with Witold Szalonek). Tuomela was a member of the working group for the experimental hypermedia opera *Korvan tarina* (The Ear's Tale; 1993), performed in autumn 1993 in the Almi Room, the small stage of Helsinki's new opera house. The independent work *Herzstück* (1992) for six singers (or chamber choir) constitutes a section of the score for the opera. The main emphasis in Tuomela's oeuvre is on chamber music and vocal works, but he has also composed a one-movement Symphony (1991/94) and the fast-paced, virtuoso chamber orchestra piece *L'échelle de l'évasion* (The Escape Ladder) for 11 instruments (1989). Tuomela has served as executive director of the Finnish Composers' Association since 1992.

The Second Neoexpressionist Generation

KIMMO HAKOLA (b. 1958), who studied with Rautavaara and Hämeenniemi, has composed relatively little as yet. His first works still show the influence of the post-serialist style, particularly that of Lindberg in the early 1980s, but by the mid '80s Hakola was going off on his own in a quest for maximum expressiveness and density. His String Quartet (1985–86) won the young composers' series in the 1987 UNESCO composers' rostrum. He proceeded to compose a series of solo works comprising . . . *sino* (1985) for solo flute, *A même les échos I–II*

(1988) for solo violin and *Loco* (1995) for solo clarinet and bass drum, compositions with an intense virtuosity and reminiscent of the maximalist 'here and now' aesthetics of Segerstam's music. His chief work to date, the monumental nine-movement Piano Concerto (1990–96) was premiered at the Helsinki Festival in 1996. It presents a highly individual blend of his earlier style with tonal elements and songful melody.

JUKKA KOSKINEN (b. 1965), who studied with Rautavaara and Aho, has also composed sparingly so far. Like Hakola, Koskinen aims at extreme intensity of expression and density of form in his chamber music works. Koskinen's String Quartet (1987), which won the young composers' rostrum in Paris in 1989, lasts only five minutes, and shirks all 'conventional' playing techniques. His most notable works in the 1990s include *Until the Deadline* (1992) for wind orchestra and the highly original *Ululation* (1994) for 12 instruments, which advances in microintervals.

Pluralism of the '90s

The modernist style and its derivatives favoured by the first 'Ears Open' generation gained such a strong hold that the young composers born in the 1960s initially had a hard time carving a niche for themselves in the Finnish music world. The fact that some of the composers of the young generation of the '80s (notably Lindberg and Saariaho) had considerable international success did not make it any easier for the next generation to emerge. New generations of composers after the Second World War have made their breakthrough at an average interval of ten years, rising up against the aesthetics of their predecessors. There was no such uprising in 1990 – it was not easy to rebel against the incontestable merits of the two previous generations. The situation for the apprentice composer had in fact deteriorated, for Finland already had such a strong and versatile contemporary music sector that it was no longer easy for a young composer to find an unexplored path to set off on.

Most of the composers who began their studies in the '80s have continued along paths staked out by their predecessors. VESA VALKAMA (b. 1963), a self-taught composer from Oulu, has attracted notice with highly complex scores built up of polyrhythmic fields.

Magnus Lindberg's style in his post-serialist period served as a model for many students. One of the composers to make his debut with modernist music in Lindbergian spirit was VELI-MATTI PUUMALA (b. 1965), a student of Heininen's. Puumala made his much-publicized breakthrough when the 1993 Helsinki Biennale dedicated a whole concert to his music. His early works were short, condensed and rich in detail, and often very difficult for the performers. Among the key achievements of this period was a trio of works for chamber ensemble: *Scroscio* (1989), *Verso* (1990/91) and *Ghirlande* (1992). In the 1990s, he seems to have turned towards less puristic musical aesthetics. His chief work to date, the effective 20-minute *Chains of Camenae* (1995–96) for chamber orchestra, is more 'pluralistic' than his previous compositions, and also more rewarding and idiomatic from the performers' point of view.

The Rise of a New Pluralism,
and the 'Second Ears Open Generation'

The new generation that followed the generation of the '80s did not really emerge until the mid '90s. The old Ears Open Society continued to function as an arranger of concerts of contemporary music, but was taken over by a whole new generation. As a rival to Avanti!, students at the Sibelius Academy established the *Zagros Ensemble*, which has concentrated largely on presenting works by composers who are still studying at the Academy. Another new competitor in the field is the *Kerberos* ensemble, established in Helsinki in 1995 by leading professional musicians of the younger-middle generation.

By the middle of the decade, most of the composers who were still studying or had completed their studies in the 1990s had abandoned orthodox modernism and were seeking new musical points of departure. Recent *Ears Open* concerts have been much more permissive in stylistic terms than similar events in the 1980s. A significant factor in producing a more relaxed atmosphere is that many of the former modernists themselves have turned towards a more traditional idiom, while some of the traditionalists and pluralists of the period between 1950 and 1980 have experienced a notable revival in the 1990s.

JUHANI NUORVALA (b. 1961) studied with Eero Hämeenniemi and went to New York in 1993–94 as a Fulbright scholar. In the 1980s, he took a particular interest in minimal music, and later also in French spectral music. Some of the key works of his early period are *Kajauksia, väreitä* (Rings and Ripples; 1985) for female voice and six musicians, *Glissements progressifs du plaisir* (1987) for chamber orchestra and the orchestral composition *Pinta ja säe* (Surface and Phrase; 1990–91), which won a prize at the Vienna Modern Masters competition in 1991. His stay in New York wrought a decisive shift and liberation in Nuorvala's music, and helped him find a distinctive style of his own;

Juhani Nuorvala has incorporated stylistic elements from minimal music, light music and jazz into his musical idiom.

his recent music shows the influence of jazz, and has less of an aestheticist and more of an urban character. Representative works from this period include two vibrantly rhythmic compositions, *Kellarisinfonia* (Garage Symphony; 1995) and *Notturno urbano* (1995–96).

MARKUS FAGERUDD (b. 1961) has a versatile background: he has played rock, worked as a theatre musician, composed music for radio plays and the stage, and performed as a pianist and percussionist in the experimental improvisation group *Free Okapi*. Fagerudd's most notable works include the radiophony *Tom Törn and the Lady in Black* (1990; also produced in German by Radio Hessen), *Yksitoista kerrosta* (Eleven Storeys; 1991) for mezzo-soprano and chamber ensemble, and the chamber orchestra work *Fresco* (1994).

Like Fagerudd, KIMMO NEVONMAA (1960–1996) and PATRICK VIDJESKOG (b. 1964) studied with Kalevi Aho. Nevonmaa's compositions give musical expression to extreme mental states. His most important works include a String Quartet (1990), which gives vent to emotions of fear and terror; the agonizingly 'painful' *Dolor nascens et efluens* (1991–92) for string orchestra, percussion and stringed instruments, and the brighter and more serene *Lux intima* (1993–94) for chamber orchestra. Vidjeskog combined neoromantic melody with a variety of more recent techniques in his early works until, in the powerful, virtuoso *Sinfonietta for String Orchestra* (1994–95), he seemed to discover his own voice.

HANNU POHJANNORO (b. 1963) studied with Rautavaara, Aho and Heininen. His varied oeuvre particularly reflects the influence of Heininen. In Pohjannoro's most recent works, such as *valo jäätynyt, kaukana tuuli* (frozen light, far away the wind; 1994–95) for flute, cello and piano, his previously somewhat introverted idiom seems to have gained expressiveness. Pohjannoro's principal work thus far is *korkeina aamujen kaaret* (high the arches of morning; 1995–96) for orchestra, composed for a concert held in conjunction with a Nordic composers' workshop in Stavanger in 1996.

TUOMAS KANTELINEN (b. 1969), a student of Eero Hämeenniemi, is basically a romantic composer. He has sought to expand his range beyond concert music proper, to cinema and the stage. The prolific and talented JUHA T. KOSKINEN (b. 1972) made his debut with the orchestral works *Eclysis* (1994) and *Fatalité* (1995); his most ambitious work is the unusual chamber opera *Velhosiskot* (The Wizard Sisters; 1995–96), to his own libretto. SEPPO POHJOLA (b. 1965) has composed formally polished and eventful chamber music and chamber orchestra works, including *Balletto* for 10 musicians (1994), the Second String Quartet (1995) and a Piano Quartet (1996). JANI KÄÄRIÄ (b. 1971) composes music with an unabashedly romantic glow, while the small oeuvre of JOHAN TALLGREN (b. 1971) approaches the aesthetics of Brian Ferneyhough. OSMO TAPIO RÄIHÄLÄ (b. 1964) attracted notice with a concert of his works in Helsinki in winter 1996. The Serbian-born JOVANKA TRBOJEVIĆ (b. 1963) studied with Eero Hämeenniemi; her most important composition to date is *Žuti Put* (1995), an intense and highly personal chamber music work. LOTTA WENNÄKOSKI (b. 1970) has demonstrated an ability to establish an unusual, delicate atmosphere in her still rather limited oeuvre.

Summary:
General Trends in Postwar Finnish Music
1940 to 1975

The immediate postwar years ushered in a lively, adventurous phase in Finnish music. For the first time since the 1920s, a new generation emerged with something to say in a language other than that of the national romantic tradition. Their aesthetic approach was modelled on that of Shostakovich, Prokofiev, Hindemith and Bartók, who represented extreme modernity in the concert repertoire of the early '50s. Sibelius still lived, a towering figure revered by all, but he was too much of a musical individualist to have given rise to any school of composition. Other composers were more important as pedagogues – Erkki Melartin was the leading Finnish teacher of composition in the 1920s and '30s, Aarre Merikanto in the '50s.

In the mid 1950s, thanks to Erik Bergman, the twelve-tone technique became known in Finland, and gradually the works of the Second Viennese School began to be performed in concert. For a brief period in the early '60s, Finnish music was dominated by modernism. Almost all composers of the middle or younger generation composed twelve-tone music, while the youngest generation of all (Erkki Salmenhaara, Henrik Otto Donner, Kari Rydman) were forceful exponents of the Continental avantgarde. Rautavaara employed total serialism in *Arabescata*; Salmenhaara applied Ligetian tone fields; there were experiments with aleatory music and happenings. Bengt Johansson composed the first Finnish tape music.

From the late '50s, Finnish composers attended summer courses of contemporary music in Darmstadt and elsewhere. In the early '60s, the leaders of the Continental avantgarde visited Finland – Stockhausen, Ligeti, Nono and Maderna came, later also Lutosławski and Penderecki.

Conservative critics mocked performances of contemporary music in the early '60s as "nursery chamber concerts". The avantgarde period was short-lived, and the new techniques of composition developed after the Second World War failed to take root in Finnish music. Most of the composers who had tried twelve-tone technique soon abandoned it for a less restrictive motivic technique and free tonality. Nonetheless, the modernist movement survived, although avoiding avantgarde extremes – of the composers who had come to the fore in the 1950s, Meriläinen and Heininen as well as Bergman represented this school. In contrast, Rautavaara abandoned avantgardism and constructivism and briefly became an intuitivist and hyper-romantic. The leading composer and teacher of the '60s was Kokkonen, while Rautavaara took over as the most important Finnish teacher of composition in the early '70s.

The next new generation of composers appeared in the late 1960s and early '70s (Segerstam, Nordgren, Aho). The position of new music had been gradually growing stronger in concert programmes, with the Radio Symphony Orchestra making a particularly important contribution. On the initiative of Seppo Nummi and others, the first Finnish summer festival, the Jyväskylä Arts Festival, had been started back in 1956; from the 1960s on, it concentrated on music. The most renowned of all the Finnish summer events, the Savonlinna Opera Festival, was launched in 1967. With the appointment of the singer Martti Talvela as artistic director in 1972, this festival soon rose to international fame. The next summer music festival to gain an international reputation, the Kuhmo Chamber Music Festival, was established in 1969. There are currently some twenty top-quality music festivals in Finland (cf. pp. 203–205). From the 1960s on, the network of music institutes has gradually spread throughout the country, resulting in a remarkable rise in the standard of musical performance.

1975 to 1996, and Where We Stand in 1996

There is a good case for the assertion that the heyday of Finnish music began in 1975: in this year, both Aulis Sallinen's *Ratsumies* and Joonas Kokkonen's *Viimeiset kiusaukset* received their first performance. Both operas had a resounding success; Kokkonen's work, in particular, achieved the status of a new 'national opera', and significantly helped dispel the general public's prejudices against new Finnish music in general. By 1975, the composers who had emerged in the early 1970s had established their position on the Finnish music map.

The next, modernist generation of composers appeared on the scene only a few years later.

A salient feature of the musical trends since the latter half of the 1960s is that whereas previously Finnish music had been dominated by a single figure, pluralism now seemed to become a permanent state of affairs: rather than one dominant personality, there were now several major composers of equal stature. In the 1970s, Aulis Sallinen gained an international reputation rivalling that of Kokkonen, while Einojuhani Rautavaara, though not yet as well-known, also made something of a name for himself abroad. Whereas Rautavaara had been the leading teacher of the 1970s, by the end of the decade and in the 1980s the young composers were taking the cue from the music and classes of Paavo Heininen. This generation also adopted Erik Bergman as their spiritual (though not stylistic) model; Bergman himself had never given rise to a school of his own as a teacher. The young composers rebelled against the trend represented by Kokkonen and Sallinen, and contemptuously styled their works "fur cap operas".

The surprising feature of this new wave of Finnish modernism, however, was that in fact the 1980s only rediscovered the very same trends that had already been presented in Finland once before, in the early '60s. The guests and other frequently performed composers at the Helsinki Biennale were the very same people who had already visited Finland in the 1960s, or figured prominently in the musical debate of those years – Stockhausen, Ligeti, Nono, Berio, Lutosławski... Again, like the avantgarde composers of the '60s, the young modernists of the '80s began to seek a new connection with tradition at the end of the decade, criticizing the Continental avantgarde of the '50s for their rejection of history.

The dictatorship of a single aesthetic approach could be fatal to the creative music of a small country. Fortunately, however, a certain pluralism survived in Finland in the '80s because all the various trends were represented by a sufficient number of strong, individualistic composers, and indeed because the personalities of the leading composers were so different. A plurality of creative styles continued to flourish, and few composers have felt unjustly overlooked. Those composers who have not been admitted to the contemporary music biennales have had their works performed at other venues, at least so far. Thus there has been no danger of Finnish music being cast in a single mould, nor is it threatened by excessive national complacency. In fact, many Finns have sought to combine homespun and international elements into a synthesis transcending national borders. Moreover, the hegemony of modernism seems to have come to an end in the early '90s.

This is the first of several reasons why creative composition is currently (August 1996) flourishing like never before in the history of Finnish music. Never before has this country had so many notable composers at any one time. The second reason is that Finland has such a short musical history, and the music scene in general is so new, that only now do composers have their first opportunity to develop and create a living Finnish music tradition.

Third, contemporary Finnish music is performed relatively frequently in concert. Thus, the Helsinki Festival (which is not a festival of contemporary music) featured no less than eleven Finnish premieres in 1990. Performances of contemporary international music are also quite frequent: the 1992 Helsinki Festival featured the first performances of compositions by eleven different Baltic composers.

Fourth, Finnish composers cannot afford to isolate themselves too far from the general music public, as the Finnish population is so small. In the largest music metropolises or virtually closed elite communities (such as American universities), a small target audience may be found for virtually any kind of new music; in Finland this is not possible. On the other hand, since some living composers are so popular, the Finnish general public is not as biased against contemporary music as tends to be the case elsewhere – audiences are basically receptive to new ideas.

Fifth, it is relatively easy for Finnish composers to get even their longer works requiring a large ensemble performed, obviously a factor of great importance.

Sixth, the government grant system has relieved most composers from financial worries and enabled them to concentrate on their creative work. Music grants for one, three or five years are awarded to composers who have shown their mettle; from 1982 to 1994 the State even awarded 15-year grants. These grants take the form of an untaxed monthly sum comparable with a salary, and sufficient to cover basic living expenses. The composer is not required to produce any specified number of works while receiving a grant – it is enough to show that one has been artistically active during the period.

Seventh, as a result of the dense network of music institutes, the quality of musical performance in Finland is currently very high, an essential factor for new music to thrive. In this context, special mention should be made of Finnish singers and conductors, who enjoy a worldwide reputation. Many of the star conductors hold positions as chief conductors of foreign orchestras or otherwise make frequent guest appearances abroad – the best-known names include Paavo Berglund, Jorma Panula, Leif Segerstam, Okko Kamu, Osmo Vänskä, Jukka-Pekka Saraste and Esa-Pekka Salonen. Together they have played a major role in consolidating the international reputation of contemporary Finnish music. Among Finnish orchestras, particular attention has been attracted by the two Helsinki ensembles, the Radio Symphony Orchestra and the Helsinki Philharmonic; the Lahti Symphony Orchestra, which has won international record prizes and made phenomenal progress in the 1990s; and the Ostrobothnian Chamber Orchestra under Juha Kangas, held by some to be the best Nordic string orchestra.

Eighth, the Finnish Music Information Centre (MIC), founded in 1963, has played a crucial role in making contemporary Finnish music known abroad. The MIC maintains a collection of scores and recordings of all notable contemporary Finnish works. It publishes brief presentations of the major composers, and it copies and distributes to individual musicians and orchestras the scores of compositions which have not been published commercially. The commercial publishing situation has also improved radically since 1980. In the early '70s, there was only one significant publisher of art music in the country, Edition Fazer. To provide an alternative to commercial publishing, Edition Pan was established in 1975 in the form of a non-profit association, which received public subsidies to publish significant compositions in which the commercial publishing houses were not interested. Pan sold its rights to Fazer in 1990, which now maintains an outstanding and highly comprehensive collection. Fazer itself changed ownership in 1993, when it was purchased by the American firm of Warner Chappell. Several smaller publishing houses, including Jasemusiikki, Modus Musiikki and Edition Love, sprang up in the 1970s and '80s.

Ninth, a great deal of contemporary Finnish music has been recorded in recent years. There are currently three Finnish record labels specializing in art music: Finlandia Records, Ondine and Alba. Ondine, in particular, has expanded significantly, signing contracts with numerous Finnish and foreign soloists and orchestras. The Swedish company BIS has also produced numerous recordings of older and more recent Finnish music, collaborating particularly with the Lahti Symphony Orchestra. Recordings of the complete major works of several composers are currently under way: BIS has already completed a series of recordings of the complete orchestral and chamber music of Joonas Kokkonen, and has started a project covering the complete works of Kalevi Aho. Ondine is planning to record all the significant works in Einojuhani Rautavaara's extensive oeuvre, and Naxos Finland is recording the principal works of Aulis Sallinen, including all his symphonies. Most of the major contemporary Finnish operas have also been recorded. As far as recordings go, the situation is thus virtually ideal.

Tenth, Finnish music has been studied in great detail (particularly by Salmenhaara and Heiniö), and a four-part history of Finnish music was recently completed, making information about our composers, music history and recent trends readily available to the ordinary music lover.

Finnish composers therefore now have the chance of a lifetime. The public is favourably disposed, and has great expectations of new works; composers only have themselves to blame if, in this unique situation, they can no longer reach their audience with music that addresses the deepest concerns of our time.

PERFORMING MUSIC

Orchestras and conductors

The first permanent Finnish orchestra was the Academic Chapel, founded in Turku in 1747. After the fire of Turku in 1827 it was transferred, along with the university, to Helsinki. There it was directed from 1835 by the German-born composer Fredrik (Friedrich) Pacius (1809–91). Disbanded in 1867, the Academic Chapel was succeeded by the Academic Orchestra (1868–926) and, from 1926, by the Helsinki University Musicians (Ylioppilaskunnan Soittajat, or YS). The oldest still-active society of music in the country, the Turku Music Society, maintained its own orchestra from 1790 to 1924, and still has its own chamber orchestra. The first public concert in Finland was held by the orchestra of the Aurora Society of Turku in 1773. In the years after 1860, a number of Helsinki theatres maintained professional music ensembles, and the Helsinki Concert Orchestra was active from 1879 to 1882. It was the composer Robert Kajanus (1856–1933) who first set orchestral music in Finland on a proper professional footing by founding the first permanent symphony orchestra in the Nordic countries, the Helsinki Orchestral Society, in 1882; it was renamed the Helsinki Philharmonic Society Orchestra in 1894 and the Helsinki City Orchestra (now also known as the Helsinki Philharmonic Orchestra) in 1914. Kajanus was its chief conductor for half a century (cf. p. 37); he was also lecturer in music at the University of Helsinki from 1897 to 1927. He was the leading conductor of the music of Sibelius in his time. Under Kajanus, the orchestra made a well-received tour of the Continent, culminating in a concert at the World Fair in Paris in 1900.

During the 'Orchestra War' of 1912–14, there were two orchestras in Helsinki. The new ensemble, the Helsinki Symphony

Orchestra, was conducted by GEORG SCHNÉEVOIGT (1872–1942). Schnéevoigt had spent his school years in Tampere and started his career as a cellist. He was a true cosmopolitan, an oft-seen guest in the music centres of Europe and America, and chief conductor of the Los Angeles Philharmonic from 1927 to 1929. He headed the Helsinki Philharmonic from 1914 to 1916 and again from 1932 to 1941, adding to the orchestra's repertoire the symphonies of Bruckner and Mahler, unusual programme choices at the time. The orchestra scored a notable success with a concert tour to London under Schnéevoigt in 1934.

The Helsinki Philharmonic was headed briefly from 1942 to 1943 by another noted Finnish conductor, Armas Järnefelt (1869–1958). Järnefelt, Sibelius's brother-in-law, moved to Sweden quite early on, and became conductor of the Royal Opera in Stockholm. Particularly esteemed as a conductor of Wagner's operas, he was appointed conductor to the royal court in 1911 and first court conductor in 1923 (cf. p. 55). MARTTI SIMILÄ (1898–1958), a noted Sibelius specialist who also took an interest in contemporary music, served as chief conductor of the Helsinki Philharmonic from 1944 to 1950. A period of technical and artistic progress began for the orchestra in 1951 with the appointment of TAUNO HANNIKAINEN (1896–1968) as chief conductor. This former cellist (who played in a trio with his brothers Ilmari and Arvo Hannikainen) had spent the years 1941–51 in the United States, serving as conductor of the symphony orchestras of Duluth and Chicago. His initially conservative repertoire gradually expanded to include modernist composers such as Schönberg and Webern. During his career, Hannikainen gave visiting performances in 26 countries of Europe, America and Asia. The Helsinki Philharmonic also served as the orchestra of the Finnish National Opera until 1963, when the opera established its own ensemble (cf. pp. 38, 201–202).

Helsinki's second major orchestra, the Radio Orchestra, was founded in 1927 by the conductor ERKKI LINKO (1893–1966). Its first chief conductor, TOIVO HAAPANEN (1889–1966) also headed

Esa-Pekka Salonen, one of the stars on the international concert circuit, whose visits to the home country are regular highlights of the Finnish music season; here conducting Avanti!

the music department of YLE, the Finnish Broadcasting Company, and was appointed professor of musicology at the University of Helsinki in 1946. Haapanen championed the music of his Finnish contemporaries and was an expert on older Finnish music. He was succeeded by SIMON PARMET (1897–1969), the former concertmaster ERIK CRONVALL (1904–79) and NILS-ERIC FOUGSTEDT (1910–1961), under whose leadership the Radio Orchestra was renamed the Finnish Radio Symphony Orchestra (which now consists of 98 musicians).

A generation shift took place in the 1960s with the rise of a group of talented young conductors. PAAVO BERGLUND (b. 1929), an expert on Sibelius, Brahms, Bruckner, Nielsen and Shostakovich, possesses the rare ability to build up performances of unshakeable symphonic logic. Berglund served as chief conductor of the Radio Symphony Orchestra from 1962 to 1971, musical director of the Bournemouth Symphony Orchestra from 1972 to 1979 and of the Helsinki Philharmonic from 1975 to 1979, and chief conductor of the Stockholm Philharmonic from 1987 to 1991, a position he has held with the Royal Danish Orchestra since 1993; he has given visiting performances around the world. JORMA PANULA (b. 1930), a colourful personality from Finland's western province Ostrobothnia, was appointed director of the Helsinki Philharmonic in 1965, expanding its repertoire with extensive Bruckner, Mahler and Schönberg cycles and performances of new Finnish music. It is largely Panula's doing that Mahler, previously little-known and undervalued in Finland, is today one of the great favourites of the Finnish concert public. Panula has also pursued a career as a composer. As professor of conducting at the Sibelius Academy from 1973 to 1993, he trained all the leading Finnish conductors of the younger generation as well as several foreign conductors. He was succeeded in this post by the well-known Estonian conductor ERI KLAS (b. 1939). In 1971, under Panula's leadership, the Helsinki Philharmonic (which now comprises 98 musicians) moved from the University to a new venue. The Finlandia Hall, designed by the celebrated architect Alvar Aalto, has a beautiful auditorium which seats an audience of 1,718, but its acoustics remain controversial. Aalto had already designed Helsinki's first large concert hall, the 1,500-seat Aalto Room in the 'House of Culture', back in 1957. It is still frequently used by the Radio Symphony Orchestra.

LEIF SEGERSTAM (b. 1944) is known best as a charismatic interpreter of the music of Mahler, Wagner and Richard Strauss. Also a prolific composer, Segerstam conducted at the Stockholm Opera and the Deutsche Oper Berlin in his early years, then served as chief conductor of the Austrian Radio Symphony Orchestra (1975–82), the Finnish Radio Symphony Orchestra (1977–87), the Rheinland-Pfalz Staatsphilharmonie (1983–89) and the Danish Radio Symphony Orchestra (1988–95). Having been appointed chief conductor of the Helsinki Philharmonic in 1995 (after the orchestra had been led by a number of controversial foreign conductors for several years) and musical director of the Stockholm Opera in 1996, Segerstam quipped that he was now "the *Generalmusikdirektor* of the North". He has given guest performances with orchestras around the world (including the Metropolitan Opera and La Scala).

OKKO KAMU (b. 1947), a member of a family of musicians, started out as a violinist, then gained a sensational victory in the first Herbert von Karajan Competition for conductors in Berlin in

1969. He was appointed chief conductor of the Radio Symphony Orchestra in 1972; after a stint with the Oslo Philharmonic, he served as artistic director of the Helsinki Philharmonic from 1981 to 1989. After several years in Denmark and Sweden (Stockholm, Helsingborg), Kamu was appointed chief conductor of the Finnish National Opera in 1996. He has conducted in numerous European, American and Asian countries, making a particular specialty of the operas and orchestral music of Aulis Sallinen.

Avanti! is a chamber orchestra consisting of young Helsinki musicians. Founded in 1983, it has given a number of exceptionally inspired performances under its co-founders ESA-PEKKA SALONEN (b. 1958) and JUKKA-PEKKA SARASTE (b. 1956) and other conductors, including its concertmaster JOHN STORGÅRDS (b. 1963). Salonen, who studied French horn and composition, made his international breakthrough as a conductor in London in 1983, when he was called in at extremely short notice to conduct Mahler's Third Symphony. He was appointed chief conductor of the Swedish Radio Symphony Orchestra in 1985 and of the Los Angeles Philharmonic in 1992; he is also chief visiting conductor of London's Philharmonia Orchestra. He has scored brilliant successes in Finland and in all the world's great music centres with the music of Bruckner, Mahler, Sibelius, Nielsen, Stravinsky, Messiaen, Lutoslawski and young Finnish composers (including Kaija Saariaho). His collaboration with Peter Sellars, the U.S. opera director and *enfant terrible*, has produced remarkable results (Debussy, Hindemith, Stravinsky). Salonen opened his stint as artistic director of the Helsinki Festival in 1995 with a strong crossover pro-gramme. He was chairman of the jury of the first international conductors' competition in Helsinki in 1995. Salonen's youthful enthusiasm and ready wit have made him the darling of the concert public. He is also a composer of avantgarde music.

Saraste, who started out as a violinist, shared first prize (with Atso Almila) in the Nordic conductor's competition in 1981. He has headed the Finnish Radio Symphony Orchestra on extensive

Jukka-Pekka Saraste and his orchestra have served up countless musical feasts to the Finnish concert public. Saraste has also had several major long-term assignments abroad.

foreign tours since 1984; in 1987 he was appointed its chief conductor. Saraste's conducting style, seemingly restrained, conceals a smouldering intensity, and under him the orchestra has made further progress, performing exceptionally impressive Sibelius and Mahler cycles and giving outstanding performances of French and contemporary Finnish music. Saraste's own tours have taken him to four continents. He served as chief conductor of the Scottish Chamber Orchestra from 1987 to 1991 and became chief conductor of the Toronto Symphony Orchestra in 1994. Saraste currently takes turns heading the Finnish Radio Symphony Orchestra with SAKARI ORAMO (b. 1965), one of the orchestra's concertmasters, who was appointed chief conductor of the Birmingham City Symphony Orchestra, starting in 1998.

OSMO VÄNSKÄ (b. 1953), a clarinetist, shared first prize in the Besançon conducting competition in 1982. Director of the Lahti Symphony Orchestra (founded 1949) since 1988, Vänskä has raised his orchestra to the Nordic elite, attracting particular notice with his interpretations of rare works by Sibelius, including the first version of the Violin Concerto in 1991 and *Skogsrået* (The Wood Nymph) in 1996, of the music of the ensemble's 'house composer' Kalevi Aho and of works by Joonas Kokkonen. The Lahti Symphony Orchestra has won several major international record awards. In 1996 Vänskä was appointed chief conductor of the BBC Scottish Symphony Orchestra. He served as chief conductor of the Icelandic Symphony Orchestra from 1993 to 1995, succeeding PETRI SAKARI (b. 1958), who was reappointed to this post in 1966.

There are thirteen professional symphony orchestras all told in Finland. The musical directors of the 82-player Tampere Philharmonic Orchestra, founded in 1930, have been EERO KOSONEN (b. 1906) from 1932 to 1969, PAAVO RAUTIO (b. 1924), ATSO ALMILA (b. 1953), ARI RASILAINEN (b. 1959) and, since 1994, TUOMAS OLLILA (b. 1965). The home of the orchestra is the grand auditorium of the Tam-pere Hall, with seating for 1,800 people, where it also plays in opera performances. Ari Rasilainen is today musical director of the Jyväskylä Sinfonia and the Norwegian Radio Symphony Orchestra. The Turku Philharmonic Orchestra is an offshoot of the previously mentioned Turku Music Society. Its concert hall was completed in 1952, and it also plays in the large-scale opera concerts and other musical events at the Turku Hall (with 10,000 seats). The orchestra's directors have included Tauno Hannikainen, Jorma Panula, Paavo Rautio, PERTTI PEKKANEN (b. 1944) and, as visiting conductor since 1995, RALF GOTHONI (b. 1946). Pekkanen, who previously also headed the Kuopio City Orchestra, is currently (since 1994) chief conductor of the city orchestras of Vaasa and Lappeenranta. Past directors of the Oulu City Orchestra, which is almost 60 years old, include the violinist ARI ANGERVO (b. 1944), who has also conducted the Finnish National Opera and the city orchestras of Rovaniemi and Lappeenranta. The Kuopio City Orchestra goes back to the turn of the century. It has an excellent auditorium with 1,064 seats in the Kuopio Music Centre, and answers for live ballet music at the international Kuopio Dance Festival. Its current conductor is Atso Almila, co-winner (with Jukka-Pekka Saraste) of the 1981 Nordic Conductors' Competition. Almila is also a trombonist, composer, conductor of the Finnish National Theatre and the Joensuu City Orchestra, chief assistant at the Sibelius Academy and director of the Jyväskylä Arts Festival. The Tapiola Sinfonietta (the Espoo City Orchestra) was established in 1988 and has already attained a high international standard; its current director is the French violinist Jean-Jacques Kantorow. The Pori Sinfonietta has been headed since 1993 by JUHANI LAMMINMÄKI (b. 1960); one of its previous conductors was HANNU KOIVULA (b. 1960), who won the Nordic Competition in 1990 and currently heads the Gävleborg Orchestra and the Danish Radio Orchestra. The Central Ostrobothnian Chamber Orchestra in Kokkola was founded in 1972 by its dynamic and talented director JUHA KANGAS (b. 1945), also an accomplished folk musician. The ensemble's repertoire extends from the Baroque to the present, with the emphasis on contemporary Finnish music. Its high artistic merit won the ensemble the music award of the Nordic Council in 1993.

In addition to these professional orchestras, Finland has several semi-professional ensembles, notably the Vivo Symphony Orchestra, comprising over 90 young musicians from all around the country. It was established in 1986 by KARI TIKKA (b. 1946), conductor of the Finnish National Opera. The Sibelius Academy Symphony Orchestra, which has performed under Jorma Panula, Eri Klas and Atso Almila, has also attained a high professional standard. The Orchestra's concert tour of China in 1996 was a great success.

There are several excellent chamber orchestras, including the Finnish Chamber Orchestra (founded 1990, no permanent conductor); the Finlandia Sinfonietta, made up of the Helsinki Philharmonic's string section; the Kuudennen kerroksen orkesteri ('Sixth Floor Orchestra'), directed by ANSSI MATTILA (b. 1953), a Baroque specialist; and the Helsinki Junior Strings, an ensemble founded and led by Géza Szilvay (b. 1943) and maintained by the East Helsinki Music Institute.

Chamber music

Chamber music in Finland goes back to the concerts given by the Turku Music Society, founded in 1790. Erik Tulindberg, a civil servant and the first Finnish composer, continued to arrange chamber music performances in Oulu when he moved there from Turku at the turn of the century (cf. p. 22). The first chamber ensemble mentioned by name, the Finnish String Quartet, played in Helsinki from 1911 to 1914; its best-known member was the cellist Ossian Fohström. The most noted and longest-lived ensemble was the Sibelius Quartet (1927–74), known at first as the Radio String Quartet (1927–33); its most regular members were Erik Cronvall, Hugo Huttunen, Erik Karma and Artto Granroth. From the 1950s to the '70s there were several comparatively short-lived quartets in which many of the most prominent Finnish string players performed: the Helsinki Quartet (1953–61), founded by the cellist Pentti Rautawaara, with Anja Ignatius as first violin; the Suhonen Quartet (1964–72), named after Professor ONNI SUHONEN (1903–87), a prominent teacher of string instrumentalists, with Okko Kamu as first violin; the Finlandia Quartet, founded in 1969, and the Voces Intimae Quartet, founded in 1970, with Seppo Tukiainen and Jorma Rahkonen as their first violins. Present ensembles include the Sibelius Academy Quartet, founded 1978 (Erkki Kantola, Seppo Tukiainen, Veikko Kosonen, Arto Noras); the Jean Sibelius Quartet, established 1980, with a married couple, Yoshiko Arai-Kimanen and Seppo Kimanen, among its members; the Finnish String Quartet, revived in 1980, first violin Jussi Pesonen; the Kerava Quartet, founded 1985, first violin Erkki Palola, with a record number of first performances to their name; and the New Helsinki Quartet and Selin Quartet, both consisting of young musicians. These last two were winners of the Concertino Praga in 1985 and 1987, respectively. The New Helsinki Quartet, complemented with woodwind instrumentalists Jorma Valjakka (oboe), Kari Kriikku (clarinet), Jussi Särkkä (bassoon) and Esa Tapani (French horn), with the addition of Esko Laine, double-bass player in the Berlin Philharmonic, becomes the redoubtable Kerberos ensemble. The Zagros Ensemble is an off-shoot of the Sibelius Academy.

The few Finnish piano trios have mainly performed only on occasion. The most active today is the Trio Finlandia, established in 1986 and consisting of women players: Marita Viitasalo, Kaija Saarikettu (at present Eeva Koskinen) and Riitta Pesola. They have toured extensively abroad.

Another mixed ensemble of strings and woodwind besides Kerberos is the improvisational ensemble Free Okapi, which uses electronic effects. Its leading figures are the clarinetist Heikki Nikula and the oboist Jorma Valjakka. A classic woodwind ensemble is the Crusell Quintet, which has comprised the foremost woodwind players of the Helsinki Philharmonic since 1935; today, Tapio Laivaara (flute), Aale Lindgren (oboe), Osmo Linkola (clarinet), Tapio Lehtonen (bassoon) and Timo Ronkainen (French horn). The leading Finnish brass players have formed several ensembles, such as the Viva Brass Quartet (first trumpet Reijo Hursti), established in 1969; the Brasstime Quartet (first trumpet Jouko Harjanne); and the Finnish Horn Quartet (first horn Timo Ronkainen). The Breath Ensemble (founded in 1982) is a chamber ensemble made up of symphony orchestra percussionists.

Some of the ensembles playing ancient music are of a very high standard. The Sonores Antiqui Ensemble from Vantaa, founded in 1967, has had the longest career. All its members (Roy Asplund, Kimmo Hakasalo, Teppo Tuominen, Arto Juusela, Herman Rechberger) play several instruments – transverse flute, recorder, krumhorn, mediaeval fiddle, viola d'amore, viola da gamba, cello, lute, guitar, vihuela, tambura, harpsichord. The ensemble specializes in mediaeval, Renaissance and early Baroque music. The Baroque ensemble Les-Goûts-Réunis was founded in 1982 (Mikael Helasvuo, Baroque flute; Timo Juntura, viola da gamba and Baroque cello; Kati Hämäläinen, harpsichord). The most recent addition is the six-member continuo ensemble Battalia, first violin Sirkka-Liisa Kaakinen. Cf. pp. 183–187.

Instrumentalists

Before the pioneer work done by the Helsinki Music Institute founded by Martin Wegelius (cf. p. 37) in 1882, few instrumentalists of note are known. One of the few was the composer Bernhard Henrik Crusell, a clarinet virtuoso born in Uusikaupunki. He played first clarinet in the Royal Chapel of Stockholm from 1793 to 1833, and was an assiduous soloist and chamber musician. The pianist ALIE LINDBERG (1849–1933), whom Liszt himself had given a word of commendation, also gave concerts extensively in Europe from the 1860s onward.

Among the earlier pianists whose work is still reflected today were ERNST LINKO (1889–1947) and ILMARI HANNIKAINEN (1892–1955). Linko, a robust interpreter of Bach, Beethoven and Brahms, served for many years as a professor and principal of the Sibelius Academy, the largest institution of its kind in Scandinavia and the third largest in Europe, which has carried on the traditions of the Helsinki Music Institute, later the Conservatory, since 1939. The Academy's other professorship for the piano was held by Hannikainen, the scion of a musical family, a sensitive and refined artist, and a composer like Linko. Other pianists who have held professorships include TIMO MIKKILÄ (b. 1912), a well-known soloist and performer of chamber music, who has played duo works with many famous violinists and cellists. TAPANI VALSTA (b. 1921), also a soloist and chamber musician of merit, was not only a professor but for many years also the organist of Helsinki Cathedral. The present professors are LIISA POHJOLA (b. 1936), member of another musical family, and known for her powerful performances of Prokofiev and other 20th-century music, and ERIK T. TAWASTSTJERNA (b. 1951), a cultivated performer who has recorded Sibelius's complete piano works and published a dissertation on Finnish piano music. He is the son of the well-known Sibelius scholar. MATTI RAEKALLIO (b. 1954), steelfingered Liszt, Prokofiev and Beethoven interpreter, is an associate professor, and was also appointed professor at the Royal College of Music in Stockholm in 1995. An earlier pianist who should be mentioned is CYRIL

SZALKIEWICZ (1914–69), an authentic performer of Sibelius, a refined lied pianist and distinguished rehearsal pianist at the Finnish National Opera.

Two Finnish pianists have achieved international fame. One of them, the versatile Ralf Gothoni, is a composer, conductor (of the Turku Philharmonic Orchestra), and the former director of the Savonlinna Opera Festival. He has an acute mind, is a particularly noted Schubert pianist, and a frequent performer of chamber music, in which he has distinguished himself particularly as the equal partner of outstanding lied singers such as Martti Talvela and Jorma Hynninen. Gothoni is a professor at the Hamburg College of Music and, since 1992, professor of chamber music at the Sibelius Academy. In 1994 he was awarded the prestigious Gilmore Prize in the United States. The other, OLLI MUSTONEN (b. 1967), was Gothoni's pupil. Exceptionally gifted from an early age, on his worldwide concert tours and as soloist for leading orchestras Mustonen has for years been giving brilliant performances of the classical and romantic repertoire, as well as of Debussy, Prokofiev and Hindemith. Mustonen is also a composer.

Since 1945 the Maj Lind Piano Competition has been held

The virtuoso technique and electric performances of Olli Mustonen infuse even the most hackneyed piano standards with new life.

regularly in Helsinki. This has provided many young pianists with a launching pad of national, and even international significance. In addition to Valsta, winners have included RISTO LAURIALA (b. 1949), a notable performer of Bach and extensive cycles of individual composers' works; EERO HEINONEN (b. 1950) – a member of the Turku school of pianists of TARMO HUOVINEN (b. 1932) – who was awarded a diploma at the Tchaikovsky Competition in Moscow in 1974, has taught many young pianists and given a series of concerts covering all Mozart's piano concertos; FOLKE GRÄSBECK (b. 1956), from a well-known musical family, known for his duets with solo instrumentalists; JUHANI LAGERSPETZ (b. 1959), performer of all Brahms's piano works, a chamber musician and concert accompanist, won a diploma at the 1982 and 1986 Tchaikovsky Competitions; ILKKA PAANANEN (b. 1960), also an accomplished soloist and accompanist, and one of the foremost musical humourists in Finland; RAIJA KERPPO (b. 1961), winner of the Nordic Piano Competition in 1989, soloist and chamber musician; ARTO SATUKANGAS (b. 1962), particularly at home with romantic music, lecturer in chamber music at Karlsruhe since 1992. Among the youngest generation, LAURA MIKKOLA (b. 1973) won second prize in the Queen Elisabeth Competition in Belgium, and the Chopin specialist JANNE MERTANEN (b. 1967) won the Darmstadt Chopin Competition in 1992.

The leading piano virtuosos specializing in contemporary music are the steely-fingered JOUKO LAIVUORI (b. 1959) and the two sisters HEINI (b. 1966) and JAANA (b. 1960) KÄRKKÄINEN. The best-known player of the fortepiano is TUIJA HAKKILA (b. 1959). The Japanese-born IZUMI TATENO (b. 1936), who lives in Finland, has done significant work in making Finnish piano music known through recordings and extensive concert tours.

Several of those mentioned above have also performed as lied pianists. PENTTI KOSKIMIES (1922–90), who specialized in this field, achieved a formidable reputation. Among those most engaged in this work are MARITA VIITASALO (b. 1948), also known as a performer of Sibelius's piano pieces; GUSTAV DJUPSJÖBACKA (b. 1950), former artistic director of the Joroinen Music Festival and now of the Joensuu Festival; and ILMO RANTA (b. 1956), known as a performer of contemporary piano music and artistic director of concert programming at the Sibelius Academy.

KATI HÄMÄLÄINEN (b. 1947), who holds a doctorate in music, MARKETTA VALVE (b. 1939), the Baroque expert ANSSI MATTILA (b. 1953), and the composer JUKKA TIENSUU have specialized in the harpsichord. Outstanding concert accordeon soloists are MATTI RANTANEN (b. 1952), lecturer at Sibelius Academy, MARJUT TYNKKY-NEN (b. 1961) and MIKA VÄYRYNEN (b. 1967), who won the Coupe Mondiale in Lucerne, Switzerland in 1989.

Professor TAUNO ÄIKÄÄ (b. 1917), highly respected by the elite among international organists, has given many concerts in Europe and America, and has had a long career as a church organist and teacher. ENZIO FORSBLOM (1920–96), professor at the Sibelius Academy from 1969 to 1986, won special recognition as a Bach interpreter (playing the harpsichord as well as the organ) and scholar. The pianist-organist Tapani Valsta has already been mentioned. KARI JUSSILA (b. 1943) has come to the fore particularly as a performer of Messiaen and other modern composers. KALEVI KIVINIEMI (b. 1958) is known for his improvisations and for expanding the conventional organ repertoire. He has won international recognition both as a performer and as director of the Lahti Organ Festival since 1990. In this position he succeeded AIMO KÄNKÄNEN (b. 1922), on whose initiative the event was first held in 1973. The most notable winners of the organ competition held in connection with the festival are OLLI PORTHAN (b. 1957), at present a professor at the Sibelius Academy, and the concert organist MAIJA LEHTONEN (b. 1962). Among church organists with the most ambitious artistic aims we may mention three Helsinki musicians, TAPIO TIITU (b. 1944), PERTTI EEROLA (b. 1950), who is the founder and director of the Chamber Orchestra and Choir of St. John's, and SEPPO MURTO (b. 1955), also an accomplished choirmaster.

The artistic and technical standard of Finnish violinists has been weighed above all by the Sibelius Violin Concerto, the most important Scandinavian composition for the instrument. It has been the obligatory final piece for the international Sibelius violin competition in Helsinki, started in 1965, and the national competition in Kuopio, first held in 1967. The first internationally-known Finnish performer of this concerto was ANJA IGNATIUS (1911–65), a professor at the Sibelius Academy from 1955 to 1978. ARNO GRANROTH (1909–87), a representative of the French school of violin-playing, was also a distinguished teacher. TUO-MAS HAAPANEN (b. 1924), a professor and principal of the Sibelius Academy, trained the Academy Chamber Orchestra to an international level. HEIMO HAITTO (b. 1925) was a child prodigy who won a violin competition in London in 1939 and lived for a long period in the United States.

Among the winners of the Kuopio Violin Competition, SEPPO TUKIAINEN (b. 1939) is a chamber musician and a professor at the Sibelius Academy. KAIJA SAARIKETTU (b. 1957), whose repertoire includes modern concertos, has been a Sibelius Academy professor since 1995. She also teaches at the Edsberg Music Institute in Sweden. HANNELE SEGERSTAM (b. 1943), ERKKI PALOLA (b. 1957), JARI VALO (b. 1961) and PEKKA KAUPPINEN (b. 1966) are concertmasters of the principal Finnish orchestras, as well as soloists and chamber musicians. Palola and Valo (of the Opus 135 Quartet) also play the first violin in quartets. MIKKO-VILLE LUOLAJAN-MIKKOLA (b. 1953), who has played in the Metropolitan Opera Orchestra, has for many years been a leading light in the Savonlinna Opera Festival Orchestra. JAAKKO KUUSISTO (b. 1974) achieved in 1990 the best position of a Finnish player up to then in the Sibelius Violin Competition (fourth prize). His brother PEKKA KUUSISTO (b. 1976) was the first Finn to win this event in 1995. Other violinists who have been successful in competitions are MANFRED GRÄSBECK (b. 1955), concertmaster of the Finnish National Opera Orchestra and winner of the Nordic Violin Competition in 1977, and EEVA KOSKINEN (b. 1961), senior teacher, who won four second prizes between 1982 and 1986 – in Switzerland, the Nether-

Pekka Kuusisto pulled off what Finland's top violinists before him could only dream of, wresting a place for himself at the top.

lands, Chile and Tokyo. SAKARI ORAMO (b. 1965) and JOHN STORGÅRDS (b. 1963) are equally talented as violinists and conductors. Mention should also be made of the fine young artist JAN SÖDERBLOM (b. 1970).

The foundations for the high level of cello-playing in Finland were laid by OSSIAN FOHSTRÖM (1870–1952) and YRJÖ SELIN (1894–1965), both Sibelius Academy professors and solo cellists of the Helsinki Philharmonic. Selin's work as a professor has been continued by ERKKI RAUTIO (b. 1931), one of a well-known series of musical brothers, principal of the Sibelius Academy from 1990 to 1993, and an interpreter of Bach and new Finnish music, and ARTO NORAS (b. 1942), one of the best-known Finnish musicians internationally, winner of the second prize in the Tchaikovsky Competition in 1966, chiefly a performer of classical and romantic music, and artistic director of the Naantali Music Festival (which he established in 1980). Among the fine players who have been solo cellists of the leading Finnish orchestras are ESKO VALSTA (b. 1924), SEPPO LAAMANEN (b. 1928) and VEIKKO HÖYLÄ (b. 1935). Younger players include RISTO POUTANEN (b. 1954), who won the national cello competition of Turku in 1972; MARTTI ROUSI (b. 1960), who shared second prize in the 1986 Tchaikovsky Competition, is artistic director of the Turku Music Festival and has been a Sibelius Academy professor since 1995; JAN-ERIK GUSTAFSSON (b. 1970), who won fourth prize in the first international Paulo Cello Competition (held in Helsinki in 1991 on the initiative of Arto Noras) is one of the finest young Finnish instrumentalists. His duets with the pianist Heini Kärkkäinen are of particularly high quality. ANSSI KARTTUNEN (b. 1960) is a virtuoso of avantgarde cello music; he is currently artistic director of the Avanti! Chamber Orchestra. MARKKU LUOLAJAN-MIKKOLA (b. 1957) has specialized in the gamba.

Double-bass soloists and chamber musicians include JORMA KATRAMA (b. 1936) and ESKO LAINE (b. 1961), winner of the Munich Competition in 1985 and since 1985 the first Finnish member of the Berlin Philharmonic. JANNE SAKSALA (b. 1967) later became the leader of this orchestra's bass section. The foremost classical guitarist is TIMO KORHONEN (b. 1964), winner of the Munich Competition in 1982.

Thanks to the network of excellent music schools that has spread throughout Finland, the artistic standard of young Finnish musicians, and thus their success in international competitions, has risen quite dramatically in recent decades. Contrary to the situation in the early days of Finnish orchestras, practically all the orchestral wind players today are Finns, as indeed are the other players, too. The present high standard of horn players in Finland is largely due to Professor HOLGER FRANSMAN (b. 1909), "the father of Finnish horn playing" and for many years the solo French horn player of the Helsinki Philharmonic, and his pupils TIMO RONKAINEN (b. 1945) and KALERVO KULMALA (b. 1947) – also a conductor. Among the winners of the Mikkeli Horn Competition, ESA TUKIA (b. 1958) and ESA TAPANI (b. 1968) are also notable soloists. The latter has had success in international competitions, including that of Munich. Other winners of international competitions are the trumpet players LAURI OJALA (b. 1918) and JOUKO HARJANNE

(b. 1962), the artistic director of the Lieksa Brass Festival; the flautist PETRI ALANKO (b. 1963), artistic director of the Helsinki Chamber Orchestra; and the clarinetist ANNA-MAIJA KORSIMAA (b. 1964). Mention may also be made of such other wind players as ILPO MANSNERUS (b. 1943), flautist and conductor; MIKAEL HELAS-VUO (b. 1946), flautist, specialist in Baroque and contemporary music, and a Sibelius Academy professor; the oboists JOUKO TEIKA-RI (b. 1938) and AALE LINDGREN (b. 1951); KARI KRIIKKU, clarinetist, amazing avantgarde virtuoso, artistic director of the Crusell Week in Uusikaupunki (which also features a woodwind competition); and the bassoonists JUHANI TAPANINEN (b. 1935) and HARRI AHMAS (b. 1957) – also a composer.

Singers

The first international Finnish singer was the bel canto soprano JOHANNA VON SCHOULTZ (1813–63), who was engaged by the Italian Opera in Paris from 1833 to 1835. The baritone FILIP FORSTÉN (1852–1932) sang at the Stockholm Opera from 1883 to 1887 and was a professor of singing in Vienna from 1894 to 1925. The soprano ALMA FOHSTRÖM (1856–1936) performed at the Metropolitan Opera in New York during the 1888–89 season, and the soprano MAIKKI JÄRNEFELT (1871–1929) at the Bayreuth Wagner Festival in 1899. From 1876 on, HORTENSE SYNNERBERG (1856–1920) sang mezzo-soprano roles at Covent Garden, London, in Rome, Moscow and South America. But Finland's first real star singer was the soprano AINO ACKTÉ (1876–1944), prima donna of grand opera in Paris from 1897 to 1903 and soloist at the Metropolitan from 1904 to 1906, and a frequently-seen guest at Covent Garden. Her most brilliant parts were the leading ladies in *Salome*, *Tosca* and *Faust*. In 1911 she was one of the founders of the 'Native Opera', later named the Finnish Opera and today the Finnish National Opera, which she directed from 1938 to 1939. This fiery artist organized five opera festivals in Olavinlinna (St. Olof's) Castle at Savonlinna in the summers from 1912 to 1916 and in 1930. This cultural achievement, quite extraordinary in the circumstances then prevailing, anticipated the present Savonlinna Opera Festival. Her mother, the soprano EMMY STRÖMER-ACHTÉ (1850–1924), and her sister IRMA TERVANI (1887–1936), contralto at the Dresden Court Opera, were also singers of note. HANNA GRANFELT (1884–1952), a distinguished Richard Strauss soprano, was engaged in Mannheim, Berlin and at Covent Garden. The soprano AULIKKI RAUTAWAARA (1906–90), member of a well-known family of musicians and a highly-regarded performer of Mozart and Sibelius, won extensive success as a concert singer and performed at the Glyndebourne and Salzburg Music Festivals and against the background of the Visby ruins in Sweden. LEA PILTTI (1907–82) was a soloist at the Vienna State Opera from 1938 to 1943. The contralto ANTONIETTA TOINI (1901–90) sang at La Scala in 1929 and 1934 and in the Arena, Verona; she later directed the Tampere Opera. The soprano LIISA LINKO-MALMIO (b. 1917), besides her work at the Finnish National Opera, had a distinguished international career as an opera and concert singer from 1943; since 1963 she has been a highly-respected teacher at the Sibelius Academy.

The bass singer KIM BORG (b. 1919) is something of a legend. He started out as an engineer, but moved on to an impressive singing career lasting over thirty years and extending to every continent; he was the first Finnish male singer to appear at the Metropolitan Opera, from 1959 to 1962. From 1972 to 1989 he was a professor at the Royal Academy of Music in Copenhagen, and he has both composed music and written about it with his own inimitable brand of humour. The baritone MATTI LEHTINEN (b. 1922) is an incomparable interpreter of contemporary Finnish music. He began his career by winning the Geneva Singing Competition in 1950, sang at the Cologne Opera from 1952 to 1955, and has created unforgettable character roles at the Finnish National Opera and in Savonlinna (the title role of Aarre Merikanto's *Juha*, and the lovable Papageno in *The Magic Flute*). He is also a notable singer of lieder and oratorio. From 1963 to 1987 he was a professor at the Sibelius Academy. Another highly impressive stage personality was the baritone USKO VIITANEN (b. 1928), of whom the great Tito Gobbi himself spoke words of praise. Viitanen mastered many great Italian roles, as did the tenor JORMA HUTTUNEN (1907–79) and later VEIKKO TYRVÄINEN (1922–86), a fine singer and actor in such roles as Lensky in *Eugene Onegin*. He toured several times in the Soviet Union.

The real international breakthrough of Finnish singers (especially men) started in the late 1950s. MIKKO PLOSILA (1914–94), a dramatic tenor who had studied economics – one of many Finnish singers with an academic degree – was a soloist at the Wuppertal Opera from 1958 to 1963, and a visiting performer on many European stages. The tenor VEIJO VARPIO (b. 1928) sang for nearly twenty years in various German and Austrian opera houses, and was the memorable executive director of the Helsinki Festival from 1980 to 1994. The baritone TOM KRAUSE (b. 1934) started in Berlin and went on to Paris, the Met, La Scala and Bayreuth; he is a regular performer in Savonlinna and a distinguished interpreter of Sibelius's songs. The baritone PEKKA SALOMAA (b. 1933) also started out at the Deutsche Oper Berlin, conducted international opera courses in Bayreuth from 1975 to 1983, and since 1979 has been professor of opera training at the Sibelius Academy. His son, the baritone PETTERI SALOMAA (b. 1961), is an oratorio soloist much in demand, was for some years a soloist at the Frankfurt Opera, and has for several years sung Mozart roles at the Drottningholm Palace Theatre in Sweden.

The worldwide opera career of the bass MARTTI TALVELA (1935–89) began in Stockholm and continued in Bayreuth, Berlin and La Scala, and from 1968 at the Metropolitan. In Savonlinna he gave unique performances: in *The Magic Flute*, *Boris Godunov*, *Viimeiset kiusaukset* (Last Temptations) by the Finnish composer Joonas Kokkonen, *Don Carlos*. As artistic director of the Savonlinna Festival from 1972 to 1979, he raised its artistic level and made it universally known. Before his sudden death Talvela had been proposed as the chief director of the Finnish National Opera from 1991. After Talvela the Savonlinna Festival was directed by TIMO

MUSTAKALLIO (1928–84), who had sung big dramatic tenor roles at the Düsseldorf-Duisburg Deutsche Oper am Rhein from 1965 to 1976. In 1974 he established a foundation that organizes singing competitions in connection with the Festival. KARI NURMELA (1937–84), winner of the Brussels Competition in 1962, sang dramatic roles in Stuttgart and Zürich. The tenor MATTI PIIPPONEN (b. 1936), a highly individualistic lied specialist and singer of character roles, has been a soloist in Düsseldorf and Frankfurt, and was for some years the professor of opera training at the Sibelius Academy. PEKKA NUOTIO (1929–89), a scintillating tenor with the Finnish National Opera, extended his repertoire from Italian opera to Wagner, singing at the Met from 1966 to 1967 *Tannhäuser*, *Tristan and Isolde* and at the opening of the Sydney Opera House in 1973 (*Tannhäuser*), as well as on several occasions at the Glasgow Opera. After Nuotio the most prominent singer of Italian tenor roles at the Finnish National Opera has been PETER LINDROOS (b. 1944), whose voice has an exceptionally Italian colouring. Lindroos has also pursued an extensive nternational career in Europe (La Scala, Covent Garden, Vienna) and in both North and South America.

Among women singers, ANITA VÄLKKI (b. 1926) has had the most brilliant career. Her heyday was in the 1960s, when she made a name for herself especially as a Wagner soprano, but also in Puccini and Richard Strauss. Between 1961 and 1966 she achieved striking artistic success at Covent Garden, the Met, the Vienna State Opera and in Bayreuth. From the '70s to the present she has sung mezzo-soprano roles, and has been a distinguished teacher at the Sibelius Academy, as have the contralto AILI PURTONEN (b. 1928), who sang in German-language opera houses in the '60s and '70s, and the mezzo-soprano RAILI KOSTIA (1930–90). The soprano RITVA AUVINEN (b. 1932) has sung many different types of role (including Wagner mezzo-soprano parts) at the Finnish National Opera; one of her most important roles was as Riitta in *Viimeiset kiusaukset* when the Finnish National Opera visited the Met in 1983. She has performed in various Finnish productions, including Savonlinna, and has given many concerts in Europe and the United States. The soprano TARU VALJAKKA (b. 1938) is equally at home in the Italian, German, Russian and Finnish repertoire, including the part of Riika in the Finnish composer Aulis Sallinen's *Punainen viiva* (The Red Line) in the Finnish National's visit to the Met in 1983. One of her specialities is contemporary vocal music. She has given concerts and guest performances throughout Europe, and in North and South America. In 1995 she was appointed a professor at the Academy of Music in Tallinn, Estonia. HELJÄ ANGERVO (b. 1940), for long a mezzo-soprano soloist at the Finnish National, nowadays an assistant director, had success in international singing competitions in the 1960s, and sang at the Hamburg State Opera in 1974–75 and in Bayreuth in 1974. MAIJA LOKKA (b. 1946) has sung the main soprano roles in many Italian (especially Puccini), German (including Wagner), Slavic (including Janáček) and Finnish operas. The soprano MARGARETA HAVERINEN (b. 1952) won the Geneva Competition in 1978; her special field is French songs. She has been a

Matti Salminen has been one of the leading performers at the Savonlinna Opera Festival since 1968; in the picture, as Daland in *The Flying Dutchman*.

guest performer at the Norwegian Opera and the Welsh National Opera.

MATTI SALMINEN (b. 1945) began his career in 1972 as first bass at the Cologne Opera. He has become a star bass singer in many of the leading opera houses – La Scala, Covent Garden, Berlin. Between 1976 and 1988 he played nine roles and gave over 150 performances at Bayreuth, and since 1981 he has sung a dozen or more roles at the Met. His broad repertoire includes German, Italian and Russian opera. He has been one of the most popular lead singers in Savonlinna since 1968, singing in Sallinen's *Ratsumies* (The Horseman), *Don Carlos*, *The Magic Flute* and *The Flying Dutchman*. His distinguishing features are uncompromising artistic quality, a tremendously expressive voice and complete immersion in the character of all his roles. HEIKKI SIUKOLA (b. 1943), who began his career at the same time as Salminen, has become a notable Wagner tenor in Germany, Vienna and France, while the Mozart specialist KIMMO LAPPALAINEN (b. 1944) was the first lyric tenor at the Stuttgart State Opera from 1972 to 1985. The baritone TERO HANNULA (b. 1946) sang in the same opera house for several years; on his visits to Finland he has delighted audiences with his comic facility. The soprano RAILI VILJAKAINEN (b. 1954), winner of the 's Hertogenbosch Competition in 1977, also sang at Stuttgart from 1978 until she moved to the Finnish National Opera in 1988.

Two notable baritones and opera directors acquired international experience from the 1970s onward. One of them, WALTON GRÖNROOS (b. 1939), has been soloist at the Deutsche Oper Berlin since 1975, served as director of the Savonlinna Opera Festival from 1987 to 1991 and as chief director of the Finnish National Opera from 1992 to 1996, and was appointed director of the Stockholm Opera in 1996. He is also a distinguished concert singer. The other, JORMA HYNNINEN (b. 1941), is one of the most respected Finnish musicians; he was artistic director of the Finnish National Opera from 1984 to 1990, and has occupied the same position for the Savonlinna Opera Festival since 1991. He

Jorma Hynninen's roles span an amazing range, from Debussy's fragile young Pelléas to tragic heroes such as Sallinen's Kullervo, depicted here.

was a professor of the arts from 1990 to 1995, and has been a Sibelius Academy professor since 1996. In Finland Hynninen has given many profound interpretations in the operas of Verdi, Mozart, Hindemith and Tchaikovsky and recitals of Schubert lieder and Sibelius songs, and sung in the Passions of Bach. He has been a guest performer in Vienna, Munich, Berlin, Paris, at La Scala and since 1984 at the Met, and has given concerts in Europe, America and Asia. The tenor SEPPO RUOHONEN (b. 1946) became a soloist at the Frankfurt Opera in 1978 and at the Deutsche Oper Berlin in 1981; since 1988 he has been the principal of the Varsinais-Suomi Music Institute in Turku. An unusual phenomenon is PENTTI PERKSALO (b. 1929), who made his debut as a Wagner tenor at the Finnish National Opera at the age of forty-one, and from 1976 sang dramatic roles in various parts of Europe and at the Seattle Opera. The Wagner tenor MATTI KASTU (b. 1943) and the bass MARTTI WALLÉN (b. 1948) have made international careers, chiefly at the Stockholm Opera; the latter gave one of the most intense renderings of the role of Paavo Ruotsalainen in *Vii-*

meiset kiusaukset (Helsinki, Savonlinna), but is also an exuberant comic singer.

The bass JAAKKO RYHÄNEN (b. 1946) is one of the chief soloists at the Finnish National – he gave a charismatic performance of the principal role in *Viimeiset kiusaukset* when the Finnish National visited the Met in 1983. In the 1980s and '90s he has built up a constantly expanding international career, singing Mozart, Wagner, Verdi and Tchaikovsky at La Scala, in Munich, Paris and Chicago. He has been a soloist at the Vienna State Opera since 1991 and is a popular performer in Savonlinna. From 1994 to 1996 he was professor of singing at the Sibelius Academy. The tenor RAIMO SIRKIÄ (b. 1951), with his powerful masculine voice, is equally impressive in Italian opera and in Wagner. After singing in many German opera houses, he was engaged by the Düsseldorf Opera in 1991. He is one of the popular favourites at Savonlinna, as is the lyric tenor JORMA SILVASTI (b. 1959), who has also frequently appeared in Germany. At present Silvasti is giving outstanding performances as singer and actor at the Finnish National. JYRKI NISKANEN (b. 1956), who has given guest performances of Wagner in Paris and elsewhere, has reinforced the notion of the broad and high international standard of Finnish tenors. The strong contingent of Finnish baritones abroad includes HANNU NIEMELÄ (b. 1954), soloist at the Mainz Opera, who had a particular success in the title role of *Macbeth* in Savonlinna; JUKKA RASILAINEN (b. 1956), a macho performer of rough parts in Düsseldorf; and JUHA KOTILAINEN (b. 1955), engaged at the Essen Opera. The giant young bass JOHANN TILLI (b. 1967), who was singing in Savonlinna at the age of twenty and has sung at the Hamburg State Opera since 1990, is today also a soloist at the Deutsche Oper am Rhein, because of the many Finnish soloists there sometimes playfully called the "Finnische Oper am Rhein".

The bass-baritone ANTTI SUHONEN (b. 1956) has sung in many German opera houses, and has recently created many delightfully comic character roles at the Finnish National. The heroic baritone

All set for a brilliant international career, Karita Mattila has already sung in many of the leading opera houses of Europe and America.

ESA RUUTTUNEN (b. 1950) has played rough male roles in Wagner and tormented Finns (Paavo Ruotsalainen in *Viimeiset kiusaukset* and the title role in *Juha*, including a guest performance in Essen). In 1996 he performed in a rare opera by Enescu, *Œdipe*, in Berlin. Other baritones include TAPANI VALTASAARI (b. 1941), SAULI TIILIKAINEN (b. 1952) and RAIMO LAUKKA (b. 1954), both frequent guests on Scandinavian opera stages, and HEIKKI KEINONEN (b. 1945), who has made an invaluable contribution to contemporary Finnish opera in Heininen's *Silkkirumpu* (The Damask Drum), Aho's *Avain* (The Key) and, in 1996, Aho's *Hyönteiselämää* (Insect Life).

The soprano KARITA MATTILA (b. 1960) belongs to the international elite. Winner of the Singer of the World Competition in Cardiff in 1983, she has sung Mozart, Verdi and Tchaikovsky, has been a guest performer several times at Covent Garden, and has sung in Brussels, Paris, Hamburg, Vienna and at the Met; she has also appeared as a soloist with many famous orchestras. The soprano SOILE ISOKOSKI (b. 1957) won singing competitions at The Hague and in Tokyo. Her career as a recitalist and opera singer is rapidly advancing in Europe. The mezzo-soprano MONICA GROOP (b. 1958), a specialist in the Baroque, has performed extensively as a concert and oratorio singer, and sung in opera at Covent Garden, in Los Angeles and in Amsterdam (*Pelléas et Mélisande*). The mezzo-soprano ULLA SIPPOLA (b. 1959), another soloist at the Deutsche Oper am Rhein, made her Bayreuth debut in 1995 as Venus in *Tannhäuser*. Women singers at the Finnish National Opera include the sopranos MERJA WIRKKALA (b. 1954), who sang in 1980–81 at the Vienna State Opera, RITVA-LIISA KORHONEN (b. 1960), a sparkling comedienne, KAISA HANNULA (b. 1960), artistic director of the Rauma Festivo Music Festival, and the lyric soprano RIIKKA HAKOLA (b. 1962); and the mezzo-sopranos EEVA-LIISA SAARINEN (b. 1952), ANNA-LISA JAKOBSON (b. 1956) and PÄIVI NISULA (b. 1961). Many young singers' road to success has begun from one of the many Finnish national singing competitions: the Lappeenranta Singing Competition, the Savonlinna Mustakallio Competition, Kangasniemi, the Toivo Kuula Competition, the Oskar Merikanto Competition or, most important, the international competition in Helsinki founded by the singer MIRJAM HELIN (b. 1911) – held every fifth year since 1984. First prize in the 1994 event went to the dramatic soprano KIRSI TIIHONEN (b. 1963); the second prize was awarded to LILLI PAASIKIVI (b. 1965), a mezzo-soprano. The co-winners of the 1996 Lappeenranta Competition were JOHANNA RUSANEN (b. 1971) and CAMILLA NYLUND (b. 1968), who is engaged at the Hanover Opera. Cf. pp. 201 and 202.

Choirs

Choral singing in Finland has had a strongly social significance as a leisure pursuit in various walks of life (students, teachers, workers, churches, etc.). There are only two professional choirs, the Finnish National Opera Choir (choirmaster ERIC OLOF SÖDERSTRÖM, b. 1957) and the Radio Chamber Choir (no choirmaster at present). In addition there is a number of other choirs of high standard which have won numerous awards in international competitions. Gregorian chant was sung in the Middle Ages, especially in Turku Cathedral. The *Piae Cantiones* collection (1582 and 1625) is a monument of Latin choral song. The first Finnish choir in the modern sense was established at the Turku Academy in 1819. After the fire of Turku in 1827, the choir was reassembled in Helsinki, where Fredrik Pacius staged performances of large vocal works (cf. p. 28) and founded the oldest still active choir in Finland, Akademiska Sångsällskapet (The Academic Song Society), today the Akademiska Sångföreningen (AS, cf. p. 30). Among its later choirmasters the best-known is Erik Bergman, the composer. Pacius's work was continued by another German-born musician, Richard Faltin. Academic choral singing was in Swedish; it was only later that the elementary school teachers trained by E.A. HAGFORS (1827–1913), "the father of Finnish choir singing", spread Finnish-language singing in choirs all over the country. Hagfors taught in Jyväskylä, as did P.J. HANNIKAINEN (1834–1924), who founded a male choir of Finnish-minded singers who had left the AS. This fine choir, Ylioppilaskunnan Laulajat (or YL; the Student Singers), with its extensive tours in several continents, has been under the leadership of Heikki Klemetti, MARTTI TURUNEN (1902–79), ENSTI POHJOLA (b. 1928), HEIKKI PELTOLA (b.1943) and MATTI HYÖKKI (b.1946), teacher of choir conducting at the Sibelius Academy. Heikki Klemetti, composer and music historian, gave special attention to voice control, purity of tone and artistic expression, and was thus a pioneer in the history of Finnish choral singing (cf. p. 59). In 1900 he founded a choir called Suomen Laulu (Finland's Song), which became a mixed choir in 1907; later choirmasters have included OSSI ELOKAS (1904–91), Martti Turunen, Ensti Pohjola, the cathedral organist SEPPO MURTO (b. 1955) and TIMO NUORANNE (b. 1963). The choir has chiefly sung big vocal works, as has Akateeminen Laulu (Academic Song; founded 1953) of Helsinki, its leaders including REIJO NORIO (b. 1934), Matti Hyökki, Atso Almila and Seppo Murto, and the Helsinki Cathedral Choir, founded by the composer and tenor EERO ERKKILÄ (b. 1941) in 1970 and led by him until 1987; the present choirmaster is Risto Raikaslehto. A similar choir in Turku is the Chorus Cathedralis Aboensis, directed by JUHA KUIVANEN (b. 1961). The Savonlinna Opera Festival Choir, replaced by a new choir led by KYÖSTI HAATANEN (b. 1947) in 1992, continues its work under the name Finnish Philharmonic Choir, directed by Juha Kuivanen. One of its former directors, HEIKKI LIIMOLA (b. 1958), today directs the Tampere Philharmonic Choir and the Tampere Opera Choir.

Besides the AS and the YL, well-known male choirs in Helsinki include the Laulu-Miehet (Men of Song; founded 1914), whose directors include Klemetti, L. ARVI P. POIJÄRVI (1900–86), Martti Turunen, Ensti Pohjola, HEIKKI SAARI (b. 1935) and URPO RAUHALA (b. 1955), Amici Cantus (founded 1983), directed, e.g., by SAKARI HILDÉN (b. 1954) and HANNU NORJANEN (b. 1964), and the Polytechnic Choir (founded 1904), successful in tour abroad and choir competitions; its directors have included Ossi Elokas, Heikki Saari and the composer TAPANI LÄNSIÖ (b. 1953). Poijärvi, a school teacher and encyclopedist, was also one of the leaders of the distinguished Finlandia Male Choir on its tour of North America and Europe in 1939. Turku has the male choir Laulun Ystävät (Friends of Song; founded 1914), led by MATTI APAJALAHTI (b. 1965) and two academic choirs, Brahe Djäknar and the female choir Florakören, both long directed by composer Gottfrid Gräsbeck.

The Finnish reformer of the chamber choir movement in the 1950s and '60s was HARALD ANDERSÉN (b. 1919), teacher and director of the church music department at the Sibelius Academy. He was director of the Academy's Cantemus Chamber Choir and the chamber choir of the Klemetti Institute, established in Orivesi in 1953 for training choirmasters. He brought to Finland a rarefied style of singing without vibrato, suitable for both old and the most recent choir music, but causing a 'choir war' by antagonizing the traditionalists' views on choral singing. Chamber choirs of high standard emerged: the Radio Chamber Choir (1961), directed by Andersén, ILMO RIIHIMÄKI (b. 1946) and Erik-Olof Söderström; Cantabile (1971), founded by YLERMI KUULA (b. 1928), at present directed by Hannu Norjanen; the Dominante Polytechnic Chamber Choir (1975), directed by Seppo Murto; the Tapiola Chamber Choir (1983), directed first by Söderström and now by

Juha Kuivanen; and the Finnish Chamber Choir (1984), directed by Söderström. The mixed choir of the Southern Finland Students' Club (EOL, founded 1931), successful in the competition in Llangollen, Wales, is now also a chamber choir. Its previous directors include Elokas, Poijärvi, Hildén and Liimola, as well as ILKKA KUUSISTO (b. 1933) and HEIKKI HALME (b. 1942), who today teaches choral direction at the Kuopio Conservatory.

Finland's youth choirs are of exceptionally high quality. The Tapiola Choir (1963), founded and directed until 1994 by ERKKI POHJOLA (b. 1931), is a symbol of the Finnish youth choir movement. It has achieved artistic triumphs under Pohjola's leadership in many countries all over the world; the present director is KARI ALA-PÖLLÄNEN (b. 1940). Cantores Minores, the Helsinki Cathedral Congregation boys' choir (founded 1953), led by the Germans Heinz Hofmann and today Christian Hauschild, has made extensive concert tours in the United States. There are also Candomino, the Espoo youth choir (1967), directed by TAUNO SATOMAA (b. 1936); Jubilate (1967), founded and directed by ASTRID RISKA, which has won competitions in Llangollen and elsewhere; Itämeren tytär (Daughter of the Baltic; 1982), the East Helsinki Music Institute's choir directed by Iris Sundberg; Vox Aurea, the Jyväskylä music classes' choir (1968), previously directed by Ala-Pöllänen and at present by the composer PEKKA KOSTIAINEN (b. 1944); and Campanella, a Tampere girls' choir (1974) directed by AINO LOPPELA (b. 1928).

The choir festivals of Tampere, Espoo and Vaasa and the Helsinki Chamber Choir Festival are international events. Cf. p. 203.

Opera

The German Karl Gottlieb Seuerling Company gave the first opera performances in Finland in 1768. Regular tours by foreign companies began in the 1820s. Many operas were played in Finland only a few years after their first performance. The first Finnish production, performed chiefly by amateurs, was *The Barber of Seville* in Helsinki, 1849, and the first performance of a

Finnish opera (though to a libretto in Swedish) was *Kung Karls jakt* (King Charles's Hunt) by Friedrich Pacius, in Helsinki, 1852. Under the direction of a distinguished man of the theatre, the manager KAARLO BERGBOM (1843–1906), the Finnish Theatre – the first Finnish Opera – flourished for a few years, but closed down because of financial difficulties (cf. p. 32). But the work of Bergbom, the founder of Finnish opera, later bore fruit: over a period of six years 32 operas were performed in Helsinki, Viipuri and Turku, all in the Finnish language. The principal star and director was often EMMY STRÖMER-ACHTÉ (1850–1924) and the conductor was LORENZ NIKOLAI ACHTÉ (1835–1900), parents of the star-to-be, Aino Ackté. After some stray attempts at opera, the first performances of Wagner were given in the Finnish National Theatre in 1904–05, organized by the conductor Armas Järnefelt and his wife, the singer Maikki Järnefelt.The first original Finnish-language opera, *Pohjan neiti* (Maid of the North) by Oskar Merikanto, was first performed in Viipuri, 1908.

The impresario EDVARD FAZER (1861–1943), the singers Aino Ackté, WÄINÖ SOLA (1883–1961), EINO RAUTAVAARA (1876–1939) and WILLIAM HAMMAR (1875–1951), and the composer Oskar Merikanto founded the Native Opera in 1911; the name was changed in 1914 to the Finnish Opera, and in 1956 to the Finnish National Opera. In 1921 Fazer established its ballet company, today the Finnish National Ballet. The company performed in a former Russian garrison theatre, the Alexander Theatre (seating 540). Despite these comparatively modest circumstances, the Opera managed to cultivate an extensive repertoire. Thus all Wagner's great music dramas were performed as early as from 1919 to 1924 and 1930 to 1935, and remained fixtures of the repertoire up to the 1970s. The management made one disastrous mistake, however, when it turned down Aarre Merikanto's brilliant opera *Juha* (1922) on the grounds that it was too difficult and too modern. Since its long-delayed first performance in Lahti, 1963, the excellence of the work has been unanimously admitted (cf. p. 67). After the managements of Fazer and Ackté, the baritone

OIVA SOINI (1893–1971), Sibelius Academy professor, steered the Opera through difficult years (1939–52). A distinguished Wagner tenor, ALFONS ALMI (1904–91), was director/chief director from 1955 to 1971; from 1946 onward he took the ensemble on nationwide tours, and later set up extensive tours abroad for the Ballet. Almi also organized international opera and ballet festivals from 1957 to 1971. In 1963 he established the Opera Orchestra (today with 112 players). This powerhouse of Finnish opera extended the repertoire with contemporary works, and later played a vital part in ensuring for Finland its new opera house. During the directorship of JUHANI RAISKINEN (b. 1937) in the 1970s and '80s, new Finnish works by Joonas Kokkonen and Aulis Sallinen came strongly to the fore, and were performed on many successful tours abroad, including the Metropolitan in 1983. Under the directorship of Raiskinen and his successor Ilkka Kuusisto – with Jorma Hynninen as artistic director – productions demanding a big orchestra and stage (e.g. Wagner) were largely abandoned, and expectations were directed towards the new opera house. The inauguration was in 1993, and with Walton Grönroos as chief director (1992–96) it has won exceptional popularity: the grand auditorium (seating 1,350) has regularly been sold out. Modern repertoire (with the exception of contemporary Finnish operas) has been played in the smaller Almi Room. The desire to see prominent Finnish singers who mainly work abroad has not been entirely fulfilled. For financial reasons some works intended for performance in the 1995–96 season were shelved, or transferred for future production. The diverse offerings of the National Ballet have been the responsibility of the well-known dancer and choreographer JORMA UOTINEN (b. 1950). In 1996 Grönroos moved to the post of director of the Stockholm Opera, and Juhani Raiskinen returned to the helm at the Finnish National after several years as director of the Gothenburg Opera in Sweden.

The list of chief conductors at the Finnish National Opera is a distinguished one: from 1929 to 1959 the Slovenian-born LEO FUNTEK (1885–1965), also a notable conductor of Bruckner, and professor of violin at the Sibelius Academy; from 1926 to 1936 Armas Järnefelt, brother-in-law of Sibelius, as both first conductor and artistic director; JUSSI JALAS (1908–87), son-in-law and authentic interpreter of Sibelius, whose tremendous repertoire over almost thirty years extended from Monteverdi to Shostakovich; ULF SÖDERBLOM (b. 1930), conductor from 1957, chief conductor from 1973 to 1993. Söderblom's work has been exceptionally praiseworthy in the field of new Finnish opera (Aarre Merikanto, Kokkonen, Sallinen, Bergman), both at the National and at the Savonlinna Opera Festival. From 1996 the chief conductor is Okko Kamu. Other conductors include the beloved song composer Oskar Merikanto, MARTTI SIMILÄ (1898–1958), and recently Kari Tikka and Markus Lehtinen (b. 1959), winner of the Nordic Competition in 1987, who also conducts in Scandinavia and Hamburg. Directors of productions have included Wäinö Sola, leading tenor in the early days, YRJÖ KOSTERMAA (b. 1921), SAKARI PUURUNEN (b. 1921), distinguished especially for honing the singers' acting skills, and JUSSI TAPOLA (b. 1946); SEPPO NURMIMAA (b. 1931) has been chief set designer for many years now.

Tampere is a city well-known for its interest in theatre. Its theatres have plenty of experience in operetta, a popular genre everywhere in Finland. In 1946 Tampere was the first city to form its own opera society. The imposing Tampere Hall, completed in 1990, with the largest opera auditorium in Scandinavia (seating 1,800), has further reinforced the city's image as a leading centre of music. Since the 1950s more than a dozen semi-professional opera societies have been established (in Lahti, Vaasa, Kotka, Kuopio, Turku, Oulu, Jyväskylä, Mikkeli, Pori, Joensuu, Espoo, Seinäjoki, Vantaa, Kerava, etc.). Their central organization, the Association of Finnish Operas, has a 'bank' of soloists for the needs of its member societies. The rise of the regional opera system has been one of the most gratifying developments in Finnish music. The auditoriums most suitable for opera, besides Tampere, are the music centres in Kuopio, Mikkeli and Espoo, and certain theatres (e.g. Turku, Pori and formerly Lahti). Among the most enthusiastic organizers of regional opera are Irma Rewell (Vaasa), Seppo Silvan (Tampere), and the former opera bass singer HANNU HEIKKILÄ (b. 1922, Lahti). Important stage directors include ILKKA BÄCKMAN (b. 1945), LEENA SALONEN (b.1945, Oulu) and JUHA HEMÁNUS (b. 1966). The Sibelius Academy Opera is today very active, under the direction of Professor Pekka Salomaa. It performs in the Alexander Theatre, Helsinki's old opera house. The Savonlinna Opera Festivals are the crown of Finnish opera life. Ambitious folk opera is performed at Ilmajoki in Ostrobothnia. Cf. pp. 187–198.

Music Festivals

The earliest Finnish summer music festivals were general song and music events, organized on nineteen occasions between 1884 and 1926 by the Society for Culture and Education in various parts of the country – the first were held in Jyväskylä. The festivals helped to develop the technical and artistic competence of choirs and musical ensembles, and to encourage awareness of national identity. They included singing and instrumental playing competitions, performances in the *Kalevala* tradition, and sometimes opera and symphony concerts. The first workers' festival was held in 1910, the first Swedish-speakers' festival and church music festival in 1927; the SULASOL (Finnish Amateur Musicians' Association) festivals began in 1934. Early pioneer work was done at the five opera festivals in the mediaeval Olavinlinna Castle of Savonlinna, organized by Aino Ackté between 1912 and 1930 (cf. p. 187); these were terminated owing to lack of funds and government interest. The first sign of a revival came with the Savonlinna Music Days, held in 1955 on the initiative of Yrjö Kilpinen, composer and academician. It was not until 1967, however, that the first Savonlinna Festival in its modern form was held. The opera played was *Fidelio*. The hallmark of the Festival is the high international standard of both Finnish and foreign soloists, the Opera Festival Orchestra and Choir. In addition to the standard repertoire, many contemporary Finnish operas have been performed. There have also been performances in the underground concert hall of the Retretti Art Centre (seats 1,050) in the nearby Punkaharju, and in the huge wooden church of Kerimäki. The artistic and other directors of the Festival have been Ulf Söderblom, Martti Talvela (cf. p. 189), Timo Mustakallio (the singing competition bearing his name is held in connection with the festival), Ralf Gothoni, Veijo Varpio, Walton Grönroos and PENTTI SAVOLAINEN (b. 1930), writer of a history of the Festival. The present directors are Jorma Hynninen (artistic director) and, since 1993, PAAVO SUOKKO (b. 1944).

The central body of Finnish music festivals is Finland Festivals, with 45 summer festival events connected with music as its members. Opera festivals include, besides Savonlinna, the Ilmajoki Music Festival, with big folk opera performances (held since 1975, director Lasse Lintala). Among the six general music festivals is the Helsinki Festival, preceded from 1951 to 1968 by the Sibelius Festival, and combined since 1981 with the Helsinki Biennale of contemporary music. The directors of the Helsinki Festival have been the composer Seppo Nummi, the cellist Seppo Kimanen, the tenor Veijo Varpio from 1980 to 1994, and the conductor Esa-Pekka Salonen from 1995 to 1996. RISTO NIEMINEN (b. 1956) has been appointed director starting 1997. Salonen rejuvenated the programme with bold surprises; in 1995 an unexpectedly large exceeding of the budget aroused attention. Other such festivals are the Turku Music Festival (since 1960, directed by the cellist Martti Rousi); the Jyväskylä Arts Festival, founded 1956 on the initiative of professors PÄIVÖ OKSALA (1907–74) and TIMO MÄKINEN (b. 1919) and Seppo Nummi (currently directed by Atso Almila); the Joensuu Festival (since 1981, directed by the pianist Gustav Djupsjöbacka); the Mikkeli Music Festival (since 1993, chief performers are the Mariinsky Theatre opera company from St Petersburg under the direction of Valeri Gergiyev; and the Sysmä Summer Sounds (since 1986, directed by the opera singer Ilkka Vihavainen). The best-known among the 11 chamber music festivals are the Kuhmo Chamber Music

Festival, founded in 1970 and directed by Seppo Kimanen; the Naantali Music Festival, founded in 1980 and directed by the cellist Arto Noras; the Korsholm Music Festival in Mustasaari and Vaasa, founded in 1983 and a joint project with the Umeå Festival across the Gulf of Bothnia in Sweden; the Viitasaari Time of Music (contemporary music, founded 1981, directed by the composer Jarmo Sermilä); the Summer Sounds of the Avanti! Chamber Orchestra in Porvoo (founded 1986 and directed by the conductors Esa-Pekka Salonen and Jukka-Pekka Saraste); the Kangasniemi Music Festival with its competitions for singers and lied pianists (founded 1983, directed by the baritone and professor at the Sibelius Academy 1988–94 MATTI TULOISELA, b. 1931); the Crusell Week in Uusikaupunki, with its woodwind competition (founded 1982, directed by the clarinetist Kari Kriikku). Other music festivals include the Tampere Biennale for new, mostly Finnish music (founded 1986, directed by the composer Usko Meriläinen), and the Kaustinen Folk Music Festival (founded 1968), with a strongly international programme. In addition there are the Kuopio Dance and Music Festival (founded 1970, directed by Jukka O. Miettinen), with Finnish and foreign ballet and dance ensembles, as well as eight jazz and three rock festivals. Cf. pp. 189–194.

POPULAR MUSIC

Home Sweet Home

Finnish popular music arose from the merging of the three 'parent traditions' of art music, folk music and Afro-American music. During the 19th century, when Finland was an autonomous part of the Russian Empire, the political climate favoured internationalism. In its new role, Finland was able to form new contacts, via East and West, with the Continental entertainment business. Meanwhile, incipient urbanization and industrialization produced new public entertainments, including restaurants, ballrooms, the *soirées dansantes* of various clubs and associations, operettas and musical plays, the circus, amusement parks, variety shows and the performances of street musicians. The time was ripe for the emergence of a new, urban form of entertainment – popular music, as distinct from art music and folk music.

Perhaps the crucial turning-point in the history of Finnish folk music occurred during the 19th century, as the ancient musical tradition often referred to as 'Kalevalan', comprising rune-singing, dirges and playing of the five-string kantele, withered. With the spread of a Western way of life, the pentatonic modality associated with a shamanistic culture based on hunting and slash-and-burn farming gave way to rhymed verses, traditional and broadside ballads, *rekilaulut* (roundelays) and dance songs, and protestant hymns, all governed by functional harmony. Only the nomadic reindeer herders of Lapland, the Sámi, have preserved the magic power of the pentatonic *joiku* chant to the present day.

Continental functional harmony began its conquest of Finland in the 17th century, starting from the western parts of the country. Its roots were in court music and military music, blended with a dash of Baroque and Classicism. European *contredanses*, the polska (polonaise), march and minuet, were already being danced at rural Ostrobothnian celebrations during the 18th century. The most common instruments were the violin and clarinet. Curiously, one of the most popular dance tunes was the *Lampaan polska* (Sheep's Polska), a variant of the *folia*. Finnish fiddlers' variations on this theme were based on Corelli's well-known work.

More recent folk music also had a direct influence. The travelling performers touring the markets of St Petersburg, Stockholm and Tallinn set the example. Along with the Italian and German organ grinders, street balladeers and players of three to five-row accordions (such as Pietro Frosini and Pietro Deiro), there was a striking number of harp players. German harpists began to tour markets and fairs in the 1830s, giving concerts wherever they could. Sometimes they were accompanied by guitar, flute, mandolin or zither. This tradition explains the success of KREETA HAAPASALO (1822–90), a kantele player from Kaustinen. The wife of a tenant farmer, Haapasalo was the first Finnish itinerant folk musician. She started by playing at the fairs of Ostrobothnia, was discovered and fussed over by Finnish patriots on account of her 'national instrument', and even performed at the courts of Stockholm and St Petersburg. Haapasalo became a national icon in the spirit of Herderian romanticism: portraits were painted of her, depicting her as an example of a 'genuine' woman of the people. Her stylistic forebears, however, were far removed from the *Kalevala*. Instead of the five-string kantele, she played a large instrument which could produce triads like a harp and pick out bass notes. Her repertoire was taken mostly from the first publication of Finnish folk tunes, *Suomen Kansan Laulantoja*, edited by A.A. Reinholm and published in 1849. Haapasalo's most popular number, her own song *Kanteleeni* (My Kantele), was a borrowing from Sir Henry

Bishop's upper-class idyll, *Home Sweet Home* (1829). Thus, too, was folk music turned into popular music.

The appearance of new, foreign material also resulted from reforms in Finnish art music, from the setting up of orchestras to basic music education, sheet music sales and instrument shops. Here, too, the Continental system served as the model. Virtually no distinction was made between art music and popular music. Foreign conductors and musicians were worth their weight in gold as directors of new philharmonic and choral societies and as conductors of dance orchestras and military bands. Even the repertoire, consisting of small-scale classical and romantic instrumental music, was largely the same at the popular restaurants and the *soirées sérieuses* in the concert halls.

The German-Russian influence continued to strengthen after 1850. From the early years of the century, entertainments in Helsinki, Turku and Viipuri had begun to be adapted to the taste of tourists from St Petersburg. At this time, *salon* orchestras became fixtures at the 'spas' and 'casinos' of the Finnish bathing resorts. These ensembles came from St Petersburg and Germany. Before the Crimean War (1854–55), several German *Stehgeiger* played at the Kaivohuone baths in Helsinki. One of them, the violinist and composer KARL GANSZAUGE (1820–68), stayed in Finland. As an assistant of Fredrik Pacius, he tried to take charge of the lagging orchestra and opera societies. At the time of his death, he was organist of Helsinki's Old Church. In 1844 a new dance, the *polka*, was all the rage among Helsinki society, as is shown by a collection of fifty-odd polkas for piano produced by Ganszauge and other musicians, including the Finns Karl Collan, C.G. Wasenius, Rafael Sjögren and the German-born Heinrich Wächter.

Military bands and amateur septets (comprising an E flat cornet, two B flat cornets, alto, tenor, baritone and bass horn) had a lowlier status than the ballroom orchestras, playing a similar repertoire in park concerts and at dances: overtures, opera fantasies, song arrangements, marches, polkas, waltzes

and mazurkas. Some new pieces were also composed. ADOLF
LEANDER (1833–99), the 'Father of Finnish Horn Players', produced folksong potpourris and composed waltzes and marches
in German-Russian style. One of the evergreens, in arrangements for septet and for ballroom orchestra, was the potpourri
Suomalaisia säveleitä (Finnish Tunes; 1871) by the theatre conductor Emil Pahlman.

By the end of the 19th century, the Helsinki entertainment
scene had close contacts with the Continent. The new, upper-
class restaurant, many of which had German, Swedish or
Russian owners, hired women's orchestras, 'Wiener-Damen-
Kapellen', Tyrolean groups, Serbian *tamburitza* bands, Russian
Gypsy choirs, Hungarian string ensembles and Romanian *lautar*
bands, and so forth. The first Afro-American 'negro comedians',
or minstrels, visited Finland en route to St Petersburg in the
1860s. A group of Sioux travelling with a circus gave a demonstration of their way of life in Viipuri.

All these were features of the new Continental popular culture, which Finland gradually adopted. A coherent, German-
Russian conception of music became the received norm
throughout the country. By the end of the century, the cornerstones of the repertoire of salon orchestras, brass bands, organ
grinders and accordionists alike were the *Schrammel* melody,
governed by functional harmony and favouring chromatic passing notes; melody-accompaniment-obbligato texture; medley-
type miniature forms, such as the potpourri; a romantic delivery,
favouring rubatos and glissandos; and a tinkly sound.

Hot

Afro-American music has been the leading influence on popular
music, in Finland as elsewhere, throughout the 20th century. The
new, mechanized production techniques – first the gramophone record, then radio and cinema, later the electronic media
– were the vital factor that made the spread of ragtime, jazz
and rock possible. The fascination of the music itself stemmed

from its new approach, differing from European music, with polyrhythmics (swing), expressive use of the voice (hot, blue note modality), improvisation and an emotional intensity coupled with high volume.

1910–1940: Ragtime, Tango, Jazz, Oom-pah

The new music was preceded by fashionable dances, popular hits and new instruments. The first saxophones appeared in army bands began at the turn of the century; music shops began to stock banjos; the cakewalk, "an original comic negro and cowboy dance", was demonstrated by the entire Ciniselli Circus troupe in Helsinki in 1905. Other syncopated novelty dances included the one-step and two-step in the 1910s and the fox-trot, charleston and black bottom in the 1920s. The tango, the latest craze in 1913 – though only danced on stage at the time – produced a commercial boom, with tango apparel, tango shoes and tango candy selling like hot cakes.

The reign of jazz began after the First World War. Its first manifestations in Finland were German cabaret jazz, a noisy ragtime comedy and instrumental circus in the style of the Louis Mitchell Jazz Kings and James Reese Europe. From autumn 1921 on, "original King of Jazz ensembles straight from the Berlin Kleinkunstbühne" played at the Oopperakellari and Fennia restaurants. The public – notably represented by a young group of modernist writers known as the 'Torch-bearers' – was entranced, seeing jazz as the harbinger of a new age of futurism, expressionism and machine culture. Restauranteurs were also ecstatic, as public dances at restaurants were well-attended even in the midst of Prohibition. The first Finnish 'salon jazz orchestras' (with names like Zamba, Melody Boys and Mr. François's Salon-Jazz-Orchestra) were formed at the height of the jazz boom. In typically European fashion, their instrumental makeup was still mixed: besides saxophonists, banjo players and *jazzers* (=drummers), the ensembles might include a Hungarian *cimbalom* player and *primas* violinist, a Russian balalaika player and Finnish salon musicians on violin, flute, cello and piano. The standard repertoire consisted of German *Schlager*, music hall couplets, tangos and Boston waltzes.

Among the foremost Finnish representatives of this style, which can perhaps best be defined as a kind of ragtime, was GEORGE GUNAROPULOS (1904–68), leader of the Melody Boys, who performed at the Fennia and Kaivohuone restaurants. The son of a Greek family in St Petersburg, Gunaropulos emigrated to Finland, studied composition with Erkki Melartin, and eventually composed two saxophone concertos, a cello concerto and a handful of other late romantic orchestral works. His ambitious, meticulous arrangements of four Finnish folk songs were recorded in 1929; they included ragtime versions of *Suomalainen rapsodia* and *Isoo-Antti*, a blues version of *Raatikkoon* and a foxtrot adapted from *Minä seison korkealla vuorella*. Probably the first Finnish jazz recording, the record was too sophisticated to make a popular hit.

The jazz scene changed in the mid 1920s. Young army musicians ferreting out the secrets of 'special arrangements', and music students who had picked up hints from BBC broadcasts, set out for New Orleans and Chicago, the centres of hot jazz. Tommy Tuomikoski, a Finnish-American saxophonist, was one of the key figures in this movement. He arrived in Finland in 1926 on the *S/S Andania*, played for several years in a variety of dance ensembles, and taught Finnish jazz hopefuls, even publishing a saxophone tutor. Many of the 'jazz pioneers' of the period later became prominent figures in Finnish popular music. Trumpeter Eugen Malmstén headed the *Rytmi-Pojat*, the leading big band playing swing in the 1930s, and trombonist Klaus Salmi led the *Ramblers* orchestra. The pianists Harry Bergström, George de Godzinsky and Toivo Kärki made a career in the film, radio and record business.

Along with ballroom jazz and hot jazz, a more rustic style, 'accordion jazz', or oom-pah, developed in the 1920s. Its leading exponent was the *Dallapé* orchestra. Founded in 1926, this

The Dallapé orchestra and Georg Malmstén at their head-
quarters, the Heimola assembly hall, in their heyday in 1936.

ensemble started modestly by playing at dance joints on the
working-class fringes of Helsinki. Dallapé played waltzes, polkas
and their homespun variant (*jenkka*), German *Schlager* in the
band's own translations, and its own foxtrots. The use of folk
music elements, primarily the accordion, helped bridge the class
divisions sharpened by the recent civil war (1918), while recordings, tours of rural Finland and published sheet music helped
establish the band's reputation. By the 1930s, Dallapé was the
bestknown dance orchestra in Finland, a 13-player ensemble
boasting the country's hottest musicians, including pianists
Aarre Koskela and Asser Fagerström, sax players Tommy Tuomikoski and Matti Rajula, trumpeter Alvar Kosunen, drummer
Ossi Aalto and sousaphonist/bassist Eero Lauressalo. The vernacular tradition was represented in this crowd by world champion accordionist Viljo Vesterinen, violinist Helge Pahlman, xylo-
phone player Eino Katajavuori and solo singer Georg Malmstén,
the no. 1 singer and composer of popular songs in his day.

The transitional years around 1930 marked a turning-point in the history of Finnish popular music. Two worlds clashed violently, as jazz supplanted the salon orchestras from the restaurants and the brass septets from the dance halls. There was bitter antagonism between old and new, Finnish-European and Afro-American, art music and popular music.

1940 and after: Swing, Bebop, Free Jazz, Fusion

The Second World War interrupted the advance of jazz. The musicians were called up for service, dances were banned, and right-wing radical circles began to call for the ethnic cleansing of music: "We must put a stop to negro music." The dance schools of Helsinki still offered a haven for swing and jitterbug. A new generation of musicians, including bassist Erik Lindström, pianist Valto Laitinen and guitarist Herbert Katz, learned to play the music of the Western allies by listening to BBC and AFN broadcasts. Jaakko Fuhrmann's swing band played at the 'Peace Dance' at Helsinki railway station in 1945. Big band jazz (Erkki Aho, Ossi Aalto) re-established its position in dance halls. Back in 1942, the Rytmi record label had released a Finnish collection of big band standards (*St. Louis Blues*, *Stardust*, *Dinah*, *As Time Goes By*). The arrangements were made – some of them while camped in a dugout at the front – by Toivo Kärki, who had won the 1939 Melody Maker competition with the piece *Things Happen That Way*. The main postwar innovators were the bass players Erik Lindström and Olli Häme, who directed their own bands as well as the Radio Dance Orchestra (1957–72), the big band of the Finnish Broadcasting Company (YLE). Towards the end of the '50s, bebop began to gain ground in Finland, initially outside the capital in Turku, Tampere and Hämeenlinna, hometowns of prize-winning bands in jazz competitions arranged by *Rytmi* magazine. The Kotka region, heartland of the Finnish wood-processing industry, produced an exceptional number of professional jazz musicians (including pianist Pentti Ahola, trumpeter Heikki Rosendahl, flutist Esa Pethman and guitarist Heikki Laurila). Pianist Jaakko Salo, the multi-instrumentalists Pentti

Lasanen and Rauno Lehtinen and the trumpeters Ossi Runne and Jörgen Petersen from Denmark all moved to Helsinki from the provinces, and wound up as studio conductors and arrangers. Also in the '50s, pianist Erkki Melakoski and saxophonist Ossi Malinen sought a cool sound in the spirit of Miles Davis and Lennie Tristano; this style was taken up in the '60s by the bands of Esa Pethman, Christian Schwindt and Otto Donner.

With the advent of bebop and free jazz, Finnish jazz began to attract international attention. The Pori Jazz Festival, established in 1966, helped set up new contacts. The Eero Koivistoinen Quartet won the Montreux competition for ensembles in 1969, Seppo 'Paroni' (the Baron) Paakkunainen's and Edward Vesala's *Tuohi Quartet* in 1971. Performing with Jan Garbarek, Arild Andersen and others, Vesala made a name for himself as an aggressive modernist. Paakkunainen built up a reputation as a multi-instrumentalist in the George Gruntz Concert Jazz Band and other ensembles. Also major names in the '70s were pianist Heikki Sarmanto, the composer of numerous orchestral and vocal works, Sakari Kukko and his ethnic jazz group Piirpauke, and Jukka Tolonen and Pekka Pohjola, playing a fusion style incorporating elements from rock, jazz and concert music.

Established in 1975 and sponsored by YLE, the arts committee of Uusimaa Province and the City of Helsinki, the UMO (New Music Orchestra) big band enables its members to play jazz professionally and is worth its weight in gold to Finnish jazz composers and arrangers. Over the years, its members have included Simo Salminen, Kaj Backlund and Esko Heikkinen (trumpet), Juhani Aalto, Tom Bildo and Mircea Stan (trombone), Juhani Aaltonen, Pekka Pöyry, Eero Koivistoinen, Pentti Lahti and Kari Heinilä (saxophone), Heikki Sarmanto, Olli Ahvenlahti, Jarmo Savolainen and Jukka Linkola (piano), Pekka Sarmanto (bass) and Esko Rosnell (drums). The band's first conductor was the pianist ESKO LINNAVALLI (1941–91); he was followed by Markku Johansson, Rich Schemaria and Eero Koivistoinen. New ensembles established in the 1990s which have already made an international reputation include Raoul Björkenheim's *Krakatau*, Iiro Rantala's *Trio Töykeät*, Tapani Rinne's *Rinneradio* and the Perko-Pyysalo-Poppoo, all of which toured Europe, the United States and Asia during the '95–'96 seasons.

Jazz training was organized in the 1960s, contributing to an improvement in the quality of musicianship and a growing general interest in jazz. The Oulunkylä Pop/Jazz Institute (Conservatory since 1986), a project outlined by Klaus Järvinen, was founded in 1972. The Sibelius Academy established a jazz department in 1983, headed since 1986 by drummer Jukkis Uotila. Its first graduate, in 1986, was sax player Jari Perkiömäki. Among international training institutions, the Berklee College of Music has been particularly important to Finnish jazz musicians ever since the 1970s. As jazz has extended its scope, the meaning of the term itself has expanded. The chase for fads and novelties has given way to a new tradition-consciousness, producing a conservative revitalism, as represented by the Downtown Dixie Tigers (DDT) and two swing ensembles, the Lasanen-Sarpila duo and the UHO trio, but also producing a creative critical approach. Jukka Haavisto founded the Finnish Jazz Archives in 1989. Although jazz performances, broadcasts and recordings have never had a large following, its vitality as a crucial genre of popular music has been consolidated by small-scale concerts, festivals and clubs.

Orchestral Music

A new generation of jazz musician-cum-composers began to emerge in the 1970s. They sought to produce a new fusion of stylistic elements from avantgarde art music, jazz and rock. The pioneer of this school was OTTO DONNER (b. 1939), who introduced happenings and collage to art music in the 1960s. The new generation of art music composers, emphasizing a permissive pluralism as a reaction against academic serialism, also took a certain interest in popular music. Donner's post-serialist *XC* (1969) for choir and orchestra culminated in a massive percussive beat "à la Elvin Jones". A similar gesture appeared in the *Symphony of Modern Worlds* (1969) by KARI RYDMAN (b. 1936). The *Otto Donner Treatment* workshop recorded an extensive vocal suite to a poem by Pentti Saarikoski entitled *En soisi sen päättyvän* (I Wish It Would Never End) in 1970. A similar cross-over tendency can be heard in Donner's music for many radio plays and films and in his orchestral works, including *Strings* (1976) and *Dalens ande* (Spirit of the Valley; 1987). The pianist HEIKKI SARMANTO (b. 1939), who has settled in New York, started out by composing instrumental works for his own quartet (e.g. *Flowers in the Water*, 1969), then moved on to intimate vocal music. Many of his songs for soprano Maija Hapuoja, including the cycle *Syksy ja muita lauluja* (Autumn and Other Songs; 1976), are based on Finnish poetry from the early 1900s. His most extensive chamber music-type works, featuring elements reminiscent of Prokofiev and even of national romanticism, are *The New Hope Jazz Mass*, first performed in New York in 1978, *Suomi, sinfoninen runo jousiorkesterille ja jazzyhtyeelle* (Finland, a Symphonic Poem for String Orchestra and Jazz Ensemble; 1984), and *Passions of a Man*, commissioned by the Joensuu Song Festival for a ballet performance on a *Kalevala* theme. ESA HELASVUO (b. 1945), a pianist, has composed music for radio plays and film scores. His chamber music frequently opposes polytonal orchestral texture to mischievous jazz piano improvisations, as in *Think-Tank-Funk* (1973), *Q* (1977) and *The Singing Grand Piano* (1987). Similar patterns appear in the music of PIRJO (b. 1939) and MATTI BERGSTRÖM (1938–94), with instrumental and electronic sections merging to form free pulsative fields. Examples include *Free and Easy* (1976), *The Forgotten Horizon* (1980) and *Northern Light on Stage* (1996).

MATTI RAG PAANANEN (b. 1939) made the Guinness Book of Records with the world's longest jazz suite, comprising 366 movements dedicated to the days of the leap year. Another mammoth project was *Tuhannen ja yhden yön lauluja* (Songs of a Thousand and One Nights; 1977–93), literally comprising

Pirjo and Matti Bergström have composed a great deal of electroacoustic ballet music to which the celebrated dancer-choreographer Jorma Uotinen has performed throughout Europe.

1001 songs. Paananen's principal works are symphonies with a programmatic background, frequently with a humanitarian message: the *Vaskoolisinfonia* (Gold Pan Symphony; 1975–77), *Sinfonia Robinson Crusoelle* (Symphony to Robinson Crusoe; 1986) and *Save Amazonia* (1993).

SEPPO PARONI PAAKKUNAINEN (b. 1943) has focused on ancient Finnish music, rune melodies, dirges, Karelian instruments and particularly on the Sámi *joiku* chant. Paakkunainen and Vesala set up the pop group *Karelia* in 1971, one of the first rock groups to use Finnish folk music as raw material. The group was involved in two ambitious orchestral suites by Paakkunainen, *Tanomania* (1981) and *Sápmi lottázan*; especially the latter work succeeds in closely integrating folk instruments with a symphony orchestra. The colourful orchestral texture rests on an extended pentatonic chord. The birchbark pipe (*tano*), the five-string *kantele* and the archaic *joiku* floats in a primal sea formed by harp clusters, flageolet fields and dark carpets of sound produced by the brass. The use of ethnic wind instruments, the repetitive use of miniature motives, and an ecological approach characterize all of Paakkunainen's recent music, from incidental music via orchestral and big band music to children's songs. Cases in point include *Nunnu* (1971), *Whale Conphony* (1974), *Kissapa Uu* (1977) and *Ethnic Conphony, Kalevala-draama* (1985). ILPO SAASTAMOINEN (b. 1942), a fellow musician of Paakkunainen's from Karelia and other groups, works with similar ethnic material. His main compositions are the oratorio *Karhunpeijaiset* (The Bear Feast; 1987) and the opera *Veiho* (The Wizard; 1993). Saastamoinen's works for amateur performers and his own rock group *Pohjantahti* turn the rough amateur delivery to advantage, employing extensive aleatory choral fields produced by controlled improvisation. The saxophonist EERO KOIVISTOINEN (b. 1946) made his breakthrough as a composer in 1968, when he released two records, the literary *Valtakunta* (The Realm) and the jazz rock album *Football*, made together with the Hasse Walli Blues Section. He followed up a collage period with a neoclassical, ascetically Bartókian phase making spare use of chromaticism in the ballet work *Äiti Maa* (Mother Earth; 1981), the two orchestral works *Sea Suite* (1983) and *Picture in Three Colours* (1987) and the incidental music to *Vincent van Gogh* (1988). Pianist JUKKA LINKOLA (b. 1955) has produced an extensive oeuvre including music for the stage, chamber music, vocal works, compositions for big band and ambitious orchestral works, including *Grand Mystery* (1985), *Structures* (1987) and the First Trumpet Concerto (1988). *Crossings*, a work commissioned for the 1983 Helsinki Festival, explores antithesis and fusion. The juxtaposed elements include a massed, free tonal sound for the orchestra and an improvisatory saxophone part written for Juhani Aaltonen; bright pentatonic and dark chromatic melodic material; rubato and alternating polyrhythmic beat divisions. As a composer, EDWARD VESALA (b. 1945) is miles removed from his musician's role as an aggressive free jazz percussionist; pieces like *Nan Mandol* (1974), *Satu* (A Fairytale; 1976) and *Lumi* (Snow, 1987) have a chamber music character.

Many of his works are studies of sonority, with a delicately transparent, oriental touch. Vesala has composed for his own instrumental ensemble, *Sound and Fury*, since 1984. One of its members in the early years was guitarist RAOUL BJÖRKENHEIM (b. 1956), who has succeeded, perhaps better than any other Finnish composer, in releasing the latent energy in the fusion of jazz and rock in the massive works *Primal Mind* (for Krakatau and UMO; 1991) and *Apocalypso* for 30 electric guitars, 6 bass guitars and 4 percussionists.

Rock

The impact of rock music in the 1960s can be compared to that of jazz in the 1920s. This time, the opposition was between jazz musicians and rock (and pop) musicians; different stylistic aims, social differences and a generation gap were at the root of the conflict. The common Afro-American foundation of both musics, however, has also produced a fruitful fusion of styles from time to time.

The early years of Finnish pop consisted of outright imitation and applications of Anglo-American precedent (The Shadows, The Beatles, The Rolling Stones). *Rautalankamusiikki* ('steel wire music'), played with amplified electric guitars, together with the acoustic folk music performed by amateur groups, paved the way for later professionals. Among the pioneers, Johnny (& The Sounds), Danny (& The Islanders), Irwin and Kirka ended up as pop singers, Eero & Jussi (Raittinen) and their group, The Boys, branched out into folk rock, while HECTOR (Heikki Harma) built up a distinctive singer/songwriter image modelled on Bob Dylan and Leonard Cohen. Among his songs, *Lumi teki enkelin eteiseen* (The Snow Made an Angel in the Hall) is already a Finnish evergreen. The most ambitious trends in the 1970s were progressive rock and fusion. *Blues Section*, founded by HASSE WALLI back in 1968, was the first Finnish rock-jazz group; *Asamaan*, Walli's project of the '70s, was a pioneer of ethno-rock, the fad of the '90s. Guitarist JUKKA TOLONEN and bassist PEKKA POHJOLA, the leading musicians in the groups *Wigwam* and *Tasavallan Presidentti*, later won fame in Scandinavia and on the Continent with their complex fusion music.

The *Suomi-Rock* style that emerged in the 1970s was a crystallization of earlier trends. Aspiring singer/songwriters began to compose their own pieces, in Finnish. Some existential and counter-cultural background was provided by what little underground there had been in the '60s, and by the left-wing 'New Song' movement. The humorous satires of JUICE LESKINEN (b. 1950) have earned him both a State award and a public statue. His song *Syksyn sävel* (Autumn Tune) has already entered the Finnish folk canon. Folk rock is the domain of singers such as Dave Lindholm, Mikko Alatalo, Mikko Perkoila and Liisa Akimoff. Bands playing straightforward rock'n'roll include Remu Aaltonen's and Albert Järvinen's *Hurriganes*, Pate Mustajärvi's *Popeda* and *Hanoi Rocks*, headed by Mike Monroe (Matti Fagerholm) and Andy McCoy (Antti Hulkko). *Honey B. & T-Bones* has a blues orientation and *Pelle Miljoona* (Petri Tiili) plays punk. 'Phenomenon' groups include Martti Syrjä's *Eppu Normaali*, *J.(uhani) Karjalainen ja Mustat Lasit* and, most notably *Dingo*, headed by Neumann (Pertti Nieminen), whose neo-modal idiom enjoyed a hysterical success in the mid '80s. The most ambitious contribution to progressive rock was made by Ismo Alanko's *Sielun veljet*, whose repetitive use of miniature motives occasionally suggests associations with Ugric shamanism. The music of *Tuomari Nurmio*, Alanko's kindred spirit, is characterized by a chromatic and chaotic musical background to a simple song line. The best-known representatives of Finnish rock today are the *Leningrad Cowboys*. This "world's worst rock group" cultivates parody and satire, and has become famous from Aki Kaurismäki's films *Leningrad Cowboys Go America* and *Leningrad Cowboys Meet Moses*. The group's brainwave was the idea of working with the Russian Red Army Chorus; the collaboration began with a carnivalistic concert in Helsinki in summer 1993. Finnish rock groups aiming at one or other of the myriad new subgenres, such as ambient, rap and techno-pop, include *4 R(oses)*, *22-pistepirkko*, *Waltari*, *Aikakone* and *Movetron*. Electronically produced borrowings, quotations and allusions complete the picture of an increasingly disjointed, postmodern rock world.

Hit

The antithesis to the Afro-American avantgarde is the hit song, the most popular of all sub-genres of popular music. Translated cover versions of international hits, and domestic hit songs in particular, present a conservative escapism which fuses innovative external elements into earlier national ones. Originally, in the 19th century, the Finnish word *iskelmä* meant a commercial breakthrough; later on it became established as the term for recorded, sung dance music accompanied by instrumental ensemble.

Who Invented Love?

Among the earliest commercial hits in terms of sheet music sales were Karl Collan's 1862 arrangement of the folk song *Tuoll' on mun kultani* (There's My Loved One), Pahlman's aforementioned potpourri *Suomalaisia säveleitä* (1871), the tango *El Choclo* and the cakewalk *At a Georgia Campmeeting* (1914), both from the A. Apostol sheet music collection. The most popular early Finnish records, made by HMV, featured Finnish-American and native Finnish couplet singers such as J. Alfred Tanner, Iivari Kainulainen and Pasi Jääskeläinen. Their songs included international music hall and cabaret favourites, folk songs and their own pieces. Especially Tanner and, later, Tatu Pekkarinen won the hearts of the Finnish people with an endearingly folksy style. The first boom period in record sales came with the 'gramophone fever' sparked off by the introduction of HMV's portable record player. The new domestic hit songs of the period, sung by Topi Aaltonen (Ture Ara) and accompanied by the Suomi-Jazz-Orkesteri and the Suomi-

Tanssiorkesteri, were *Asfalttikukka* (Asphalt Flower; composed by Ernest Pingoud under a pseudonym), the folk tune *Emma* and Georg Malmstén's *Särkynyt onni* (Broken Happiness); they sold up to 18,000 copies. Throughout the 1930s, the hit song – based on the national heritage and only with a slight hint of the Afro-American about it – ruled the record market. The Dallapé orchestra (recording for the German Odeon label) and its lead singer GEORG MALMSTÉN (1902–81) were overwhelmingly popular, selling some 80% of all Finnish records!

Malmstén, who began his career as an army bandleader and opera soloist, was a prolific composer of hit songs. His best-loved waltzes and foxtrots, which include *Leila*, *Aallokko kutsuu* (The Call of the Waves), *Kyllikki-valssi* (Kyllikki Waltz). *Katariinan kamarissa* (In Catharine's Bedroom) and *Heili Karjalasta* (My Flame from Karelia), run the whole gamut of early 20th-century styles, the early years of the century, from the Salvation Army bands' tunes to the Russian romance, the German *Schlager* and the Scandinavian folk tune. Dallapé's classic oompahs and the foxtrots *Yö Altailla* (Night in the Altai), *Keltaiset banaanit* (Yellow Bananas) and *Paavo Nurmi* by Tynnilä and Jäppilä were down-home dance tunes descending directly from the Russian military march and the *Schlager*. Austro-Hungarian *Biedermeier* and Finnish folk song were the sources for the extensive output of USKO KEMPPI (1907–94), which included hits such as *Laulu tulipunaisesta ruususta* (Song of the Scarlet Rose), *Pustan poika* (Son of the Puszta), *Vanhan merirosvon kapakassa* (In the Old Pirate's Tavern), *Ikävä* (Yearning) and *Erämaajärven mökki* (Lakeside Cottage in the Woods). The *Schlager* dominated the market for translated songs, and the German popular marches *Lili Marlen*, *Erika* (*Kaarina* in Finnish) and *Keine Angst, Rosmarie* (*Pelko pois, Rosmarie*) were big wartime hits. The war was also the heyday of the rustic humour of the trenches: the soldiers at the front aimed *Between the Eyes*, pined for the ample lap of *Big Iita* and exchanged the harem of *Ali Baba* for the icy dugouts at *Lake Eldanka*. The nostalgic waltzes of the

Tsarist period were still popular enough to give the Army leadership the jitters. Its counterstroke was to ask George de Godzinsky to compose a similar, but Finnish, waltz to compete with the Russian ones. The result was *Äänisen aallot* (The Waves of Lake Onega). The most prolific hit song period of GEORGE DE GODZINSKY (1914–94), HARRY BERGSTRÖM (1910–89) and TOIVO KÄRKI (1915–92) began after the war. Godzinsky and Bergström composed numerous popular hits for their film scores; G. de G.: *Katupoikien laulu* (Guttersnipes' Song), *Pohjolan yö* (Northern Night), *Sulle salaisuuden kertoa mä voisin* (I Have a Secret to Tell You), *Sulle kauneimman lauluni laulan* (I Sing My Loveliest Song to You); B: *Vaimoke* (Substitute Wife), *Seitsemän tuntia onnehen* (Seven Hours to Happiness), *Saimaan valssi* (Lake Saimaa Waltz), *On lautalla pienoinen kahvila* (There's a Little Café on the Ferry). Compared with the composers of the '30s, their style was more modern, and incorporated features of swing and music hall. As studio conductors, they both recorded the best-loved songs of the Finns' favourite singers Olavi Virta, Harmony Sisters, Kipparikvartetti, Metro-Tytöt and Tapio Rautavaara. In the 1950s, Kärki became 'God Almighty of the Finnish hit song' as head of recording at the Fazer company. The standbys in the extensive postwar output of this former jazz fan include both nostalgic tango classics, such as *Siks oon mä suruinen* (That's Why I'm Sad), *Liljankukka* (Lily Blossom), *Anna-Liisa, Täysikuu* (Full Moon), *On elon retki näin* (Life's Journey) and *Hiljainen kylätie* (A Quiet Village Street), and more traditional, catchy polka, *jenkka*, waltz and foxtrot tunes. Kärki's principal lyrics writers were Kerttu Mustonen and Reino Helismaa.

In the late 1950s, the new Scandia label filled a new market niche with its successful invention of the 'jazz hit'. The company launched the teenage girl soloists Brita Koivunen, Vieno Kekkonen and Laila Kinnunen, and hired the best of the bebop musicians (Olli Häme, Erkki Melakoski, Jaakko Salo) for its studio ensembles. The songs were old favourites, either klezmer tunes or their stylized imitations, including *Sä kaunehin oot*

George de Godzinsky

Toivo Kärki

Harry Bergström

(translated from the Yiddish *Bei mir bist du schein*), *Suklaasydän* (Chocolate Heart), *Neulo kaunis morsian* (Sew, Lovely Bride) and *Pojat* (Boys); Russian romances and Gypsy tunes like *Mustat silmät* (Black Eyes) and Monti's *Czárdas*. Thus the East European heritage returned to Finnish popular music.

The traditional field began to break up in the 1960s. The production of cover versions of translated Anglo-American and Italian hits continued; still in the late 1960s, the recordings made in Finland and in Finnish by the Italian singer Umberto Marcato reached higher sales figures than Elvis. *The Discophon group* and RAUNO LEHTINEN (b. 1932) came up with the idea of the instrumental hit. The dixielandish *Muskat Ramble* and *Säkkijärven polkka*, performed by the studio ensembles Kolibri and Vostok All Stars and spliced together with Les Paul-type 'trick' recording, were standbys of the broadcasts of Sävelradio, YLE's light music department founded in 1961. Lehtinen's 1963 composition *Letkis* (from 'let's kiss') was the all-time hit in the history of Finnish popular music, recorded in no less than 92 countries. Also a versatile film and orchestra composer, Lehtinen went on to become head of musical entertainment on Finnish commercial TV, and to compose two songs chosen to represent Finland at the Eurovision song contest, *Tom-tom-tom* and *Tie uuteen päivään* (The Road to a New Morning).

Since the 1970s, the Finnish popular song has sought to strike a balance between translated cover versions, a suave middle-of-the-road style and Finnishness. Traditional hit songs, particularly tangos, are the evergreen favourites of the record-buying public. Folk and rock music have won the nation's favour only when the traditional melody in minor key could be detected behind their modish exterior. The reason must be in part sociological: the man in the street or country-dweller has a non-analytical attitude to music, and demands safe repetitiveness from songs. Period styles, such as the oom-pah renaissance in the '60s, Topi Sorsakoski's remakes of Olavi Virta's old hits in the '80s, and the imitation Slav romances tailored for Laura Voutilainen in the '90s show that a securely conservative approach is the recipe for success. Even in periods of recession, when the volume and range of record production tends to shrink, the basic popular song survives. This was proved by the oom-pah period during the depression of the '30s, by wartime 'trench populism', by the pessimistic songs of the period of rural depopulation and the 'great migration' of the '70s (Matti & Teppo, Erkki Junkkarinen, Reijo Kallio, Irwin), and again by the more optimistic 'feminine energy' of Katri-Helena and Arja Koriseva in the '90s. During fat years, the spectrum is broader. Economic trends may determine the fate of the efforts of the neo-modal movement (Dingo, Sir Elwood, Aikakone and Movetron) to break loose from the straitjacket of major-minor tonality.

Heaven and Hell

Between the opposing poles of European and Afro-American music, the Finnish minor-key popular song has proved its persistence, despite a singular lack of success in the Eurovision song contests. Its prevailing moods are anguish and nostalgia, the subconscious roots of 'arctic hysteria'. Repeated from one stylistic period to the next, they represent inseparable twin myths, the fear of hell and the dream of heaven.

The musical representation of anguish is the descending fifth, sol-do, the oppressive *katabasis* figure defined in the Baroque doctrine of affections. This motive has a history of its own in Finland. The melodic flow of the *Kalevala*, ranging over one pentachord, was always anchored in the descending fifth. This structure was bolstered by Gregorian chant, surviving the Reformation in the Gregorian-based folk chorales favoured by revivalist movements. The descending fifth now took on the meaning of anguish, and was therefore a characteristic feature in hymns describing the Passion and in funeral and war hymns. The weekly reminder of sin, the liturgical *Kyrie eleison*, is based on the same motive. By the 19th century, the *katabasis* fifth had been adopted in secular songs as the symbol of negative emotions and events – deceit, jealousy, separation and pain. This feature was passed on to the popular song via broadside ballads and *rekilaulut*. Its ultimate crystallization came in the Finnish evergreen tango *Satumaa* (Fairyland) by UNTO MONONEN (1930–68); the shadow of the *Kyrie eleison* looms behind this piece, which gives perfect expression to Finnish self-destructiveness. The same note of anxiety is struck by the 'confessional songs' of the 1970s, describing affliction, drunkenness, divorce or thoughts of suicide, such as *Et voi tulla rajan taa* (You Can't Come over to the Other Side; J.P. Lehto), *Viikonloppuisä* (Weekend Father; Jukka Kuoppamäki) and *Yksinäinen* (Lonesome; R. Lumisalmi). Among the songs of the '90s, Joel Hallikainen's smash hit *Kuurankukka* (Frost Flower; Timo Koivusalo), Irwin's hangover-befuddled *Rentun ruusu* (The Rotter's Rose; Kassu Halonen), Petri Laaksonen's *Täällä Pohjantähden alla* (Under the North Star) and Kaija K's *Kuka keksi rakkauden* (Who Invented Love?; Markku Impiö) all sprang up – willy-nilly – from the vale of tears evoked by the descending fifth.

The counterpart to the *katabasis* is the ascending minor-key sixth, sol-mi. According to Boris Asafyev, this interval was the characteristic 'intonation' of 19th-century Russian music; Finnish popular music adopted it from the military bands and

The tango is the crystallization of the Finnish soul. This Argentine dance first came to Finland in 1913, but only really became popular after the Second World War, when composers of popular songs developed a Finnish version of the tango. Compared with the macho image of the original, the Finnish tango is shy and reserved. The dance has slowed down to a walk; syncopation has given way to triads, which suit the Finnish language better. The alienation and anticipated disappointment characteristic of the tango are dressed in the garb of folk poetry and romanticism: the autumnal ennui of the full moon, red leaves and the quiet village road, on the one hand; the soothing escapism of Fairyland and the Argentine pampas, on the other. The typical tango melodies reflect the bleak spiritual landscape of 'arctic hysteria' in greater depth than the texts do: from the haunting fear of hell (the *Kalevala*-Gregorian descending fifth) to the nostalgic longing for heaven (the Russian ascending sixth).

The incarnations of the Finnish tango are still the beloved male soloists of the '50s and '60s: Eino Grön, Reijo Taipale, Henry Theel, Taisto Tammi, Markus Allan and many others. The greatest of them all was Olavi Virta (in the picture), with his soulful glissando-rubato – inherited from the Romantic era – and his Gypsy timbre still the idol of all budding tango singers.

The Seinäjoki Tango Festival is a commercial event which seeks to recapture the magic of yesteryear by arranging annual 'championships' for would-be tango kings and queens. This event provided a springboard to success for Arja Koriseva and others.

waltz-romances of the Tsarist period. As a basic ingredient of Georg Malmstén's waltzes, Dallapé's oom-pah classics, and particularly Kärki's tangos, it was assimilated into the Finnish hit song as the symbol of Chekhovian nostalgia, autumn leaves, quiet village roads and moonlit nights. It is also the principal motive of the classic tangos of PENTTI VIHERLUOTO (b. 1915), such as *Punaiset lehdet* (Red Leaves) and *Musta ruusu* (The Black Rose) as well as of two rock hits which have already entered the realm of folk song, Juice Leskinen's *Syksyn sävel* (Tune of Autumn) and Edu Kettunen's romance *Minä olen muistanut* (I Have

Remembered). Thus audiences are soothed by the immutability of the world as depicted in the conservative hit song, a form of layman's therapy emphasizing permanence, and thus making life easier to live.

Film, Theatre, Pops
The Vagabond's Waltz

The ensembles that played in Finnish cinemas in the silent film era followed international precedent by playing old standards. *Träumerei* accompanied the 'dreamlike, visionary' scene, *Ave Maria* stood for 'daydreams', and the *Egmont* Overture was played during 'noisy scenes' (from the *Fazer Cinematheque Catalogue*, 1927). Among the few early Finnish film compositions, Armas Järnefelt's suite to *Laulu tulipunaisesta kukasta* (Song of the Blood-Red Flower; M. Stiller, 1919) has been preserved. This breathlessly Wagnerian tone poem is based on Finnish folk songs about young maidens and rivermen. The programmatic style of music for silent films carried over to the era of the talking picture. A post-romantic picture-book style based on the use of leitmotifs in the spirit of Max Steiner was typical of drama films, whereas comic films approached musical comedies with their song numbers, overtures, intermezzos and finales. The leading Finnish film producer Suomen Filmiteollisuus (SF) had a trusty band of fast-working conductor-composers (Martti Similä composed 34 film scores, Tapio Ilomäki 37 and Georg Malmstén 12). Among composers of art music, Uuno Klami, Leevi Madetoja, Sulho Ranta, Helvi Leiviskä, Väinö Haapalainen and Peter Akimoff composed film music. Two enormously prolific composers of light music entered the film business in the late '30s: George de Godzinsky, who composed 53 film scores for SF and Harry Bergström, who produced no less than 78 scores for Suomi-Filmi.

The new postwar generation, notably the art composers Heikki Aaltoila (57 film scores), Einar Englund (17), Ahti Sonninen (14), Tauno Pylkkänen (14) and Tauno Marttinen (6), brought a fresh neoclassical tang to film music. Einar Englund's music to Erik Blomberg's Lapp ballad *Valkoinen peura* (The White Reindeer; 1952) is based on *joiku* themes. Bartókian alienation and understated dramatic effects made this composition a classic of Finnish film music. Godzinsky's music to T.J. Särkkä's film *Kulkurin valssi* (The Vagabond's Waltz; 1941, screenplay by Mika Waltari) was a pioneering effort. Godzinsky produced variations on the popular couplet by J.Alfred Tanner as the film's freedom theme, now in Gypsy style, now in a stylized Tchaikovsky version, and culminating in the sparkling orchestral fireworks of the happy end. The popular *rillumarei* comedy that became fashionable after the war produced similar adaptations of the dramaturgy of musical comedy. One of the pioneering works in this genre, in addition to *Kulkurin valssi*, was Harry Bergström's score – to which Toivo Kärki (42 films) put the finishing touches – for the film *Kaunis Veera* (Lovely Veera; 1950). Hit songs and unabashed underscoring were central to the film farces of the period; this tradition was revived by Jaakko Salo in his music for Spede Pasanen's *Uuno Turhapuro* farces in the 1970s.

The new film composers who emerged around 1960 – Erkki Melakoski, Pentti Lasanen, Jaakko Salo, Lasse Mårtenson and Rauno Lehtinen – were mainstream or bebop jazz musicians who stuck with the post-romantic and popular Hollywood idiom. The music to Maunu Kurkvaara's *films noirs* was diametrically opposed to this: Usko Meriläinen's scores for *Yksityisalue* (Private Property), *Juhlat* (The Party) and *Naiset* (Women) were twelve-tone chamber music, while Leonid Bashmakov adopted an improvisatory style à la Satie & Poulenc for the films *Tirlittan* and *Patarouva* (The Queen of Spades). Otto Donner, Esa Helasvuo and Eero Koivistoinen relied from the early '60s on intimate jazz vignettes and chamber music pastiches. Kari Rydman was the first to experiment with tape music and collage in his music for Jaakko Pakkasvirta's film *Yö vai päivä* (Night or Day; 1962). The most interesting recent film scores include

Antero Honkanen's electronic music for Markku Lehmuskallio's *Korpinpolska* (The Raven's Dance; 1980) and Honkanen and Meriläinen's electroacoustic music for the same director's *Skierri* (1982). Markku Kopisto's music to Risto Jarva's comedies of the '70s, *Jäniksen vuosi* (The Year of the Hare) and *Mies, joka ei osannut sanoa ei* (The Man Who Couldn't Say No), and Anssi Tikanmäki's numerous scores for the films of Aki and Mika Kaurismäki, including *Arvottomat* (The Worthless) and *Klaani* (The Clan) had a more traditional dramatic structure based on leitmotifs. Many of Tikanmäki's scores employ frequent allusions to music ranging from Shostakovich and Pärt, as in *Kaivo* (The Well; P.Lehto, 1992), to domestic popular favourites. Tikanmäki has also composed music for several classics of silent film, including *Greed* and *Potemkin*.

The Log Floaters

Musical comedy has long been the lifeline of both amateur and professional theatre. In the 19th century, Swedish amateur troupes toured Finland, while the Russian aristocracy arranged its own operetta performances. *Orpheus in the Underworld* and *La Belle Hélène* were seen in Helsinki only two years after their premieres, and Viennese operetta, particularly *The Merry Widow*, were instant hits with the Finnish music public. Exotic settings, Gypsies, Hungarians and the Orient exerted an immediate fascination. The first Finnish effort in this vein was August Tavaststjerna's musical version of Pushkin's *Zemfira* in 1870. The first of the classic Finnish musical comedies was Emil Kauppi's *Kosijat* (The Suitors; 1910), staged by the Oulu Finnish Operetta under Pasi Jääskeläinen. Sam Sihvo's *Jääkärin morsian* (The Jaeger's Bride; 1921) and *Hevoshuijari* (The Horse Coper; 1924), Oskar Merikanto's *Tukkijoella* (The Log Floaters; 1928), Ilmari Hannikainen's *Talkootanssit* (The Barn Dance; 1930) and many other rural comedies have been perennial favourites of the amateur stage and film. The operettas *Aavikon lapset* (Children of the Desert; by Martti Nisonen, 1914), *Sysmäläisiä* (Sysmä

Folk) and *Miranico* (by Toivo Palmroth; 1926 and 1929), and particularly Georg Malmstén's popular revue operettas *Lennokki* (The Model Plane; 1936) and *Vetoketju* (The Zip; 1938) had a somewhat more urban character. The first theatre in Finland to produce indigenous musical comedies was Helsinki's Swedish Theatre, for which George de Godzinsky (its musical director at the time) composed *Veronika* (1949) and *Häät preerialla* (Wedding on the Prairie; 1959). His later hit shows included *Onnenpotku* (Lucky Fluke; 1962), *Rosvo-Roope* (Robber Roope; 1960), *Kuisma ja Helinä* (1971) and *Kaksi Vihtoria* (Two Victors; 1981). In the wake of the international megahits of the early '60s, such as *West Side Story* and *Fiddler on the Roof*, Jorma Panula composed *Ruma Elsa* (Ugly Elsa; 1960) and *Syntipukki* (Scapegoat, 1963), following them up in 1970 with *Tulipunakukka* (Scarlet Flower). The theatre conductor Arthur Fuhrmann composed the musical comedies *Vieno Vainikainen* (1963), *Rakkain rakastaja* (Dearest Lover; 1966; both written by Marja Rankkala) and *Lössi* (The Gang; Kari Tuomisaari, 1965). Erkki Melakoski's *Gabriel, tule takaisin* (Come Back, Gabriel!; Mika Waltari, 1961) is one of the most popular Finnish musicals of all time. Helsinki's smaller Swedish-language theatre, Lilla Teatern, produced a number of satirical revues in the 1960s, including Erna Tauro's *Åttan* (Eight; 1964) and Otto Donner's *Var är min stora luddiga nalle?* (Where's My Big, Fluffy Teddy Bear?; Bengt Ahlfors, 1968), heralding the incipient political music theatre of the late '60s and '70s. The left-wing 'New Song' movement was launched by the rousing musical play *Lapualaisooppera* (Lapua Opera; 1966); with its carnivalistic approach, following in the footsteps of Brecht and Eisler, it soon gave rise to a new, committed type of music theatre. The Kom theatre, Agit-Prop quartet, Koiton Laulu singers, Raatikko dance theatre, radio, TV theatre and Love Records were strongholds of literary-artistic left-wing radicalism, which has come to stand as a symbol for the whole era. Chydenius — and his 'Chydenians', pianists EERO OJANEN (b. 1943), TONI EDELMANN (b. 1945) and HEIKKI VALPOLA

(b. 1946) – composed, in addition to chamber music, jazz and choral works, a sizable quantity of ballet, theatre and film music as well as songs such as *Kalliolle kukkulalle* (On the Rock, on the Hill) which have already become evergreens. Closely related to the New Song are some of the works of Otto Donner, the sensitive ballads of Kari Rydman and the literary chansons composed by TAPIO LIPPONEN for the *Muksut* group. M.A. NUMMINEN (b. 1940), the Finnish underground writer, anarchist and dadaist, turned the Finnish Army regulations on indoor duties, Wittgenstein's aphorisms and a book on sex education into humorous children's songs, "neo-vulgar Negro jazz" or parodies of the *Schlager*. The pianist JANI UHLENIUS (b. 1945) worked as Numminen's partner, accompanist and arranger for many years.

In recent years, pianist-conductor JUKKA LINKOLA (b. 1955) has introduced new ideas into music theatre. His children's musicals *Peter Pan* (1985) and *Antti Puuhaara* (Antti Treebranch; 1994; both with text by Jukka Virtanen) and *Max ja Moritz* (1987) shifted the language of the musical as well of children's music several degrees closer to jazz, rock and free tonal art music. Linkola, whose music for the stage includes the opera *Elina,* the TV-opera *Angelica* (1991) and the ballet *Ronja Ryövärintytär* (Ronia, the Robber's Daughter; 1989), won a competition for musical theatre sponsored in 1992 by the Foundation for the Promotion of Finnish Music with the work Kairatut sydämet (Drilled Hearts). The techno-musical *Hype* (1993), produced by the Swedish Theatre of Helsinki, was the most recent major hit in the genre.

Cabaret and Variety Shows

The history of cabaret and variety shows in Finland begins in the 19th century, when the music public in the capital enjoyed music performances featuring violinists standing on their heads or drummers hanging from the ceiling. The Stockholm entertainer Sigge Wulff brought the couplet, cabaret and music hall to Finland. The Finnish couplet singers Iivari Kainulainen, J. ALFRED

TANNER (1884–1927), Rafael Ramstedt, Tatu Pekkarinen and Matti Jurva performed in the new vaudeville houses such as the Helikon and Apollo, in restaurants, 'couplet cafés', during intervals between films, in circuses and on record. Their popularity waned in the years between the wars, but revived during the Second World War. The songwriter PALLE, a.k.a. the writer Reino Hirviseppä, a.k.a. as Major R.W. Palmroth (1906–92), curator of the Army Museum, recruited a new set of comedians from among frontline soldiers to serve as wartime entertainers. After the war, inspired by the example of Berlin, Palle established a revue theatre called Iloinen Teatteri (The Merry Theatre); in the days of the Allied Control Commission in Finland, however, it had to be disbanded. Performances nevertheless continued to be given until the 1960s by Ossi Elstelä's Punainen Mylly (Moulin Rouge), which featured revues by Toivo Kärki and Reino Helismaa. In the late '60s, director-writers Jukka Virtanen and Matti Kuusla, the pioneers of Finnish TV entertainment, set up a Swedish-type floor show at the Adlon and Kalastajatorppa restaurants, with pianists Jaakko Salo and Lasse Mårtenson and singer Marjatta Leppänen. The tradition was revived in 1979 by the *Uusi Iloinen Teatteri* (The New Merry Theatre), which performs in the summer season at the Peacock Theatre in Linnanmäki amusement park. A literary cabaret restaurant called Kaksi Kanaa (Two Hens) has operated in Helsinki since 1991.

The Happy Angler

Some composers of film scores and light music have also composed a certain amount of orchestral music, character pieces, rhapsodies, suites, arrangements for choir and orchestra, stylized dances, and so forth. The mainstay for this type of music from 1953 to 1966 was the Radion Viihdeorkesteri (Radio Pops Orchestra) conducted by George de Godzinsky. Its two main sources were post-romantic *salon* music, particularly Viennese tunes, and the Broadway-Hollywood tradition, with Afro-American spices. Godzinsky's own orchestral music is a prime example of the wide range of styles employed. His *Miljoona-marssi* (March of a Million), the suite *Suomen tivoli* (Finland's Tivoli) and the overture *Lystikäs matka* (A Humorous Voyage) are jovial pastiches of Viennese music. *Sininen valssi* (Blue Waltz) is a languid Boston waltz, *Syysilta Aulangolla* (Autumn Evening at Aulanko) a Tchaikovskyan concert waltz, and *Pussi-järven polkka* a take-off of the popular *Säkkijärven polkka*. Harry Bergström recycled his film scores, assembling overtures and arrangements for pops choirs from his incidental music. His independent works include the Gershwin-style piano rhapsodies *Ametisti* (Amethyst; 1954), *Topaasi* (Topaz; 1971) and *Suoma-lainen Madridissa* (A Finn in Madrid; 1968). Conductor VEIKKO HUUSKONEN (b. 1930) has composed a series of neoclassical works on Baltic themes, including the suite *Kuvia linnunradalta* (Pictures from the Milky Way) and the *Baltic Concerto* for accordion and orchestra. *Vainionpään Kallen soitto* (Music of Kalle Vainionpää) for two accordions and orchestra is Huuskonen's most streamlined orchestral work. ENSIO KOSTA (Sten Ducander, 1926–83), Finland's Erik Satie, produced a number of compact, neoclassical character pieces, including *Valse lente et triste* (1975), *À la Jequibau* (1975), and *Musiikkia Keski-Maasta* (Music from Middle Earth; 1983) to themes of J.R.R. Tolkien. Kosta's spare, often two-part texture, bitonal musical idiom and the contrasting sensitive orchestral colouring is reminiscent of the popularism practised by *Les Six*. A similar, though more full-blooded French piquancy can be found in the orchestral mini-atures of Marcus Eje (Einar Englund). ERKKI MELAKOSKI (b. 1926) cultivated the Scandinavian pastiche with works such as *Kuvia Sipoosta* (Pictures from Sipoo), *Potpuri Julinin nuottikirjasta* (Potpourri from the Julin music book; 1979) and arrangements from the P.A. Nummelin music book (1991). Esa Pethman is a composer of Leroy Anderson-style intermezzos like *Iloinen onkimies* (The Happy Angler) and *Pikku pikkolo* (The Little Pic-colo) and of Ravelesque, flute-dominated impressions such as *Serenadi aamulle* (Serenade to Morning) and *The Perfumed*

Garden. Rauno Lehtinen has composed a few suites and several miniature pieces for orchestra, including the orchestral idyll *Balaton*, and has arranged many of his favourite popular hits for large orchestra. Other jazz musicians to compose works for pops orchestra include Erik Lindström, Ossi Malinen, Nacke Johans-son, Jaakko Salo and Pentti Lasanen. The best-known of these compositions, however, is *Myrskyluodon Maija* (Maija from the Stormy Cliffs, 1964) by LASSE MÅRTENSON (b. 1934), an orchestral arrangement of the music to a popular TV film. Anssi Tikan-mäki's *Maisemakuvia Suomesta* (Finnish Landscapes; 1979) and Jukka Linkola's film music suite *Lumikuningatar* (The Snow Queen; 1987) are among the more recent works of light music for large orchestra.

World Music

Folk music fell somewhere by the wayside in the changes at the beginning of this century. The spirit of popular education fa-voured 'refined' folk music in arrangements, solo and choral songs and stereotyped folk dances. It was only in the 1960s that serious interest began to be taken in authentic ethnic music. Flamenco aficionados and fans of Andean, Irish and Gypsy music set up groups, and Love Records, as a promotor of 'alter-native music', began to publish African, Vietnamese and Finnish Gypsy music, also preparing the ground for a folk revival. The propitious moment arrived in 1968:

1968 was Europe's 'mad year' revisited, a year of revolution. It sparked off many different movements: cars burned in the streets of Paris, and in Helsinki the Old Student House was seized by students; [the populist politician] Vennamo gained thirty-three electoral seats in the presidential election, and a folk music festival held at Kaustinen had an amazing turnout. All these events were aspects of the same change.
(Heikki Laitinen, 1987)

At the heart of the Kaustinen Folk Music Festival were the

Kaustisen Purppuripelimannit group, a product of the Central Ostrobothnian fiddlers' tradition, and the fiddler-composer KONSTA JYLHÄ (1910–84). The music of Kaustinen had already gained some renown through radio and TV broadcasts and recordings. The growth of the festival from a local get-together to a national event – and soon an international one – had a tremendous therapeutic impact. Fiddlers' groups were formed throughout the country, relearned the old repertoire, and composed new pieces. Kaustinen nurtured both scholarship and art. Erkki Ala-Könni, professor of folk music, was involved from the start. The Folk Music Institute was established in Kaustinen in 1973. Its first director, HEIKKI LAITINEN (b. 1943), was a fiery proponent of both folk music research and practice. His vision brought new depth to the whole concept of folk music. The focus shifted from fiddlers' tunes to ancient Finnish music, and from instrumental music to folk song; to build bridges between popular music and folk music was no longer a sin. *Kankaan pelimannit*, *Primo* and *Nelipolviset* were some of the groups set up by Laitinen. In 1983 Laitinen became head of the new Department of Folk Music at the Sibelius Academy, where he carried on the folk music education started by professor MARTTI POKELA (b. 1924). Laitinen later worked with the dancer Reijo Kela and the Suomussalmi group, producing numerous sound and dance performances and theatre shows, including the 40-hour improvisation *Vapauden kaiho* (Longing for Freedom; 1990), the ecological dance and music act *Ansapolku Suomussalmella* (Trapper's Trail at Suomussalmi; 1990), *Yrjö Kallisen valaistuminen* (The Illumination of Yrjö Kallinen; 1995) and *Pohjalaisia* (The Ostrobothnians; 1996). Laitinen was awarded the title of professor of the arts in 1995.

In just over ten years, the folk music department has produced a spate of new professionals whose recordings have won international recognition. The axioms of their music-making are reliance on the ear, improvisation, emotional involvement and their own compositions. Among the new folk groups, *Pirnales* was already founded by Martti Pokela. *Niekku*, a group of singers and instrumentalists, covers the full range of Finnish folk music, from *Kalevala* singing to fiddlers' music. Of the group's members, Liisa Matveinen and Anna-Kaisa Liedes have also embarked on a solo career. The key figure in *JPP* (short for Järvelän Pikkupelimannit), violinist Arto Järvelä, has played in numerous different ensembles, including the burlesque duo *Pinnin pojat* with accordionist Kimmo Pohjonen. He also plays in the virtuoso accordionist Maria Kalaniemi's group *Aldargaz*, which cultivates an Astor Piazzolla style. The eight-woman a cappella group *Me Naiset* has adopted the archaic singing technique of the Ingrians (a Finnic people who formerly occupied the region surrounding present-day St Petersburg) and a polyphony based on ear and improvisation. The group sings Karelian and Ingrian rune melodies and Estonian and Mordvin songs (Mordvin is another Finnic language spoken by a Uralic people living in the middle Volga basin). *Kantele* players trained by Pokela, a virtuoso of the instrument, include Matti Kontio, Sinikka Järvinen, Timo Väänänen, Sari Kauranen, Arja Kastinen and Minna Raskinen.

Outside the Sibelius Academy, the only government-subsidized folk music group, *Tallari*, hails from Kaustinen. *Kaustisen Näppäripelimannit* is a lively 40-player school group trained by Mauno Järvelä. *Slobo Horo* of Tampere specializes in Balkan popular music ('musica orientala'). The Gypsy Ensemble *Hortto Kaalo*, founded in 1970, plays Russian and Finnish Gypsy songs and compositions by its own members. The Ostrobothnian Erkki Rankaviita specializes in the rhymed *rekilaulu* (roundelay) ballad. Folk music has a conspicuous role in the music played by many Finnish rock and jazz groups, fitting in with the global boom for "world music". The Ingrian energy of the Swedish group *Hedningarna* is provided by the Finnish singers Sanna Kurki-Suonio and Tellervo Paulasto. *Angelin tytöt*, Nils-Aslak Valkeapää and Wimme Saari sing *joiku*, either alone or accompanied by Senegalese drums and jazz and rock ensem-

Contemporary *joiku* chant: Tuuni and Ulrika Länsman of *Angelin tytöt*.

ble. The best-known Finnish world music group is *Värttinä*, whose music is a blend of Ingrian archaism, Balkan rhythms and rock. This Finnish equivalent of *Canto Gregoriano* grew via the Academy's folk music department out of a youth club group founded by Sari Kaasinen in the small Karelian village of Rääkkylä. The return of modality to popular music via folk music proves that archaism can be modern. Sound carries farthest at the grassroots level.

SELECTED BIBLIOGRAPHY

Abraham, Gerald (ed.),*Sibelius: A Symposion.* London 1947.

Aho, Kalevi, *Einojuhani Rautavaara als Sinfoniker – As Symphonist.* Helsinki 1988.

Ala-Könni, Erkki, *Die Polska-Tänze in Finnland.* Helsinki 1956.

Andersson, Otto, *Den unge Pacius och musiklivet i Helsingfors på 1830-talet.* Helsingfors 1938.

"Arctic Paradise". *Contemporary Finnish Folk Music 1966–1997,* Helsinki Music Information Centre 1995.

Collan-Beaurain, Maria, *Fredrik Pacius. Lefnadsteckning.* Helsingfors 1921.

Dahlström, Fabian, *Bernhard Henrik Crusell. Klarinettisten och hans större instrumentalverk.* Ekenäs 1976.

Dahlström, Fabian (ed.) *Bernhard Crusell. Tonsättare, Klarinettvirtuos. Hans dagböcker, Studier i hans konst, Verkförteckning.* Ekenäs 1977.

Ekman, Karl, *Jean Sibelius.* Helsinki 1935 (in English).

Fantapié, Henri-Claude & Anja, La musique finlandaise. *Boréales* 26–29 (1983).

Finnish Music Quarterly. Helsinki 1985–.

Flodin, Karl, *Martin Wegelius.* Helsingfors 1922.

Furuhjelm, Erik, *Jean Sibelius. Hans tondiktning och drag ur hans liv.* Borgå 1916.

Goss, Glenda Dawn, *Jean Sibelius and Olin Downes. Music, Friendship, Criticism.* Boston 1995.

Gronow, Pekka, *Record Industry: Ethnomusicological Approach.* Tampere 1996.

Hannikainen, Ilmari, *Sibelius and the Development of Finnish Music.* London 1948.

Hanson, Sten (ed.), *Nordiska Musikfester / Nordic Music Days 100 years.* Stockholm 1988.

Heiniö, Mikko, *Vår tids finländska tonsättare och deras bakgrund.* Tavastehus 1986.

Helasvuo, Veikko, *Sibelius and the Music of Finland.* Helsinki 1952/57/61.

Hong, B. J., *Selim Palmgren. Life and Works.* Bloomington 1977.

Horton, John, *Scandinavian music. A Short History.* London 1963/Tokyo 1971.

Jalkanen, Pekka, *Alaska, Bombay and Billy Boy,* Helsinki 1989.

James, Burnett, *The Music of Jean Sibelius.* London 1983.

Johnson, Harold E., *Jean Sibelius.* London 1959.

Korhonen, Kimmo, *Finnish Composers since the 1960s.* Helsinki 1995.

Korhonen, Kimmo, *Finnish Concertos.* Helsinki 1995.

Korhonen Kimmo, *Finnish Orchestral Music I–II.* Helsinki 1995.

Kukkonen, Pirjo, *Tango Nostalgia. The Language of Love and Longing,* Helsinki 1996.

Layton, Robert, *Sibelius.* London 1965/84.

Levas, Santeri, *Jean Sibelius. A Personal Portrait.* London 1972.

Mauke, W., *Ernst Mielck*. Leipzig 1901.

Muikku, Jari, Finnish Jazz. Helsinki, Finnish Music Information Centre 1990.

Murtomäki, Veijo, *Symphonic Unity. The Development of Formal Thinking in the Symphonies of Sibelius*. Helsinki 1993.

Mäkinen, Timo, *Die aus frühen böhmischen Quellen überlieferten Piae Cantiones-Melodien*. Pieksämäki 1964.

Mäkinen, Timo & Nummi, Seppo, *Musica fennica. An Outline of Music in Finland*. Helsinki 1965/85.

Nummi, Seppo, *Modern musik. Finlands musikhistoria från första världskriget fram till vår tid. Finland i dag*. Stockholm 1967.

Parsons, Jeremy (ed.), *Erik Bergman. A Seventieth Birthday Tribute. Festskrift för Erik Bergman / Festschrift für Erik Bergman 24.11.1981*. Salo 1981.

Parsons, Jeremy & von Bonsdorff, Lena & Heiniö, Mikko (eds.), *Vägvisaren till Det sjungande trädet*. Helsingfors 1991.

Ringbom, Nils-Eric, *Jean Sibelius. A Master and His Work*. Oklahoma 1954.

Rock in Finland. Finnish Music Information Centre, Helsinki.

Rosas, John, *Ernst Mielck*. Åbo 1952.

– *Fredrik Pacius som tonsättare*. Åbo 1949.

The Roots of Finnish Popular Music. Finnish Music Information Centre, Helsinki.

Tawaststjerna, Erik, *Jean Sibelius I* (in English). London & al. 1976.

Tawaststjerna, Erik, *Jean Sibelius II* (in English). London & al. 1986.

Tawaststjerna, Erik, *Jean Sibelius I* (på svenska). Keuruu 1992.

Tawaststjerna, Erik, *Jean Sibelius II* (på svenska). Stockholm 1991 & Helsingfors 1994.

Tawaststjerna, Erik, *Jean Sibelius III* (på svenska). Helsingfors 1968 & Keuruu 1991.

Tawaststjerna, Erik, *Jan Sibelius I* (in Russian). Moskva 1981.

Wallner, Bo, *Vår tids musik i Norden från 20-tal till 60-tal*. Stockholm 1968.

Vignal, Marc, *Jean Sibelius*. Paris 1965.

INDEX